Sport and Social Exclusion in Global Society

Social exclusion is one of the most pressing challenges in post-industrial societies, encompassing economic, social, cultural and political dimensions. This important new book critically examines the relationship between sport and social exclusion from global and cross-cultural perspectives. The book analyses sport and social exclusion by focusing on three key questions: How does social exclusion affect participation in sport? How is social exclusion (re)produced, experienced, resisted, and managed in sport? How is sport used to combat social exclusion and promote social inclusion in other life domains? To answer these questions, the authors discuss and critically reflect on existing knowledge and in-depth case studies from Europe, Australasia, Africa and Latin America. The book illuminates the relationship between sport and social exclusion in Global North and Global South contexts, addressing key issues in contemporary social science such as social inequality, worklessness, gender, disability, displacement, homelessness and mental health.

Sport and Social Exclusion in Global Society is important reading for all students, researchers and policy-makers with an interest in sport sociology, sport development, sport management, or the relationship between sport and wider society.

Ramón Spaaij is an Associate Professor in the College of Sport and Exercise Science and Institute of Sport, Exercise and Active Living (ISEAL) at Victoria University, Australia. He is also Special Chair of Sociology of Sport at the University of Amsterdam, and Visiting Professor at the Utrecht University School of Governance, The Netherlands. Spaaij has published ten books including *Sport and Social Mobility: Crossing Boundaries* (2011), *Understanding Lone Wolf Terrorism: Global Patterns, Motivations and Prevention* (2012), *The Social Impact of Sport: Cross-Cultural Perspectives* (edited, 2010) and, with Cindy Burleson, *The Olympic Movement and the Sport of Peacemaking* (2013). His main research interests are the sociology of sport and the sociology of terrorism.

Jonathan Magee is a Senior Lecturer in the School of Sport, Tourism and the Outdoors at the LIVERPOOL JMU LIBRARY ...shire and has a wide range of teaching experience regarding sport and social inclusion, sport and community, and sport development and coaching. Magee initially focused his research career on sports labour migration but has more recently published on sport and leisure experiences of young people with disabilities as well as the Homeless World Cup. Magee has co-edited a number of books, including *Women, Football and Europe: Histories, Equity and Experiences* (with Caudwell, Liston and Scraton, 2007) and *The Bountiful Game: Football Identities and Finance* (with Bairner and Tomlinson, 2005). He has also conducted evaluation work of football community projects for the Football Foundation in England. Magee has also worked as a consultant for West Bromwich Albion in the FA Premier League.

Ruth Jeanes is a Senior Lecturer in the Faculty of Education at Monash University. Jeanes has spent a decade researching equity and inclusion within a sport and active leisure context, initially focusing on gender issues and in more recent years exploring experiences of young people with disabilities. She has explored issues of social exclusion within both Global North and South contexts, conducting extensive research with young people in Zambia in the previous five years. Jeanes has co-edited (with Jonathan Magee) *Children, Youth and Active Leisure* (2011) and *The Socioecological Educator* (with Wattchow *et al.*, 2013). She has published an extensive range of journal articles and book chapters in the broad area of sport and social inclusion.

Sport and Social Exclusion in Global Society

Ramón Spaaij, Jonathan Magee and Ruth Jeanes

Routledge
Taylor & Francis Group

LONDON AND NEW YORK

This edition first published 2014
by Routledge
2 Park Square, Milton Park, Abingdon, Oxon, OX14 4RN

and by Routledge
711 Third Avenue, New York, NY 10017

Routledge is an imprint of the Taylor & Francis Group, an informa business

British Library Cataloguing in Publication Data
A catalogue record for this book is available from the British Library

Library of Congress Cataloging-in-Publication Data
Sport, social exclusion and global society / edited by Ramón Spaaij,
Ruth Jeanes and Jonathan Magee.
pages cm
1. Sports–Sociological aspects. 2. Social isolation. 3. Sports and
globalization. I. Spaaij, R. F. J. (Ramon F. J.) II. Jeanes, Ruth.
III. Magee, Jonathan.
GV706.5.S7366 2014
306.4'83–dc23
2013049211

ISBN13: 978-0-415-81490-4 (hbk)
ISBN13: 978-0-415-81491-1 (pbk)
ISBN13: 978-0-203-06658-4 (ebk)

Typeset in Baskerville
by Cenveo Publisher Services

Printed and bound by CPI Group (UK) Ltd, Croydon, CR0 4YY

To Lukas and Jonty

Contents

Figures

Abbreviations and acronyms

AFL	Australian Football League
BME	Black and minority ethnic
CALD	Culturally and linguistically diverse
CASE	Centre for Analysis of Social Exclusion
CCDS	Canadian Centre for Disability Studies
CCP	Central Communist Party
CCPR	Central Council for Physical Recreation
CDPF	China Disabled Persons' Federation
DCMS	Department of Culture, Media and Sport
ERASS	Exercise, Recreation and Sport Survey
EU	European Union
FAZ	Football Association of Zambia
GDP	Gross Domestic Product
HWC	Homeless World Cup
ICA	Instituto Companheiros das Américas
IDB	Inter-American Development Bank
MDG	Millennium Development Goals
MHU	Mental Health Unit
MUD	Moral underclass discourse
NHS	National Health Service
NGO	Non-Governmental Organization
NORAD	Norwegian Agency for Development Cooperation
NOWSPAR	National Organization for Women in Sport, Physical Activity and Recreation
OECD	Organization for Economic Co-operation and Development
PSE	Poverty and Social Exclusion
SEU	Social Exclusion Unit
SFD	Sport for development
SOE	State-owned enterprise
SPCSC	State Physical Culture and Sports Commission
SSP	Sport Steward Program
UK	United Kingdom
UN	United Nations

UN DESA	United Nations Department of Economic and Social Affairs
UNICEF	United Nations Children's Fund
UNOSDP	United Nations Office on Sport for Development and Peace
US	United States
WHO	World Health Organization

Acknowledgements

This book would not have been possible without the support and encouragement of our colleagues, students, friends and family. We are grateful to Simon Whitmore and his team at Routledge for their unwavering support and stewardship throughout this project. We owe a debt of gratitude to Dr Wendy Mee and students in the La Trobe Master of International Development where some of our theoretical ideas and considerations were first pitched and discussed. We are grateful to Mi Zhou, Amanda Vargas and Flavia Rocha Pedrosa for their outstanding research assistance for the Chinese and Brazilian case studies, respectively. We are also extremely grateful for the ongoing support provided by John Minten, Dean of School, Sport, Tourism and Outdoors, University of Central Lancashire (Uclan). Thank you also to colleagues in the Sport and Physical Activity Research Group at Monash University for their ongoing conversations and suggestions regarding the book. We thank Karen Farquharson, Sean Gorman and Dean Lusher for allowing us to draw on some of the findings from our collaborative research project 'Managing Diversity in Junior Sport' for one of the case studies. Our thanks also go to Maryann Martin, who once again provided expert editing services. Finally, we owe a debt of gratitude to the respondents in our various research projects that have shaped the empirical dimensions of the book. Without their contributions we would not have had a book, and we are thankful to these individuals for allowing us 'in' to their world and sharing their stories and experiences.

1 Introduction

Social exclusion is one of the most pressing challenges facing global society. Profound economic, social and political transformations have produced precariousness for all but the most privileged social groups (Bourdieu 1998; Bauman 2001, 2004). Social exclusion, it is argued, is a widespread and painfully felt feature of contemporary life conditions that encompasses economic, social, political and cultural dimensions (Bhalla and Lapeyre 2004), and is increasing in many parts of the world (UN DESA 2010).

In *The Exclusive Society*, criminologist Jock Young (1999) posits that the transition from modernity to late modernity entails a movement from an inclusive society of stability and homogeneity to an exclusive society of change and division. In his work, Young (1999: 7) argues that there has been a shift from 'a society whose accent was on assimilation and incorporation' to 'one that separates and excludes'. The implications of this transition are profound, in that it has transformed social exclusion into a seemingly permanent problem in which the world of the 'losers' is increasingly separated from that of the 'winners'. For Young, in late modernity social exclusion operates principally on three levels: that is, economic exclusion from the labour market, social exclusion practised among people in civil society, and the ever-expanding exclusionary activities of the criminal justice system.

The notion of social exclusion is thus seen to cover a remarkably wide range of social, economic and cultural issues that lie at the heart of politics (Sen 2000). And not just national or local politics, for at this point in the twenty-first century social exclusion cannot be fully understood without reference to its global context. According to the World Commission on the Social Dimension of Globalization (2004), globalizing processes exacerbate social inequality and its effects on people, families and local communities by dislocating traditional livelihoods and threatening environmental sustainability and cultural diversity. Although this particular interpretation of globalization is contested, such as by those who emphasize how agency and resistance mediate the relationship between globalization causes and outcomes (Guillén 2001), few observers would dispute that social exclusion has global drivers and manifestations rather than being a restricted local or national problem, even if its impact is felt most severely at a local level.

In the face of this global challenge, sport may be perceived as a rather trivial and peripheral activity. Yet the role that sport plays, or can play, in promoting social inclusion is increasingly embraced in international policy and research (European Commission 2007; Bailey 2008; Kelly 2011). National and supranational government policies have driven to an extent the emphasis on sport as a tool for addressing social exclusion. Sport has been advocated as a vehicle for a range of broader social objectives, including the empowerment of marginalized young people, neighbourhood renewal, social integration and community cohesion (Keim 2003; Coalter 2007; Spaaij 2013b). It also penetrates international development, especially in the areas of conflict resolution and health promotion (Levermore and Beacom 2009). It has been argued that the social benefits of sport extend to spheres that are 'hard to reach' through more traditional political, social and aid activities (e.g. Football Task Force 1999; Bailey 2008). As a consequence, sports programs targeting social exclusion are now widespread in both the Global North and the Global South.[1] These efforts highlight a 'will for inclusion' based on an enduring and omnipotent belief in sport's inherent worthiness and public value (Macdonald *et al.* 2012: 9).

Sports metaphors, with their language of a level playing field, fair play, winners and losers, first past the post, and getting to first base, have informed many a discussion about the economy, wealth distribution and equity. For example, in referring to international trading practices in his 2012 State of the Union Address, US President Barack Obama claims that 'if the playing field is level, I promise you: America will always win'. And in 1993 his predecessor Bill Clinton refers to his country's economic strategy as one of 'expanding markets abroad and providing a level playing field for American workers to compete and win in the global economy'.

While advocates of meritocracy refer to sport as an exemplar of how economic and symbolic rewards are – and ought to be – distributed according to individual merit, social activists draw upon sports metaphors to formulate alternative visions of a fair society. For example, the non-governmental organization (NGO) Caritas Aotearoa New Zealand (2011) states that for those on the losing side of a competitive society, it often feels as if the world is anything but a level playing field: 'Many people living in poverty feel that the rules themselves are unfair, judged by referees biased by a hostile crowd, in an environment where they cannot possibly succeed, let alone win' (Caritas Aotearoa New Zealand 2011: 7). Whereas in sport we expect that there are agreed upon rules and unbiased referees who enforce those rules, in broader society elites are often determined to be their own referees and consolidate the individual or collective gains made. In a similar vein, sociologist Pierre Bourdieu (2000: 215) argues that the meritocratic ideal of a level playing field is illusory: 'Those who talk of equality of opportunity forget that social games … are not "fair games." Without being, strictly speaking, rigged, the competition resembles a handicap race that has lasted for generations.'

However, even in sport itself the existence of a level playing field is a utopia (Kell 2000; Eitzen 2006). In a sense, sport is part of the problem, as it can serve not only as an agent of social inclusion but also to differentiate, marginalize and exclude (Elling and Knoppers 2005; Anderson 2010). Indeed, by its very nature organized competitive sport performs or at least condones the exclusion of some through its emphasis on performance and winning, and (over-)conformity to the norms of the sport ethos (Donnelly and Coakley 2002). Exclusionary processes in sports-related policies and practices are multiple and diverse, embedded as they are in existing ethnocentric, patriarchal and heteronormative systems (Marjoribanks and Farquharson 2012; Dagkas and Armour 2012). They range from explicit and active mechanisms such as institutional racism and gender-based violence to more subtle forms of exclusion associated with unequal power relations along the intersections of class, race, ethnicity, gender, sexuality, age, religion, (dis)ability and geography. While direct and manifest exclusion may have become less common in sport, the hidden, entrenched cultural processes that affect the extent to which people have access to and feel welcome and connected with a sport organization or sporting group remain as powerful as ever (Elling 2002, 2007; Lake 2013). And while in certain respects (e.g. access to sport participation opportunities) the playing field may be levelling in sport, in other ways the reverse appears to be true as expectations of growing access, opportunity and equity remain at variance with reality.

Social exclusion can occur or be challenged at any level of sporting competition, from the foundation/participation levels through to the performance/excellence levels. These different levels are visualized in the sports development continuum (Scottish Sports Council 1988) in Figure 1.1. Enoch (2010: 46) describes this continuum as 'a logical progression from learning the basic skills at foundation level to performing as an elite performer at the excellence level'. The continuum suggests that elite competitive sport is as much part of 'sport for all' (i.e. the promotion of access to sport) as the provision of community opportunities for participation (Houlihan and White 2002). As such, the continuum seeks to reconcile some of the historical tension between those promoting elite sport and those promoting grassroots participation by suggesting that these dual goals are inextricably interdependent (Bloyce and Smith 2010).

The sports development continuum depicted in Figure 1.1 is instructive for conceptualizing the relationship between sport and social exclusion. Research on sport and social exclusion, including our own, has predominantly focused on the foundation and participation end of the continuum, while scholarly attention on social exclusion at the performance/excellence end has been scant. However, the research that does exist in the latter area confirms the significance of exclusionary mechanisms in high-performance sport. Collins and Buller (2003) show that high-performance sports programs do not cater equally for all sections of the community; rather, they are mediated by social stratification, which provides a filter for who gets in at the beginning of the talent selection process. Young people with a lower socio-economic status, in

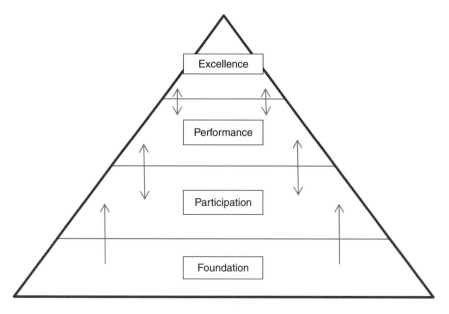

Figure 1.1 The sports development continuum.

particular, are often not being provided with equal opportunities to perform at the highest level. Hence, Kay (2000: 166) concludes that 'from the humblest levels of mass participation through to the pinnacles of performance, participation profiles are skewed away from the less privileged sectors of our society'.

Advancing the research landscape

This book critically examines the relationship between sport and social exclusion from both global and cross-cultural perspectives. In so doing, it seeks to contribute to scholarly debate on the interactions, processes and contexts that drive or alleviate social exclusion in relation to sport. While important pioneering work has been carried out on sport and social exclusion (e.g. Collins with Kay 2003), we contend that such research favours a particular focus on policy processes and relies heavily on secondary material.[2] A key aim of this book, then, is to advance intellectual and policy understanding of more subjective, 'lived' aspects of social exclusion in and through sport. It does so by providing first-hand empirical research and critical insights into the real-world experiences of participants and practitioners. In particular, the book gives recognition and voice to individuals and communities that are frequently ignored within research in this field through in-depth, empirically grounded examinations of diverse population groups' lived experiences, and the social mechanisms that affect those experiences at micro, meso and macro levels. We argue that this approach is a particular strength of the book as it advances previous research into sport and social exclusion in an innovative and distinctive way.

Further, we aim to transcend the narrow parameters of the nationally focused body of research into sport and social exclusion. This, we believe, requires more than merely bridging different geopolitical areas through the incorporation of research data from multiple and diverse parts of the world. It requires, first and foremost, a particular theoretical-analytical 'mindset', one that engages dialogically with alternative ideas and perspectives on social exclusion that challenge or complement the dominant Eurocentric approaches. The purpose of this task is to acknowledge and give voice to the diverse meanings that the term 'social exclusion' has in different global regions, as well as to uncover and formulate any possible North–South linkages (Mosley and Dowler 2003) in thinking about and directing action towards social exclusion. Our commitment to synthesizing and applying ideas and experiences from the Global South as part of the dialogue of theory development is based on the belief that social theory from the world periphery has power and relevance for understanding our changing world (Connell 2007).

The book draws on literature and case studies from across the Global South and the Global North – not equally or exhaustively, but fairly broadly, with these materials used to substantiate and illustrate the arguments made. The resulting analysis is attentive to thinking and experiences from the Global South and enables us to reflect on our theoretical and empirical bias towards the Global North. While a globally inclusive approach of this kind is still in its infancy in the sociology of sport, its potential is convincingly demonstrated in Palmer's (2013) account of global sports policy, Kay's (2009, 2012b) work on sport in international development contexts, and Spaaij's (2011) analysis of social mobility.

We admit, however, that we have only been partially successful in this effort. As noted in Chapter 2, this is largely a reflection of the relatively widespread uptake of the notion of social exclusion in Global North research, policy and practice over the past two decades, relative to its Global South equivalents. This is particularly the case in relation to sport. Moreover, as we discuss below, while a significant proportion of our recent research has been undertaken in Global South communities, other case studies discussed in this book were carried out in the countries where we have lived and worked for most of our academic careers – that is, the United Kingdom (UK), the Netherlands and Australia. Thus, while our analysis signifies an important step forward in extending intellectual and policy debates about sport and social exclusion, we also believe that more work is needed to enable a truly globally inclusive understanding of sport and social exclusion.

Key questions

Our exploration of the relationship between sport and social exclusion in global society is guided by three key questions that are pertinent to all levels of sport. First, *how does social exclusion affect sport participation and non-participation?* This question addresses the effects of social exclusion and disadvantage on one's ability to participate in sport and the nature of participation. To answer this question, it is necessary to take into account issues of access and opportunity as well as the structural and cultural conditions of sport activities or programs that may promote or inhibit social inclusion (Donnelly and Coakley 2002). However, as will be seen, non-participation does not equal social exclusion, as this occurs when people want to participate but cannot. After all, not everyone wishes to participate in sport. Most sports activities are those of choice, and participation is voluntary with the exception of compulsory physical education in schools. Hence, people may choose not to take part in sport for a variety of reasons including disinterest (Collins with Kay 2003). Given this, voluntary exclusion from sport may be a problem only when it has negative externalities, an argument we explore in Chapter 2.

The second overarching question that this book addresses is *how social exclusion is (re)produced, experienced, resisted and managed in sport.* This question is principally concerned with the processes and mechanisms of exclusion/inclusion that operate within sporting environments. Just as non-participation does not equal exclusion, so participation does not equal inclusion. Rather than merely reflecting existing inequalities, sport, via social agents' interactions with sports spaces, is actively involved in producing and sustaining inequalities and exclusions (Dashper and Fletcher 2013). Thus, sport can reinforce or exacerbate social exclusion through practices of differentiation and inferiorization (Elling 2002; Elling and Knoppers 2005). It is pivotal in this regard to explore the intersections between different markers of individual and group identity such as gender, age, race/ethnicity, class and ability, and how social exclusion can be compounded within sport as a result of such intersectionalities. At the same time, the active negotiation of sports spaces by players and other social agents, and its potential for resistance and subversion, also need to be taken seriously.

The third question that guides our analysis is *how sport is used to combat social exclusion and promote social inclusion in other life domains.* The focus here is on sport as a policy tool for addressing social exclusion in different global regions. The role that sport can play in combating social exclusion is embraced in international policy and research, yet concerns persist about the lack of robust evidence (Coalter 2007; Tacon 2007) and the potentially fatal flaws of sport as a social development tool (Darnell 2007, 2012; Spaaij and Jeanes 2013). We know that sport does not automatically contribute to transcending or breaking down the walls of exclusion, and that it can also strengthen the very social divisions that it is expected to bridge. Sport arguably presents a false front that traps the most severely excluded into a false consciousness in which they believe sport to be a ticket to a better life (Anderson 2010). From this perspective, sport is 'a sedative, a stultifying force' rather than a transformative practice (Carrington 1986: 16). In this book, we critically examine these issues as they are being played out in different global regions.

These three questions thus capture different aspects of the relationship between sport and social exclusion. The first looks specifically at the factors and processes affecting an individual's ability to participate in sport, the second at what happens to those who do enter the playing field, and the third at the wider social objectives which sports policies and programs aim to achieve. As this book will show, these issues are often closely intertwined in practice and need to be considered as different pieces of the same puzzle.

In order to address the aforementioned questions, this book draws intensively on more than a decade of research by its authors in the Global North and Global South. This research comprises a range of individual and collaborative projects that address one or more aspects of the relationship between sport and social exclusion. Here, our diverse research endeavours are brought together to present a number of case studies that have developed from our broader research platforms. While our own research (discussed in more detail below) primarily addresses social exclusion at the foundation and participation end of the sports development continuum (Figure 1.1), we recognize that exclusionary processes can be found at any level of sporting competition, and that the different levels are often interdependent in terms of the experiences, causes and consequences of social exclusion.

The case studies discussed in this book are part of a broader data set that was obtained through qualitative research methods and, occasionally, mixed methods research. The predominance of qualitative methods reflects the nature of the research objectives and questions that have driven our research endeavours, our personal expertise and training as researchers, and our own research paradigms. The bulk of our research has sought to capture the voices, experiences and meaning-making processes of the people being studied. Qualitative research strategies are particularly appropriate for obtaining this kind of knowledge. However, in some research projects we opted for a mixed methods design that involved the integration of qualitative and quantitative approaches where this was considered the most suitable methodology to achieve the objectives of the research.

Overview

In Chapter 2 we discuss the key issues and debates in the social exclusion literature to conceptualize social exclusion. Competing interpretations of social exclusion are explored and synthesized. Importantly, we contend that social exclusion is a multidimensional (set of) process(es) that is broader than merely poverty and material deprivation. In so doing, we challenge the view that material deprivation is the core of social exclusion, a long-held view in the sociology of sport. Thus, this view needs expanding to consider the fluidity and complexity of social exclusion beyond poverty – something that is core to the approach offered in this book. This approach situates social exclusion in its global context, and provides the conceptual backbone for our empirically grounded analysis of sport and social exclusion.

Following this conceptual discussion of social exclusion, Chapter 3 examines how sport and social exclusion are portrayed and addressed in public policy. The chapter has a particular emphasis on the intersections between social policy and sport policy, and as such provides a comparative analysis of three countries: the UK, Zambia and China. In Chapter 3 we highlight some of the diversities and complexities that become apparent when the intertwining of sport and social exclusion policy is considered beyond the narrow confines of the UK where the bulk of research in this area has been conducted.

Chapter 4 examines how sport excludes or marginalizes particular groups and individuals. It outlines some of the key mechanisms of social exclusion that operate within sports environments in the Global North and Global South before turning to a more detailed analysis of how these mechanisms play out in practice via a case study of sport, gender and social exclusion in Zambia. The research discussed in this case study consists of in-depth interviews with 14 female players aged between 14 and 27. Both gender and poverty have shaped the young women's engagement with sport. The women had played football for a period ranging from one to 12 years and three had participated at elite level. The research focused on exploring the lived experiences these women had of their participation in football. For the purpose of the case study we focus on data that elicited the challenges and barriers the women faced in relation to their sport participation.

Following on from the examination of mechanisms of social exclusion in sport, Chapter 5 shifts attention to the ways in which sport has acted as a domain for combating social exclusion in other life domains. Chapter 5 focuses on sport as a policy tool for addressing social exclusion in the Global North. We draw upon our research in two specific areas – mental health and worklessness – to critically examine the nature, benefits and limitations of the use of sport in these varying contexts. The first case study uses in-depth interviews to examine participants' and staff members' experiences of an ongoing sport program that was part of a broader mental health rehabilitation initiative in the UK (Magee and Jeanes 2010). Research data were collected from participants (males in their 20s or early 30s), medical staff and staff members who organized the sports activities. The second case study combined quantitative and qualitative research methods to assess the extent to and ways in which the Sport Steward Program (now City Steward Program) in Rotterdam, the Netherlands, affected the labour market attachment of participating youth (Spaaij 2009a, 2011). Our critical reflections on this case study are also informed by our evaluation of a similar program in the UK that sought to support workless young people in re-engaging with education and employment. That evaluation utilized interviews with young people, program managers, coaches and education officers to gain a holistic understanding of the experiences of those involved in the program (Spaaij *et al.* 2013).

This analysis of sport as a policy tool for addressing social exclusion is extended in Chapter 6 through an analysis of 'sport for development' (SFD), which enables us to identify parallels between the ways in which sport is used in the Global North and the Global South. The two case studies that are presented in the chapter build on primary data collected by the authors in Zambia and Brazil, respectively, to scrutinize the role of sport in achieving complex development objectives and to draw attention to the broader social processes and contexts that affect what is or is not achievable in SFD, including the influence of global drivers of social exclusion as a structuring context for local experiences. One of the main SFD initiatives studied in Brazil involved the Vencer ('To Win') program, a program aimed at improving the skills and employability prospects of disadvantaged young people. The study combined different research methods, including participant observation, semi-structured interviews and surveys (Spaaij 2012a). In Zambia, the programs under study focused on using sport as a context in which to educate young people about HIV/AIDS (Jeanes 2013). This research utilized interviews with NGO staff, young participants, peer leaders and community stakeholders in SFD programs within specific local contexts, based on our recognition that such programs are clearly not homogeneous across space and time. Thus, when considering how sport is used to combat social exclusion, we do so with an understanding of how specific initiatives are currently operationalized within particular communities in the Global South.

The process of engaging socially excluded individuals to participate in sport activities is analysed in Chapter 7. The chapter identifies how the UK social inclusion agenda has redefined the role of coaches in community sport. This development is explored through a case study of the experiences of one of the authors (Magee) as a community coach on a football program for homeless young men. Here, the relationship-building process between the coach and these individuals is central. Part of a broader data set concerning the uses and challenges of sports activities as a vehicle for improving the lives of vulnerable homeless individuals (Magee 2010, 2011; Magee and Jeanes 2013), this case study finds that sports coaches would benefit from learning from other fields and disciplines. Further, critical pedagogy is proffered as an approach that can enable sport programs, and the coaches working on them, to move beyond the goal of merely (re-)engaging participants and instead facilitate social change by collaboratively developing critical and reflective capacities.

Drawing on primary research data and evidence of good practice, Chapter 8 discusses the ways in which sports communities can be made more inclusive for all persons involved. Specific case studies include a discussion of how a bottom-up community development approach has been valuable in creating inclusive active recreation spaces for young people with disabilities, and how some sports clubs have effectively developed opportunities that appeal to people from culturally and linguistically diverse (CALD) backgrounds. The former case study builds on our research into the multilayered aspects of social exclusion experienced by young people with disabilities and their families when attempting to participate in casual active leisure and sports opportunities, and places particular emphasis on how young people with a range of disabilities can be supported in articulating their views and experiences (Jeanes 2011a; Jeanes and Magee 2011a, 2011b). The latter case study draws upon three years of ethnographic fieldwork that examined the sport involvement of people with CALD backgrounds in Australia (Spaaij 2011, 2012b, 2013a, in press). This research explored, *inter alia*, the barriers and facilitators to community sport participation as experienced by resettled refugees from the Horn of Africa. Our ongoing research into how diversity based on race/ethnicity, gender and disability is experienced and managed in community sport clubs in Australia also informs this case study (Spaaij *et al.* in press).

The final chapter draws together and critically reflects on the key issues and themes emerging from our analysis of sport and social exclusion in global society. The chapter proposes avenues for future research and considers how sport can be organized and provided more equitably to tackle individual and collective forms of social exclusion.

Notes

1 The terms 'Global North' and 'Global South' are used here to make transparent the continuing power inequalities between various regions of the world. Although not strictly accurate development markers (e.g. Australia and New Zealand), their use highlights differences in economic and social growth (English 2005; Kay and Spaaij 2012). The terms are further discussed in Chapter 2.
2 A notable exception is the work of Agnes Elling (for example, Elling 2002, 2007).

2 Social exclusion in the global age

Introduction

While the term 'social exclusion' is commonly used by policy-makers, academics and media commentators, it means different things to different people. Any systematic analysis of sport and social exclusion, then, needs to clarify the meaning of the term and define its key features and properties. The chapter commences by offering a concise history of the term from its modern roots in France to its contemporary usage in a range of policy contexts and academic fields. We then consider the definition and key features of social exclusion and discuss how it differs from and intersects with related notions of poverty and disadvantage. Following this discussion, we examine the multiple dimensions of social exclusion and the different spatial levels at which they operate, and critically scrutinize the applicability of the concept of social exclusion as a Global North construct to social realities in the Global South. The final part of the chapter outlines how the concept is used in this book. In brief, we conceptualize social exclusion as a process that negatively affects the rights, recognition and/or resources of targets of social exclusion and/or their opportunity to participate in key activities in different societal domains.

In this book, the conceptualization of social exclusion presented in this chapter is applied to sport. The relationship between sport and social exclusion is pertinent both from a policy or social action perspective and as a field of academic inquiry, as sport offers a compelling lens through which to analyse the causes, mechanisms and consequences of social exclusion as well as ways in which these can be tackled. It is within this context that the present book is situated. Critically, sport is not merely a mirror or metric of broader social processes – that is, a microcosm of society (Eitzen 2011) – but also very much part of the processes that shape society's fundamental social, cultural, ethical and political issues. For example, sport is an important setting for socialization, psychosocial development and self-expression where people learn, negotiate and challenge social norms and identities. Hence, sport provides opportunities to examine the complexities of social, cultural and economic life in local, national and global contexts and, as such, can further our understanding of the nature and effects of social exclusion in broader areas.

Sport constitutes a contested set of relational processes that involve critical issues of power and privilege within particular societal contexts at particular times (Sugden and Tomlinson 2002; Marjoribanks and Farquharson 2012). Our main focus here is on the way sport intertwines with social, political, economic, cultural and organizational forces that reproduce, exacerbate or diminish social divisions and inequalities. *Pace* Bourdieu (1978) and Pociello (1995), we consider sport as a relatively autonomous institution (or field) that has its own dynamics, rule-making and history, and which reflects and legitimates broader social inequalities. At the same time, however, the realm of sport is highly interdependent and cannot be fully understood in isolation from other social spheres such as the economic, political, social and cultural arenas discussed in this chapter. With this in mind, we now turn our attention to the concept of social exclusion.

Social exclusion: a concise history of a concept

It may seem relatively simplistic and somewhat misleading to consider social exclusion as the opposite of social inclusion, but the significance of this first step cannot be downplayed. The sense of belonging to, participating in, contributing to and accessing societal activities encompasses the notion of '*in*clusion' as opposed to '*ex*clusion' and 'feelings of being shut out … from any of the social, economic, political and cultural systems which determine the social integration of a person in society' (Walker and Walker 1997: 8). The intuitive core of the idea of social exclusion is that every member of society should be able to participate fully in it. The social ideal it expresses is one of common membership, where no one is denied access to activities and practices that are central in societal life (Gray 2000).

Unfortunately, the notion of social inclusion is no less complex and contentious than that of social exclusion (Askonas and Stewart 2000; Goodin 1996), and raises important questions such as: 'Inclusion into what?' 'On whose terms?' 'In whose interests?' As will be shown in this chapter, the relationship between social exclusion and inclusion is complex and contested. We know that not being excluded does not necessarily mean a person or group is included (Taket *et al.* 2009). Likewise, social inclusion does not necessarily imply common membership or social connectedness, which refers to the personal relationships people have with others in the community.

In order to understand how the term 'social exclusion' is employed in specific contexts, including sport, we need not only to distinguish between its utility as an academic explanatory concept and its political deployment to justify certain forms of policy intervention (Arthurson and Jacobs 2004), but also to identify the linkages between the two. Our first step in this process is a brief excursion into the historical roots of social exclusion in the social sciences and humanities as well as in a policy context.

The term 'social exclusion' relates to familiar concepts such as poverty, disadvantage, marginalization and social closure. The idea that the theme of exclusion conveys can be found in a variety of classic works, such as Aristotle's (1908) *Nicomachean Ethics*. Within sociology these include the works of Durkheim (1895), Weber (1978), Merton (1938), Simmel (1955), Goffman (1963), Becker (1963), Lemert (1967), Jahoda, Lazarsfeld and Zeisel (1971) and many others. Notwithstanding this historical continuity, it is indisputable that the contemporary usage of the term 'social exclusion' originated in France in the 1970s, where it referred to the idea of the rupturing of the social bond. The stranglehold of post-World War Two austerity had taken a firm grip on many Western European nation states as they struggled to re-establish themselves; nevertheless, by the 1960s economic fortunes were on the rise. Post-war, the French welfare state was characterized by a social insurance model that predominantly provided occupational solidarity and offered earnings-related benefits to the vast majority of the working population (Béland 2007). At the same time, social assistance programs granting genuine social rights existed to help those excluded from the labour market. It was in relation to the latter that the term 'social exclusion' emerged in French social policy and academic discourse (Béland 2007). By the 1970s, however, France's economic fortunes were in decline. High unemployment rates were seen to threaten the social fabric of the nation, and greater attention was focused on those considered to be socially excluded.

Underpinned by the French tradition of national integration and social solidarity, and specifically by the social thought associated with Durkheim (1895), René Lenoir, Secretary of State for Social Action in the Republican Government of Prime Minister Jacques Chirac (1974–76), published *Les exclus: un Français sur dix* in 1974. In this work, Lenoir focuses on societal and moral deterioration, especially with regard to unemployment as a major source of social exclusion. Social exclusion, he asserts, threatens society as a whole due to the loss of collective values and the destruction of the social fabric that binds its citizens (Taket *et al.* 2009). Lenoir's thinking was based on the idea that the French social contract does not leave individuals to fend for themselves; rather, society owes its members the means to a livelihood and, in turn, members have obligations to the larger society (Silver and Miller 2003). Lenoir (1974) identifies 'the excluded' in France as an eclectic mix of the uninsured, unemployed, people with intellectual or physical disabilities, the mentally ill, substance abusers, delinquents, single parents and other persons considered deviant. While Lenoir's publication illustrates how the notion of social exclusion is seen to cover a remarkably wide range of social issues, over time, the term has broadened even further to cover other groups perceived as excluded in one way or another (Taket *et al.* 2009).

Despite the specificities of the political and social context within which the term 'social exclusion' first emerged, it diffused rapidly throughout Europe, mainly under the patronage of the European Union (EU). By the early 1990s, the term had become a substitute for that of 'poverty' within EU policy programs. This was a significant shift, with the EU pursuing the objective of 'social action' from 1974 to 1994 through three poverty programs, which ended after the UK and Germany withdrew their support (Silver 2010). According to Silver and Miller (2003), the third EU poverty program gradually transformed into a fight against social exclusion, with long-term unemployment as the main focus. This discursive emphasis on social exclusion has continued ever since, as reflected for example in the EU's 2004–2010 Disability Action Plan, the 2007 European Year of Equal Opportunities for All, and the European Year for Combating Poverty and Social Exclusion in 2010.

The adoption of the term 'social exclusion' among politicians, policy-makers and academics in the UK is somewhat remarkable considering that, in the French usage of the term, it sits uneasily with the Anglo-American focus on poverty (Silver 1994). However, it should be remembered that the concept of poverty is itself contested (Alcock 1997) and that, in some accounts, poverty is defined in relative terms that strongly resonate with the notion of social exclusion in the French tradition. An example is Townsend's (1979: 60) influential interpretation of poverty as a lack of resources and participation in 'the activities ... which are customary, or at least widely encouraged or approved, in the societies to which [the poor] belong'.

It was the New Labour government of Tony Blair that in 1997 heralded a new era for social exclusion in UK policy discourse. That same year, New Labour established the Social Exclusion Unit (SEU), which assumed responsibility for the development of 'integrated and sustainable approaches to the problems of the worst housing estates, including crime, drugs, unemployment, community breakdown, and bad schools etc.' (Social Exclusion Unit 1998: 2). The SEU was initially concerned with the less severe forms of exclusion affecting large portions of the population; however, it increasingly focused on so-called 'deep exclusion', that is, the most entrenched, durable, and multidimensional manifestations of disadvantage (Silver 2010). Social exclusion was thus central to New Labour's social policy agenda. As Chapter 3 shows, respective policies in the UK focused on the use of sport for wider social purposes, delivering social policy through sport based on the firm belief that sport had the potential to combat various social ills (Collins with Kay 2003; Blackshaw and Long 2005; Coalter 2007). Consequently, substantial amounts of funding were released for programs that used sport to promote the wider policy agenda of addressing social exclusion.

In 2005, the SEU was closed and in 2007 Tony Blair left office, leaving a legacy of 'joined-up strategies to combat concentrations of social exclusion' (Collins 2010: 26). However, these strategies were downgraded as government attention was redistributed. The election of the Conservative-Liberal Democrat Coalition government in 2010 ultimately sealed the fate of the use of the term 'social exclusion' at a policy level in the UK. Under the Conservative-Liberal Democrat Coalition government, the rhetoric has shifted to the notions of 'active community' and 'active citizenship'. Indeed, UK policy discourse has applied the emotive terms 'moral underclass' and 'feral underclass' to those citizens who are seen to lack character and personal responsibility for their own inclusion, such as those who participated in the 2011 civil disturbances in cities and towns across the UK.

The diffusion of the term 'social exclusion' has not been restricted to Europe. In Australia, it is now a key buzz term in national and state policy discourse. Basing itself on the model of the British SEU, the South Australian government in 2002 launched the Social Inclusion Initiative, opting for the term 'inclusion' rather than 'exclusion' to promote its focus on developing holistic and innovative solutions to social exclusion as a way to assist the most disadvantaged members of the community (Silver 2010). This policy transfer was facilitated by Australia's long-standing policy affinities with the liberal Anglo-American welfare regimes, and with the Australian Labor Party's Social Inclusion Agenda that built explicitly on Britain's New Labour's approach, while adding some specific emphases (Silver 2010).

In 2007, the newly elected federal government led by Labor Prime Minister Kevin Rudd followed the South Australian example by establishing a Social Inclusion Board and a Social Inclusion Unit within the Department of the Prime Minister and Cabinet. Headed by future Prime Minister Julia Gillard as the then Minister for Social Inclusion, a list of indicators was developed to measure and evaluate progress on social inclusion, such as housing affordability, access to services and homelessness. The objective of this policy has been to create a 'stronger, fairer Australia ... [where all] participate fully in the nation's economic and community life, develop their own potential and be treated with dignity' (Australian Government 2009: 2). Its strategic focus centres on unemployment, workless households, homelessness, child poverty, mental illness and Indigenous disadvantage population.

Overall, the Australian situation is one where the term 'social exclusion' arrived relatively late, and with some distinctive features (Silver 2010; Hayes *et al.* 2008). However, with the election of Julia Gillard as Prime Minister in 2010, the quest for social inclusion in Australia arguably took a more central position on the political stage to make up for its late arrival and relative lack of progress when compared to Europe. Reflecting this development, social exclusion is now also a significant area of academic and policy research in Australia (e.g. Saunders 2003, 2008; Smyth 2010). Yet, the political currency of the notion of social inclusion/exclusion remains fragile in Australia. In one of its first post-election actions, in September 2013 the newly elected Coalition government disbanded the Social Inclusion Board.

The notion of social exclusion has also diffused to the Global South. As noted in Chapter 1, the terms 'Global North' and 'Global South' are used here to make transparent the continuing power inequalities between various regions of the world. The Global South can be seen to comprise the nations of Africa, Central and Latin America, and most of Asia; as such, it includes more than half of the recognized states in the world. Still, the terms 'Global North' and 'Global South' are not strictly accurate development markers as they conceal the myriad geographies and internal diversity of the Global South (consider, for example, the stark contrasts between China and Zambia, as discussed in Chapter 3). Further, Australia and New Zealand are obvious deviations from the geographical categorization of North and South (Rigg 2007). However, their usage in this book highlights persisting differences in economic and social growth and the distribution of wealth (English 2005). It also serves to emphasize that both North and South are, together, drawn into global processes. The Global North and Global South consist of social worlds that while closely interconnected are constituted differently. Hence, they are not two discrete, internally bounded worlds facing each other (Tucker 1999).

The diffusion of the term 'social exclusion' to the Global South was driven primarily by international development agencies and supranational government institutions (Rodgers 1995; Gore and Figueiredo 1997). The notion of social exclusion has been particularly influential in Latin America as an extension of the study of poverty and marginalization, and it has also been taken up, albeit to a lesser degree, in Sub-Saharan Africa and South East Asia. Nonetheless, alternative concepts, notably poverty and vulnerability, are still more widely embraced in at least some parts of the Global South (Popay *et al.* 2008). One reason for this is that the direct application of the notion of social exclusion as formulated in the Global North to problems of poverty and exclusion experienced in the Global South has a number of pitfalls (Hashem 1995). At the same time, however, there are also conceptual connections between these separate debates and across geographical boundaries between North and South (O'Brien *et al.* 1997). These pitfalls and possible connections are discussed in depth further on in this chapter.

From the preceding discussion it is clear that social exclusion has diverse intellectual roots with different meanings in different nations across different times. This context specificity should be kept in mind when evaluating the myriad definitions of social exclusion that have been developed and applied in academic research in different global regions. It is to these definitions that we now turn.

Defining social exclusion

Social exclusion is difficult to define. Its meaning and measurement are contested among scholars: for example, whether it should be viewed as a state or a process, as a cause or an effect. However, most scholars would agree that in a broad sense social exclusion refers to a lack of participation in societal activities. Schuyt (2006: 69) describes social exclusion as 'not being allowed to participate; not being able to participate; not (or no longer) wanting to participate'.

The conceptual vagueness of social exclusion can be illustrated by the diverging definitions and frameworks that scholars have proposed in the past two decades. The influential definition of social exclusion proposed by researchers at the London School of Economics Centre for Analysis of Social Exclusion (CASE) provides a useful starting point for discussion: 'An individual is socially excluded if he or she does not participate in key activities of the society in which he or she lives' (Burchardt *et al.* 2002: 30). The focus in this definition is on the individual as the primary unit of analysis and on the state or condition of being excluded rather than on exclusion as a process. This definition posits a rigid dichotomy: a person is either included or excluded. In contrast, as will be seen below, many scholars now view social exclusion as a more fluid picture of people along a continuum of exclusion, rather than a clear division between those who are 'in' and 'out'. Burchardt *et al.* (2002: 31) admit that social exclusion 'is clearly a matter of degree' and that, strictly speaking, their definition should refer to being 'socially excluded to a greater degree' and 'the less the extent of participation'.

The CASE definition has also been criticized for not paying adequate attention to agency in the exclusion process – the idea that people are excluded by the acts of others or through choices of their own. Thus, it is not non-participation itself that constitutes social exclusion, but rather the lack of the *opportunity* to participate in activities that people have reason to value (Saunders 2008). Indeed, an earlier CASE definition explicitly addressed the issue of (lack of) agency:

> An individual is socially excluded if (a) he or she is geographically resident in a society, (b) he or she cannot participate in the normal activities of citizens in that society, and (c) he or she would like to so participate, but is prevented from doing so by factors beyond his or her control.
>
> (Burchardt *et al.* 1999: 229)

An analytical distinction is made here between self-exclusion and enforced exclusion caused by external factors. It is questionable whether voluntary social exclusion is unjust or harmful given that it does not involve a lack of opportunity to participate, but instead arises from free choice (Barry 2002). However, a person's choice to exclude him/herself can arguably still be problematic if it threatens social solidarity, has negative externalities, or when it has negative consequences for the long-term future and wellbeing of the individual involved (Richardson and Le Grand 2002; Le Grand 2003). There is, however, another compelling reason why we ought to take self-exclusion seriously: apparent self-exclusion is often a function of restricted opportunities to participate or a response to the experience of discrimination or moral rejection (Schuyt 2000; Morgan *et al.* 2007). We therefore need to ask: what are the underlying social mechanisms that drive self-exclusion? This question is directly relevant to sport. While individuals may simply choose to absent themselves from sport commitments or from particular sports (Macdonald *et al.* 2012), research also shows that self-exclusion from sport often cannot be separated from available opportunities and experienced material or socio-normative barriers; for example, it can be a response to a perceived lack of opportunity or acceptance (Elling 2002, 2007).

Gated communities and other forms of residential segregation in large parts of the world are a striking example of how self-exclusion on the part of the powerful can have severe externalities both for those 'left behind' and for society as a whole. In his well-known account of the obstacles to societal participation faced by African Americans in the 1940s, Myrdal (1944) stresses the role of residential segregation in perpetuating racial inequality and social exclusion. Myrdal finds that residential segregation prevented African Americans from associating with other social groups in activities founded on common neighbourhood. It further permitted any prejudice on the part of public officials to be freely vented on African Americans without affecting other citizens. While urban fortresses have emerged in various forms for many different reasons, they seem to have similarly damaging effects on social solidarity, inequality and community cohesion (Blakely and Snyder 1997). For example, Atkinson and Flint (2004) characterize gated communities as 'havens of social withdrawal' that are used by the powerful to insulate against perceived risk and unwanted encounters. In Chapters 4 and 8 we examine how self-exclusion occurs within sports contexts. For example, we describe how minority ethnic sports participants may prefer to play in teams with persons of similar ethnic backgrounds because they feel more comfortable and secure within these spaces. While the majority of ethnic sports club personnel tend to perceive this as a personal choice, research shows the complex mechanisms of social exclusion that lead minority ethnic participants to feel like outsiders within such clubs in the first place (Bradbury 2011; Spaaij 2013a, in press).

Social exclusion as a dynamic process

This example of residential exclusion suggests that social exclusion is a process driven by power relations, an argument that has become quite widely accepted among scholars (e.g. Gough *et al.* 2006; Popay *et al.* 2008). Despite this, policy-oriented notions of social exclusion frequently focus on the state or condition of being excluded rather than on the processual dynamics of social exclusion. The UK government's definition of social exclusion is a case in point. It defines social exclusion as: 'a shorthand term for what can happen when people or areas suffer from a combination of linked problems, such as unemployment, poor skills, low incomes, poor housing, high crime, bad health and family breakdown' (Social Exclusion Unit 2001: 10).

This definition is problematic, however, because it makes no reference to the social mechanisms that create, condone or exacerbate the identified problems. A danger of defining social exclusion as a static condition is that it can be used to moralize about the excluded and blame the individual for their own plight, rather than exposing structural and socio-normative processes largely outside the control of the individual. It thus has the potential to further stig-matize the excluded. In this context, Gough *et al.* (2006: 4) make the impor-tant point that the term 'social exclusion' may suggest that individuals are responsible for integrating themselves into a society that is itself fundamen-tally sound, whereas, in reality, 'it is precisely normal society which creates social exclusion'. A fundamental concern here is that social inclusion policies typically seek to adapt socially excluded people to the needs of prescribed mainstream institutions of society, rather than to regulate or change these institutions to accommodate the needs of those experiencing social exclusion (Labonte 2004). An example of this, discussed in Chapter 3, is disability sport in China. While the Chinese state increasingly recognizes the disadvantage and stigma experienced by many people with disabilities, its disability sport policy tends to place the responsibility for social inclusion on the shoulders of individuals with disabilities themselves, rather than tackle the structural and socio-normative barriers to social inclusion that these individuals face.

Indeed, one school of thought views individuals' behaviour, character and welfare dependency as the primary cause of social exclusion. The classic example of this position is Charles Murray's (1982, 1996) underclass thesis. Notwithstanding the fierce criticism that Murray's position has attracted (Murray 1996), it has inspired Conservative political leaders in several countries in the Global North. Murray's viewpoint features prominently in the moral underclass discourse (MUD) that has influenced political and policy debate in the UK and the US (Levitas 2005). Hence, MUD shifts the focus from the structural basis of poverty and exclusion to the moral character and behaviour of the excluded themselves. This discourse presents those experiencing social exclusion as culturally distinct from the 'mainstream' and emphasizes their lack of morals or character (Levitas 2005). This discourse also operates in sport, with many sports programs aimed at addressing social exclusion based on the belief that the targeted participants have deficits. Rather than being defined in terms of the need for social justice or empowering young people to be effective agents of social change in their communities, such programs typically define positive development in terms of providing socialization experiences that compensate for what is lacking or missing in the lives of disadvantaged young people (Coakley 2011).

Examples of this viewpoint abound more broadly. In September 2012, the then US presidential candidate Mitt Romney told a private gathering of donors that 47 per cent of American voters have an entitlement mentality and do not take personal responsibility for their plight. These citizens, argued Romney, believe that they are victims and that government has a responsibility to care for them in terms of healthcare, subsistence, housing, and so on (Mother Jones 2012). Another recent example of a moral underclass discourse relates to the civil disturbances that occurred in towns and cities across England in August 2011. Prime Minister David Cameron rejected any attempt by those implicated in the civil disturbances to justify their behaviour by blaming it on something other than their own criminality, by arguing for 'pockets of our society that are not just broken but, frankly, sick' (Eaton 2011). He identified the 'root cause' of the disturbances as being:

> ... a complete lack of responsibility in parts of our society, people allowed to feel the world owes them something, that their rights outweigh their responsibilities and their actions do not have consequences ...

Restoring a stronger sense of responsibility across our society in every town, in every street, in every estate is something I am determined to do.

(Eaton 2011)

From this viewpoint, there are no social or political grievances that can legitimate the types of behaviour displayed during the civil disturbances. Other commentators have instead sought to draw attention to the complex and multiple underlying causes of the disturbances. For example, the Riots Communities and Victims Panel (2012) points to the low aspirations of young people implicated in the disturbances, with many young people speaking of a lack of hopes and dreams for the future due to the absence of employment opportunities. The Panel also notes the widespread distrust and antipathy towards the police as a driving force behind the disturbances. However, in similar terms to Prime Minister David Cameron, the Panel stresses the lack of shared values and a sense of personal responsibility, and that the disturbances could ultimately be ascribed to a lack of character on the part of the perpetrators. The Panel recommends a new approach to building character, in which schools and parents should take a lead role by instilling character in children and young people so that they make the right choices in life. However, the need to reduce social inequality and its effect on many, particularly young men, remains underemphasized in this and many other accounts of the disturbances (Eaton 2011).

Whereas the MUD tends to be narrowly focused on a lack of personal responsibility as the principal cause of social exclusion, a particular strength of the concept of social exclusion is its concern with the processes and actions by which people are excluded (Rodgers 1995; De Haan 1998). Many scholars who use the language of social exclusion consider the dynamic analysis that it encourages to be a major step forward. Its processual character is emphasized, for example, in the European Foundation's (1995) definition of social exclusion as 'the process through which individuals or groups are wholly or partially excluded from the society in which they live'. A process approach to social exclusion implies that something or someone is excluding someone else (Lister 1998; Silver and Miller 2003); thus, such an approach enables us to identify who or what is doing the excluding, and how these actions operate, are legitimated or condoned (Saunders 2008).

The process character of social exclusion features centrally in the comprehensive definition proposed by Levitas *et al.* (2007: 25):

Social exclusion is a complex and multi-dimensional process. It involves the lack or denial of resources, rights, goods and services, and the inability to participate in the normal relationships and activities, available to the majority of people in a society, whether in economic, social, cultural or political arenas. It affects both the quality of life of individuals and the equity and cohesion of society as a whole.

This definition explicates the idea that social exclusion is broader than poverty, embracing issues such as the denial of rights and non-economic dimensions. While poverty and deprivation may also be seen as multidimensional phenomena (Townsend 1993; Morgan and Baker 2006), the multidimensional viewpoint occupies a more central position in definitions of social exclusion. Key here is the concept's perceived ability to link together both material and non-material deprivations, encompassing 'not only the lack of access to goods and services which underlie poverty and basic needs satisfaction, but also exclusion from security, from justice, from representation and from citizenship' (Rodgers 1995: 50). Still, social exclusion clearly overlaps with poverty and deprivation, and some definitions of poverty and deprivation appear more or less indistinguishable from those of social exclusion (Gough *et al.* 2006; Morgan *et al.* 2007). For at least some analysts (e.g. Collins with Kay 2003; Collins 2012), poverty is still the core of social exclusion, where social exclusion can be understood as the process by which poverty and material deprivation are created and reproduced.

The definition by Levitas and her colleagues (2007: 25) draws attention to the fact that social exclusion is felt not only at the micro level, but also at the macro level ('the equity and cohesion of society as a whole'). This multilevel perspective can also be found in the Social Exclusion Unit's (2001: 5) recognition that the human costs of social exclusion affect society as a whole through 'reduced social cohesion, higher crime and fear of crime, and higher levels of stress and reduced mobility'. Indeed, research consistently shows that the effects of social exclusion are almost wholly negative, both for people's psychological and material wellbeing and for the communities in which they live, creating conditions that give rise to conflict, increased inequality and mistrust (Abrams *et al.* 2005).

Levitas *et al.*'s (2007: 25) reference to 'normal' relationships and activities available to 'the majority of people in a society' signals another key feature of social exclusion, namely *relativity*. Social exclusion refers to a particular time and place, and can only be judged within that specific context (Atkinson 1998). Burchardt *et al.*'s (2002: 30) reference to 'key activities of the society' similarly emphasizes the relativity of social exclusion, much in the same way that poverty is now considered a relative phenomenon (Townsend 1979). Both definitions suggest that it is impossible to define or measure social exclusion using a single, universal and unique criterion or indicator. Rather, social exclusion needs to be considered in the light of prevailing social and cultural norms as countries differ and change in their understanding of what social exclusion/inclusion means and what 'normal' activities and relationships are perceived to be (De Haan and Maxwell 1998; Bhalla and Lapeyre 2004). While this appears to be an empirical question, it is also a normative one. The prioritization of which activities are 'normal' or desirable involves a judgement, one that is likely to change over time as expectations and opportunities change.

Degrees and dimensions of social exclusion

Social exclusion is inherently relational. Over time, thinking about social exclusion has moved beyond a simple included/excluded dichotomy or fixed polarity of being 'in' or 'out' (Nevile 2007). Instead, social exclusion is a fluid continuum, a sliding scale that is subject to changes over time (Breman 2004; Steinert 2007a, 2007b). The boundaries separating the included from the excluded are fluid and emergent, and they arise from the interactions and interdependencies between social actors with unequal power. Where only a binary distinction is recognized, the excluded are discursively positioned outside society and attention is drawn away from the inequalities and differences among the included (Levitas 2005). This renders the powerful and the privileged invisible because they are subsumed under the 'normal and ordinary' (Byrne 2005: 57). In this context, Pease (2009: 37) notes that the concept of social exclusion 'has done little to address those of us who benefit most from existing social divisions and inequalities'. As Chapters 3 and 4 will discuss in greater detail, while social exclusion policy rhetoric has been interwoven with sport for a number of years, this has not significantly challenged the question of who controls and governs sport. Responsibility for this remains within the hands of the dominant groups, usually white middle-class males.

Social exclusion is typically experienced in degrees rather than in all-or-nothing forms. Very few people ever reach the end of the imagined trajectory of absolute social exclusion (Silver 2007), because in almost all cases at least some relational links with wider society or with one's own group or community remain intact. For this reason, some scholars consider social exclusion along a continuum, with intermediate steps of precariousness and vulnerability (e.g. Paugam 1991; Minujin 1998). In its most severe manifestations, social exclusion involves 'deep exclusion' across multiple domains or dimensions, resulting in profoundly negative consequences for quality of life, wellbeing and future life chances (Levitas *et al.* 2007). Wessels and Miedema (2007) refer to this as severe isolation from one or more of the commonly known formal and informal institutions and patterns of association. They distinguish severe exclusion from intermediate or mild degrees of social exclusion. For example, 'preliminary exclusion' is experienced by those who face minor and often temporary disruptions but are still able to participate in key societal domains. In relation to sport, we know that complete social exclusion from sport participation is rare because of the breadth of sport opportunities in organized and unorganized settings (Elling 2007), especially in the Global North (see Chapter 4). For example, in Chapter 8 we explore how those who feel under-served or marginalized by the mainstream sport sector have alternative sport participation opportunities at their disposal, such as alternative sports competitions and leagues that cater specifically for social groups with a history of stigmatization and exclusion, such as gay and lesbian, minority ethnic groups and people with disabilities.

While conceptualizing social exclusion as a continuum is instructive, there is a danger that the term becomes used in a cover-all sense to describe almost any kind of social disadvantage, in which case it loses its value as an analytical construct. Room (1999: 171) argues that if the notion of social exclusion is to be useful as an analytical concept, then we should use it only when we speak of:

> ... people who are suffering such a degree of multi-dimensional disadvantage, of such duration, and reinforced by such material and cultural degradation of the neighbourhoods in which they live, that their relational links with the wider society are ruptured to a degree which is to some considerable degree irreversible.

In this interpretation, the process of exclusion can become a state when, over time, it is repeatedly reproduced and reinforced through social relations and practices. In a similar vein, Estivill's (2003: 39) analysis of the complex 'itinerary to exclusion' speaks of 'chronic exclusion' when 'barriers are so insurmountable and distances so great, both symbolically and in reality, between those inside and those on the outside that the insiders no longer *see* the outsiders, who lose any opportunities and hopes of a possible return'. For Estivill, the chronic state of social exclusion marks the situation in which exclusion is at its most obdurate. This approach resonates with the French notion of social exclusion as a rupture of the social bond, where the process of exclusion involves a downward spiral of cumulative and multidimensional disadvantage, almost to the point of no return (Gallie and Paugam 2000). In this context, recent research on the sport experience of people with disabilities highlights how multiple levels of constraints affect their ability to negotiate access to organized sport (Jeanes and Magee 2011b). These range from physical access barriers and cost of participation to negative attitudes towards their participation and a lack of support from friends and family. These factors combine to create powerful mechanisms of social exclusion.

Although one might question whether a narrow focus on abject or chronic exclusion is analytically helpful, the reference to multidimensionality is critical here. In the aforementioned narrow definition proposed by Room (1999), different dimensions of social exclusion are closely intertwined. From this perspective, social exclusion refers to mutually reinforcing processes of deprivation that lead to the gradual erosion of resources, capabilities and opportunities (Bhalla and Lapeyre 2004). An individual or group is more likely to be vulnerable to exclusionary processes when they experience difficulties in multiple societal domains (Percy-Smith 2000). However, while different dimensions of social exclusion are interrelated, they are also independent in that each dimension represents a process and/or an outcome considered important in its own right (Burchardt *et al.* 2002). Individuals or groups may be excluded in some dimensions or contexts and for some time and not in others. Steinert (2007a: 5) refers to this as 'sectoral exclusions'. He argues that social exclusion can be broken down into an array of situations of possible exclusion that may or may not be correlated. In many instances these dimensions can be viewed as relatively autonomous: people are excluded from one social system only and can compensate and counteract this by mobilizing the other resources they still have (Abrams *et al.* 2005). For Steinert (2007a: 4), the 'normal' model of being excluded is the 'dynamic, contested, episodic threat of exclusion that the person can fight against and often compensate'. Again, the importance of agency is highlighted. This view of social exclusion also recognizes that the positioning of any individual or group at a particular time in a particular context can be characterized as a multiple and dynamic combination of inclusion and exclusion (Taket *et al.* 2009).

The multidimensionality of social exclusion: competing frameworks

A myriad of analytical frameworks have sought to capture and measure, each in its own way, the multidimensional nature of social exclusion. When taken in conjunction, however, the main scholarly approaches cover five broad dimensions of social exclusion that are outlined in Figure 2.1. While the focus here is on scholarly, theoretically informed approaches rather than policy-oriented models, we recognize that this distinction can be fuzzy, for example where a framework has been specifically developed to inform policy, as in the case of the Poverty and Social Exclusion (PSE) Survey that is discussed below.

Figure 2.1 Dimensions of social exclusion.

In one of the earlier theory-driven accounts of the multidimensionality of social exclusion, Madanipour (1998) identifies three broad dimensions of exclusion: economic, political and cultural. The economic dimension refers to access to resources, most notably employment. In the political arena, social exclusion refers to a lack of political power and representation, for example, the complete or partial exclusion from political decision-making. Madanipour's (1998) reference to the cultural arena as a dimension of social exclusion is particularly noteworthy because this dimension is under-explored in many of the later analytical frameworks. For Madanipour, the main form of exclusion from the cultural arena involves marginalization from symbols, meanings, rituals and discourses. He argues that the forms of cultural exclusion vary widely, such as that experienced by minority ethnic groups whose language, appearance, religion or lifestyle are different from those of the majority ethnic group in a society. While different social groups may experience varying degrees of these different but interrelated forms of exclusion, the most acute forms of social exclusion occur when economic, political and cultural exclusion coalesce. In a similar vein, Schuyt (2000, 2006), whose work highlights, *inter alia*, the moral dimension of social exclusion, speaks of the cumulative nature of social exclusion. For Schuyt, the moral dimension of social exclusion refers to pejorative judgements and stigmatization, either hidden or explicit, of those who are perceived to be different and outside of the norm.

A similarly concise, yet more operational, multidimensional framework is offered by Bhalla and Lapeyre (2004), who also distinguish three broad dimensions: economic, social and political. The economic dimension refers to questions of income and production and access to goods and services. The social dimension involves three main aspects: (1) access to basic public goods such as health, education, clean drinking water and sanitation; (2) access to the labour market; and (3) the opportunity for civic participation, for instance in trade unions or local associations. Finally, political exclusion refers to the denial of human and political rights. In this model, the distinction between the economic and social dimensions of exclusion is blurred as they refer to broadly similar phenomena.

Three conceptual frameworks have been particularly influential in shaping social exclusion research in Western Europe, and especially in the UK. These are the work undertaken by CASE (Hills *et al.* 2002), the Poverty and Social Exclusion (PSE) Survey (Gordon *et al.* 2000; Pantazis *et al.* 2006), and the Bristol Social Exclusion Matrix (Levitas *et al.* 2007). The CASE researchers identify four dimensions of social exclusion: consumption (the capacity to purchase goods and services); production (participation in economically or socially valuable activities); political engagement (involvement in local or national decision-making); and social interaction (engagement with family, friends and community) (Burchardt *et al.* 2002). These four dimensions strongly resonate with the framework proposed by Bhalla and Lapeyre (2004), albeit that it divides the economic dimension into 'production' and 'consumption'. The CASE researchers are also more successful in their analytical separation of the economic and the social, as in Bhalla and Lapeyre's framework these dimensions overlap significantly due to their incorporation of access to the labour market (or production) as a key aspect of the social dimension.

While the frameworks proposed by Bhalla and Lapeyre (2004) and the CASE researchers (Burchardt *et al.* 2002) include a political dimension, PSE does not. The PSE Survey distinguishes four dimensions of social exclusion: impoverishment, labour market exclusion, service exclusion and exclusion from social relations (Gordon *et al.* 2000). Impoverishment relates to exclusion from adequate income or resources, a form of exclusion that is also at centre stage in the other two frameworks and reflects the British tradition of poverty research. Unlike the CASE researchers, however, PSE incorporates 'service exclusion' as a dimension of social exclusion. This dimension refers to people's use of public and private services as well as the perceived availability of these services. Their incorporation of 'perceived availability' as an indicator of social exclusion, in addition to actual usage, strongly resonates with Bhalla and Lapeyre's (2004) focus on the issue of access (i.e. to services, good and the labour market) and indicates a disconnect between the concept of social exclusion and the indicators used in most measurement tools. Social exclusion is typically framed in terms of the *opportunity* to participate; however, existing frameworks and indicators almost invariably measure *actual* participation or non-participation. Put differently, social exclusion relates to things that people cannot do, whereas most of the data used to study exclusion describe what people actually do or do not do (Saunders 2008). As Burchardt *et al.* (2002: 41) rightly note: 'We neither know whether the (non-)participation is regarded as problematic by the individual, nor whether he or she has other options.'

The aforementioned frameworks are relatively concise with regard to the number of identified dimensions of social exclusion. In contrast, some scholars propose a far more expansive model. For example, one widely cited research collection distinguishes seven dimensions of social exclusion: economic, social, political, neighbourhood, individual, spatial and group (Percy-Smith 2000). While we agree that neighbourhood, spatial and group dimensions are critical in that some persons are more vulnerable or exposed to exclusion due to who they are (seen to represent) and where they live (see Chapter 6 for the Zambian case study), we also believe that this approach conflates the societal *domains* in which exclusion occurs with the *levels* at which it operates. We will return to this issue further on in this chapter.

The Bristol Social Exclusion Matrix is arguably the most comprehensive framework for operationalizing and measuring social exclusion. The matrix identifies no fewer than ten dimensions of social exclusion that fall within the three main areas of resources, participation and quality of life (Levitas *et al.* 2007). Resources comprise three dimensions: material/economic resources (e.g. income); access to public and private services (e.g. housing, transport);

and social resources (e.g. social support). The second area – participation in economic, social, cultural and political life – is at the core of many definitions and theories of social exclusion, including the aforementioned frameworks. For Levitas and her colleagues (2007), this area covers four dimensions of social exclusion: economic (e.g. paid and unpaid work); social (e.g. participation in common social activities); culture, education and skills (e.g. literacy, access to education); and political and civic participation (e.g. citizenship status, voluntary activity). Finally, quality of life is broadly concerned with health and wellbeing, living environment (e.g. housing quality, neighbourhood safety), and crime, harm and criminalization (e.g. objective and subjective safety, exposure to bullying and harassment, discrimination).

Scholarly approaches to the multidimensionality of social exclusion are not restricted to Europe. In Canada, Galabuzi's (2004, 2006) work on social exclusion among minority ethnic groups stands out for its emphasis on issues of access and opportunity. Galabuzi (2004) identifies four dimensions of social exclusion as it relates to minority ethnic groups:

- Exclusion from social production: denial of opportunities to contribute to and participate actively in society;
- Economic exclusion: unequal or lack of access to normal forms of livelihood;
- Exclusion from civil society: disconnection through legal sanctions, institutional mechanisms or systemic discrimination based on race, ethnicity, gender, disability, sexual orientation or religion;
- Exclusion from social goods: failure of society to provide for the needs of particular groups, such as adequate housing and language services, and sanctions to deter discrimination.

These four domains of exclusion closely correspond to the production, consumption, social relations and services dimensions discussed above, but have an explicit focus on institutional mechanisms and discrimination as drivers of social exclusion. This emphasis is one of the main strengths of Galabuzi's (2004, 2006) approach as it explicitly addresses the question of who, or what, is doing the excluding.

Despite their differences, the frameworks discussed in this section share a commonality in their recognition of social exclusion beyond poverty. This multidimensional understanding of social exclusion challenges the view that poverty is *the* core of exclusion, a view that is held by Collins and Kay (2003) in their influential account of sport and social exclusion. Another commonality among the different frameworks is that they all emanate from the Global North where the concept of social exclusion originated. However, the challenges and pitfalls of applying a concept or theory of social exclusion developed in the post-industrial states of the Global North to industrialized, newly industrialized or pre-industrial countries in the Global South are multiple. It is to this issue of North–South comparison that we now turn.

Social exclusion and the Global South

The above-mentioned approaches to social exclusion can be conveniently grouped together under the umbrella term of 'northern theories' in that they were invariably produced in post-industrial societies in the Global North and mainly reflect the social issues facing these societies. Northern theories of social exclusion have been exported to the Global South through a global network of institutions including universities, scholarly journals, international development agencies and supranational government institutions. While we use the term 'northern theories' to refer to this general process, we recognize the internal diversity of social exclusion theory and research within the Global North. This diversity is evident, for example, in Silver's (1994) typology of social exclusion paradigms, which shows that different scholarly approaches to social exclusion and the different political uses of the term emanate from competing social science paradigms and political ideologies. In other words, there is no such thing as a single, unified northern theory of social exclusion in the singular.

The question remains, however, of what (if any) relevance Global North approaches to social exclusion have for countries in the Global South that often face qualitatively different economic, political and social realities. This is a multi-layered question. At one level, it recognizes the need to contextualize epistemic knowledge into the local cultural, political and economic context (Apffel-Marglin and Marglin 1996). At a deeper level, it relates to the funda-mental critique of northern social science that alternative ways of thinking about the world are marginalized, with little dialogue and little recognition. This critique posits that the production of knowledge about the Global South has taken place as an integral part of the unequal power relationship between the North and South, where the Global North is seen to have the power to articulate and project itself and its worldview on to others (Tucker 1999).

In *Southern Theory*, Connell (2007) argues that even where it addresses global inequalities, mainstream social science still works through categories produced in the Global North and fails to engage to any real degree with the knowledge produced by the Global South. Social science in the Global South can inject themes and ways of thinking about the modern world that are rela-tively uncommon or neglected in northern thought. To encourage a process of mutual influence, it is pivotal that scholars in the Global North pay closer attention to work from the Global South and engage with it dialectically to develop multiple perspectives (Tucker 1999). As Connell (2007: xii) puts it:

> ... colonised and peripheral societies produce social thought *about the modern world* which has as much intellectual power as metropolitan social thought, and more political relevance. Since the ground is different, the form of theorising is often different too. Work needs to be done to develop the connections, as well as the contrasts, between these bodies of thought and those of the metropole.

In the field of social exclusion research, some groundwork has indeed been undertaken to identify such connections and contrasts. Gore and Figueiredo (1997) were among the first to consider whether the concept of social exclusion formulated in the Global North could be applied in different types of societies. They argue that while social exclusion occurs within all societies, it has different meanings and manifestations and therefore 'does not permit easy generalization and comparisons' (1997: 9). Still, they recognize that the notion of social exclusion offers opportunities for dialogue and two-way learning between North and South. In a similar vein, De Haan and Maxwell (1998: 8) find that although the particularities of place and history remain important, there is 'great scope' for global communication across geographical boundaries considering that poverty and social exclusion debates have strong resonance in different global regions. Bhalla and Lapeyre (2004) similarly conclude that the concept of social exclusion has universal relevance and validity even though its particular features and prevalence may differ between particular countries and global regions.

Others, however, are not so sure. There are a number of reasons why it may be difficult to apply the term to Global South contexts in any meaningful way. Commencing with Lenoir's (1974) use of the term in France, social exclusion in the Global North has been strongly associated with a lack of access to paid employment in the organized workforce and with the loss of rights associated with work and social welfare. It is defined first and foremost in relation to the welfare state and formalized labour market, against standards considered the norm in developed countries at particular points in time (Saith 2007). Where social exclusion is defined in terms of the denial of the opportunity to participate in 'normal' relationships and activities available to 'the majority of people in a society' (Levitas *et al.* 2007: 25), this implicitly refers to norms that are in many respects Eurocentric. In many developing countries it is difficult to define exclusion in these terms due to profound differences in social security and labour market arrangements (Saith 2007). In the Global South, informal and casual employment is the rule, and seasonally determined irregular employment the norm.[1]

In the Global North, the assumption is that when we refer to social exclusion, we are speaking about a marginalized minority who are unable to participate in the normal range of activities, or acquire a sufficient standard of living, relative to most citizens. In 1970s France, Lenoir (1974) calculated that this applied to about 10 per cent of the population. Even in more alarming estimates, such as the recent estimate that 23 per cent of the EU's population is 'at risk of poverty or social exclusion' (European Commission 2012), the underlying assumption holds that there is a majority from which a small or more sizeable minority is excluded in some form. In contrast, and judged by the same standards, the excluded may form the majority in many countries in the Global South, where they are living in poverty, are excluded from formal labour markets, and/or have little, if any, entitlement to social protection from the state. In essence, then, this would require a complete analytical reversal of the majority–minority relationship that underpins northern notions of social exclusion. One of the dangers here is that if used merely to describe a static condition or to identify specific groups that are being excluded, the concept of social exclusion may be 'a broad screen, a curtain', which hides rather than makes visible problems of severe destitution in countries where such problems are in fact part of normal life (Popay *et al.* 2008: 44).

We concur with Kay (2012b: 221) that comparing how the concept of social exclusion is applied in Global North and Global South countries is 'a useful exercise in highlighting how these settings differ as economic, political and social contexts'. Moreover, Global South approaches to social exclusion offer important insights for scholars in the Global North. First and foremost, they bring to the fore important differences in understandings about the nature of the problem and the form or conditions of inclusion that are deemed important in particular societies or by particular groups within those societies. Four distinct themes stand out in Global South conceptualizations of social exclusion: civil and political rights; social recognition and human dignity; violence and personal security; and global power relations. These themes are discussed below.

Much of the European writing on social exclusion focuses on non-participation in paid employment and economic activity. In contrast, a rights-based understanding of social exclusion is more strongly established in the Global South (Mathieson *et al.* 2008), where the denial or systematic violation of political, civil or social rights is often considered a key, defining feature of social exclusion. Exclusion from basic rights can include a lack of access to public services such as healthcare, education, housing, water supply, sanitation and social security (Gore and Figueiredo 1997; Breman 2004). Exclusion from land rights or native title is another pressing form of social exclusion that affects many Indigenous peoples across the globe, including those in Latin America and Australia (Hunter 2008; Popay *et al.* 2008).

Rights-based approaches to social exclusion are concerned not only with economic exclusion and inequality, but also with cultural forms of injustice that stem from 'who you are' and 'where you are from' (Kabeer 2000). Economic and cultural exclusion are often intertwined, sometimes inseparably so, such as when stigmatization leads to a denial of access to employment or public goods (Correa-Velez *et al.* 2013). Cultural forms of exclusion are 'manifested in the ways in which dominant social groups invisibilise, seek to impose dominant values, or routinely devalue or disparage certain categories of people' (Kabeer 2000: 4). This interpretation resonates with the aforementioned cultural realm of exclusion theorized by Madanipour (1998) in relation to European cities, as well as with Galabuzi's (2004) analysis of the exclusion from civil society experienced by minority ethnic groups in Canada.

In Global South approaches, cultural exclusion is often expressed in terms of a lack of social recognition and human dignity (Fraser 1997). In Brazil, for instance, the urban poor refer to their lack of recognition and visibility and their status as 'second-class citizens', a social reality they confront on a daily basis (Dagnino 2005; Perlman 2010). Human dignity, which many urban poor consider a central component of citizenship (Wheeler 2005), refers to being treated with respect and without discrimination or prejudice in everyday life. The Brazilian case, discussed in depth in Chapter 6, suggests that the formal assertion of political and social rights does not automatically alleviate the pervasive sense of exclusion in everyday life experience, where large segments of the population can be effectively marginalized from active partic- ipation in the public sphere. Northern theories of social exclusion tend to underplay the importance of human dignity and social recognition as central components of social exclusion. It could be argued, however, that within the context of systematic human rights violations, 'social recognition' might be a more appropriate term than 'social inclusion' (O'Brien *et al.* 1997).

Another theme that is undervalued in northern approaches to social exclusion is the role of violence and personal insecurity as a contributing factor to, and effect of, exclusionary processes (Valencia Gutiérrez 2001; Valencia Agudelo and Cuartas Celis 2009). Where violence is seen as a consequence of social exclusion, the emphasis tends to be on the restricted range of resources and social support available to people, which may include criminal activities and gang membership. In areas experiencing deep social exclusion, gang membership and violent behaviour can be among the very few means of gaining power and recognition as well as providing important coping mechanisms for the people involved, including economic livelihoods and social support (McIlwaine and Moser 2001; Barker 2005). At the same time, violence contributes to and exacerbates exclusionary processes in that it reduces the dignity and wellbeing of other human beings and restricts their full and equitable participation in public spaces. In the Global South, sport is frequently used as a place where safe public spaces can be developed for those that struggle to access them else- where (Meier and Saavedra 2009); however, at the same time, sports spaces can themselves be violence-inducing (Daimon 2010). In reality, such violence disproportionately affects the lives of marginalized people who have themselves not resorted to violence (Berkman 2007). Residents of socially excluded communities often cannot depend on institutions such as the police and the justice system to protect their civil and human rights (Arias 2006). These issues are central to the lived experience of social exclu- sion of many people in the Global South.

Exclusion or adverse inclusion?

In addition to directing our attention to social issues that are especially salient in Global South contexts, a global perspective on social exclusion shifts atten- tion from internal structures and relationships within nationally bounded societies towards an appreciation of the forms of social exclusion that reside in the relations between nations and global regions. This perspective casts a different light on the questions 'Exclusion from what?' and 'Inclusion on whose terms?' As we have seen, scholars often address the first question by identifying the main dimensions of social exclusion – economic, social, political and cultural. The more critical among them problematize the very notion of social inclusion because of its narrow focus on participation in the modern capitalist system that, in their view, can never be truly inclusive (Gray 2000; Byrne 2005). Bowring (2000: 320), for example, contends that the social inclusion debate eschews a critique of the dominant roles, norms and practices from which marginalized people are excluded, and therefore is 'in danger of leaving the cultural hegemony of capitalism intact'. Others argue that, by definition, social inclusion implies exclusion, as there can be no inside without an outside. Thus, the notion of social exclusion/inclusion necessarily fixes attention on boundaries and margins, on what differentiates one class of persons from another (Goodin 1996).

An important insight that can be gleaned from a global perspective is that the central issue is not the false dichotomy between inclusion and exclusion, but rather the terms and conditions of social inclusion (Mathieson *et al.* 2008). As noted earlier, a key concern is that social inclusion relates only to involvement in prescribed mainstream institutions of society that reproduce or reinforce the status quo. This insight has led some scholars to propose the term 'adverse incorporation' (Du Toit 2004; Hickey and Du Toit 2007), based on their belief that the key to understanding social exclusion is to come to grips with how marginalized people are actually incorporated within broader social and economic formations of power in ways that exploit and marginalize them and undermine their ability to control and impact the systems into which they are locked.

The most notable differences between the concepts of adverse incorporation and social exclusion relate to issues of power and the extent to which poverty is understood in relational as opposed to residual terms (Hickey and Du Toit 2007). The social exclusion discourse has been criticized for emphasizing the residual rather than relational aspects of poverty, thereby moving analytical attention away from an understanding of how power relations within society underpin poverty. The notion of exclusion may be ill-equipped to deal with issues concerning the adverse terms of inclusion or relations that do exist between people and various political, economic and social processes and structures (Byrne 2005). However, in recent years attempts have been made to capture these relational aspects through the lens of social exclusion by drawing attention to causal processes and embedding those explanations within an understanding of the larger relational structures within which people are inserted (Gough *et al.* 2006; Popay *et al.* 2008). For example, we now know that marginalizing or exploitative processes operating in the global political economy graft themselves on to the dynamics of exclusion operating at local and national levels (Beall 2002). These developments have led some to explore the synergies between the two concepts in the analysis of poverty in the Global South (Hickey and Du Toit 2007).

Spaces of social exclusion

In this book, we draw on the aforementioned theories and approaches to conceptualize social exclusion as a (set of) process(es) that negatively affects the rights, recognition and/or resources of targets of social exclusion and/or their opportunity to participate in key activities in different societal domains. This process operates across different spatial scales, ranging from the interpersonal level through to the global level. In its more extreme forms, social exclusion results in a person or group being effectively 'shut out' from the social, economic, political and/or cultural systems that operate in particular spaces and times (Walker and Walker 1997).

Our approach presents social exclusion as a relational, multidimensional, multilevel process – features that have been extensively discussed in this chapter. It is well attuned to a global perspective on social exclusion by enabling an analysis of the processes that marginalize or unfavourably include individuals, families, groups, localities, nations and global regions in terms of a fair share in social, economic, cultural and political resources and social recognition (Sen 2000). The focus on relational exclusionary processes entails a 'strong' conception of social exclusion that forces attention on to inequality and emphasizes the role of the agents or institutions that are doing the excluding (Veit-Wilson 1998). This conception challenges the dominant policy focus on the 'weak' concept of social exclusion, that is, one that explains social exclusion as an outcome of an individual's handicaps and character. Our approach also recognizes temporality as a key element in the dynamics of social exclusion. Temporality refers not only to the fact that patterns of exclusion develop and change over a long course of time, but also to the idea that exclusionary processes are often historical, in some cases to the point where they become defined culturally in terms of a 'natural essence' of the excluded parties and seen as inevitable (Abrams *et al.* 2005). In other words, social exclusion can become consolidated, structurally and culturally, over time.

Our understanding of social exclusion is informed by the World Health Organization (WHO) Social Exclusion Knowledge Network (Popay *et al.* 2008), which identifies different spatial scales at which social exclusion operates. These different scales are mutually constitutive; hence, in general, exclusionary processes at the more abstract levels provide a context and pretext for the more specific and concrete levels (Abrams *et al.* 2005). Exclusionary processes operating at the global level may be seen to articulate with exclusionary axes at the national, local or community level. However, while these different processes can be mutually reinforcing, they can also mitigate or counteract each other's effects. As such, we view social exclusion as a *glocal* phenomenon that involves the mutual, interdependent shaping of local struggles and global forces (Robertson 1992). The results of this interplay between exclusionary processes at different spatial scales will be different for different localities or groups and at different points in time.

It is beyond the scope of this chapter to consider in detail the multitude of processes that give rise to or exacerbate social exclusion at these different levels. However, a number of drivers of social exclusion at neighbourhood, institutional, national and global levels have been referred to throughout this chapter. There is now a vast literature on exclusionary processes in a context of globalization (e.g. Jordan 1996; Bhalla and Lapeyre 2004; Breman 2004). The bulk of this literature focuses on economic and labour market transformations, welfare state retrenchment and formal institutions as the core mechanisms of social exclusion. These mechanisms can be seen to intersect with cultural and symbolic processes that differentiate and stigmatize particular groups, nations and global regions (Estivill 2003). These intersections will be examined in relation to sport throughout this book.

By portraying social exclusion as a dynamic and relational process, we argue that both parties involved in the relationship – targets and sources – have the potential for influence. Recent theory and research emphasize the structural conditions and institutional mechanisms that create, condone and exacerbate social exclusion. While this approach is of vital import in addressing the question of who/what is doing the excluding, any fine-grained analysis of social exclusion also needs to take into consideration the agency and subjectivity of those who face exclusionary processes (Vobruba 2000; Marsh 2004). Indeed, people who are being excluded are not simply passive victims. They may be resourceful in coping with given circumstances by drawing on the material, social or psychological resources they still have, or conversely they may play an active role in their own exclusion. The process of social exclusion is actively constructed, negotiated and resisted in the interactions between sources and targets of exclusion, especially in situations where the targets are aware of the interdependencies involved (Abrams *et al.* 2005). Here, again, the interplay between different spatial scales is critical to our understanding of the nature and effects of social exclusion. In Chapter 3, we examine this interplay with specific reference to sport, social exclusion and public policy.

Note

1 We owe this important observation to Dr Wendy Mee.

3 Sport and social exclusion in public policy

Introduction

The previous chapter conceptualizes social exclusion as a process that negatively affects the rights, recognition or resources of targets of social exclusion, and/or their opportunity to participate in key activities in one or more societal domains. Underpinning this definition is the welfare of individuals and groups and their ability to experience core social activities in a meaningful and equitable way. Public policy has a responsibility to promote inclusive and welcoming environments in sports clubs and programs that receive government funding. This challenge is also central to sport policy given its core business of sport participation (Elling 2007). In this chapter, we examine how social exclusion and its link with sport are portrayed and addressed in public policy, with a particular focus on the intersections between social policy and sport policy.

The analysis will focus on three countries – the United Kingdom (UK), Zambia and the People's Republic of China (China) – that represent diverging policy approaches to social exclusion. In focusing on these three countries, we do not aim to provide an exhaustive overview of the myriad policy approaches to social exclusion in different global regions. Rather, by building on the conceptual framework presented in Chapter 2, we seek to identify some key patterns of similarity and difference in prevailing policy approaches to social exclusion and sport in the Global North and Global South. A focus on China and Zambia helps us to problematize the dominant UK-focused view on sport and social exclusion, which draws attention to long-standing government involvement in sport as a way to address social exclusion. The Chinese and Zambian experiences outlined here present very different realities in terms of both the intersections between sport policy and social policy, and the wider welfare context within which these intersections are situated. Thus, this chapter will highlight some of the diversities and complexities that become apparent when sport and social exclusion policy is considered beyond the confines of the UK.

The UK is included in this discussion as it initiated the modern public welfare system modelled by many Western nations throughout the nineteenth and twentieth centuries (Blakemore and Griggs 2007). After decades of abstaining from interference in sport policy, the UK government in the 1960s began to invest in sport as a vehicle to address wider social issues, including social exclusion (Coghlan 1990; Polley 1998; Collins with Kay 2003; Keech 2003). Hence, the UK policy approach provides a 'benchmark' to examine the policy experiences of other countries. Zambia, a former colony of the British Empire that has been independent since 1964, provides an example of a Global South country that is positioned very differently within the global political economy. As will be seen, social inclusion policies in Zambia typically fall within the broader rhetoric of development and, as such, present important insights into supranational vectors of social exclusion and how these affect local realities, including sport policy. Finally, the inclusion of China here is determined by its distinctiveness in global political terms as a single-party state and its diversified yet inconsistent welfare system (Chan *et al.* 2008; Li 2005). Despite China's global economic and political impact, including in the realm of high-performance sport, relatively little is known about the nature and extent of linkages between its social policy and sport policy. This makes China particularly interesting as a case study in sport and social exclusion policy.

Sport and social exclusion in the UK: fading policy fad or enduring reality?

The UK is considered the birthplace of the public welfare system (Blakemore and Griggs 2007; Hill 2003), with the Poor Law of 1601 being one of the earliest forms of institutionalized social policy. In ensuing centuries, the UK government assumed a more active and central role to improve public health and alleviate poverty. While the economic downturn of the 1920s and 1930s increased policy intervention, World War Two provided the impetus for a significant reconstruction of policies underpinning the social welfare system. The immediate post-war period witnessed the coming of age of state welfare as many Western countries followed the UK and extended or consolidated their social welfare provision (Page 2001; Blakemore and Griggs 2007).

In the UK, post-war reforms were based largely on a report by Sir William Beveridge (1942), whose social policy designs were intended to defeat what he called the 'five giant social evils' – want, disease, ignorance, squalor, and idleness. His revolutionary plan recommended universal coverage and a wide range of benefits without means testing (Blakemore and Griggs 2007). The resulting welfare state was founded upon the 'Big Five': income maintenance and social security; health services; personal social services; education and training; and employment and housing (Alcock *et al.* 2004). Subsequent UK governments throughout the post-war decades maintained the welfare system and the role of state as provider. This notion that social welfare can be best achieved through significant government intervention dominated governments for quite some time, with the state being seen as a benevolent force (Kearns 1997). However, as outlined below, this position has come under fierce criticism in recent decades.

The association between social policy and sport policy in the UK is characterized by duality, that is, government's involvement in sport both extends social citizenship rights and emphasizes the wider social benefits presumed to be associated with sport participation (Coalter 2007). This duality, Coalter (2007: 8) notes, 'is a common characteristic of most social policies, where the extension of social rights has mostly been accompanied by social obligations and duties'. This is not a recent trend, as the UK government's involvement in leisure – of which sport is a fundamental component – can be traced to moral reforms of the nineteenth century and the quest for healthy lifestyles (Bailey 1978; Holt 1989). As Roberts (1992: 9) rightly notes, 'tackling social problems using leisure provision as a subsidiary strategy has a long history'. For example, Haywood *et al.* (1990) identify policy innovations and interventions of respective UK governments up to the end of World War Two that focused mainly on the control of popular recreation forms and leisure time of the masses. Post-war, leisure policy documents surfaced in the form of *Leisure for Living* (Labour Party 1959) and *The Challenge of Leisure* (Kerr *et al.* 1959), against the backdrop of political concern about at-risk youth (Roberts 1983; Haywood *et al.* 1990).

Until the 1960s, there was limited systematic central government interest in sport due in large part to a prevailing amateur sports ethos that did not warrant its attention (Houlihan and White 2002; Green 2004). In that decade, however, the UK government formally recognized the social benefits of sport and amended policy to include its use for wider social purposes. Hence, in subsequent decades the sport policy landscape changed significantly.

In 1935, growing national health concerns influenced the establishment of the Central Council for Physical Recreation, and in 1957 Sir John Wolfenden was commissioned to chair a committee on the position of sport within UK society. The Wolfenden Report, delivered in 1960 against a backdrop of a poor performance at the 1960 Olympic Games, identified that provision for youth sport was lacking in the UK, with post-school involvement lower than in other European countries. The report particularly targeted young people, and advocated increased participation through better facilities and coaching within a wider improvement in how sport was organized, delivered and administered (CCPR 1960). While the Wolfenden Report focused on the role of 'sport for sport's sake', it also identified the prospective contribution of sport to build character, albeit reservedly. The potential role that sport could play in the alleviation of broader social problems was also couched in cautionary terms; for instance, 'the causes of criminal behaviour are complex, and we are not suggesting that it would disappear if there were more tennis courts or running tracks' (CCPR 1960: 25). While not all of the report's recommendations were agreed with or acted upon by the then Conservative government (such as establishing an autonomous organization to oversee the development of sport), the report's importance should not be underestimated. In 1964, the newly elected Labour Prime Minister Harold Wilson cemented the future contribution of sport as part of the government agenda by declaring it to be 'essential to Britain's economic and social development which had not been given priority in the past' (cited in Polley 1998: 21).

With UK national policy in the 1970s and 1980s focused on increasing opportunities for sport participation (Houlihan and White 2002), sport providers became increasingly sophisticated in targeting disadvantaged, low participation groups (Roberts 1992). Increased facility provision occurred alongside policy development that resourced particular under-represented groups, such as women, people with disabilities, and minority ethnic groups. This targeted policy approach should be understood against the backdrop of political concerns about social unrest in inner-city areas such as in Liverpool, Bradford and Bristol, with sport being perceived as a potential solution to social problems (Bloyce and Smith 2010). For example, there was significant public investment in sport and leisure facilities in Northern Ireland, predominantly in Belfast, as a strategy to reduce sectarian tension between Protestant and Catholic communities (Sugden and Bairner 1986, 1993). However, the impact of these initiatives appears to have been limited, largely because facilities were located in areas that reinforced ethno-sectarian segregation. This created what Bairner and Shirlow (2003) term a 'fear of leisure': that is, people's fear of using a leisure centre in the 'other' religious community even if it was the closest facility.

The establishment of the Action Sport program in 1982 evidenced the UK government's intention to use sport to target particular community sectors for wider social policy purposes. Action Sport provided 15 local authorities with significant funding to co-organize sport development programs for under-represented and socially excluded groups, in particular the unemployed (Houlihan and White 2002). By supporting local authority strategies, Action Sport was able to provide an impetus for the development of a more strategic approach to sport management that had hitherto been lacking (Collins 2010). However, this developing government policy attention towards mass participation in sport was largely reversed from 1992 under Prime Minister John Major. His government's 1995 sports policy strategy, *Sport: Raising the Game*, was the first in two decades to focus on elite sport and its contribution to national identity at the expense of the central role of local government to promote social citizenship and mass participation in sport, which was effectively ignored during this period (Coalter 2007).

Sport and social exclusion under New Labour

From 1997, Tony Blair's New Labour government addressed core economic and social problems using a Third Way approach. This approach involves restructuring traditional social democratic doctrines to respond to globalization and the knowledge economy, emphasizing citizens' social responsibilities in addition to their social rights (Giddens 1998). The Third Way advocates a mix of private and public welfare in an approach much more receptive to solutions based on the market and civil society than traditional social democracy. Hence, social investment is generated and distributed not wholly through the state, but by the state working with commercial, voluntary and informal agencies. This welfare pluralism focuses on coordination and collaboration through public-private partnerships as a way to align interests, leverage resources and solve implementation problems (Hill 2003). Civic society, community regeneration and social inclusion are central components of the Third Way approach to public governance. Giddens (1998: 108), a key Third Way proponent, refers to social exclusion as 'mechanisms that act to detach groups of people from the social mainstream', a view reflected in New Labour's social exclusion mandate. As noted in Chapter 2, the Social Exclusion Unit (SEU) was established in 1997 to develop integrated and sustainable approaches to the problems of social exclusion and community breakdown.

New Labour advocated sport as having the potential to combat various social problems and achieve wider social outcomes; as such it was afforded a more central place on the UK's social policy agenda (Collins with Kay 2003; Blackshaw and Long 2005; Houlihan 2011). In so doing, New Labour sought to direct sport policy around social inclusion, equality and diversity. Specifically, New Labour contended that sport could enhance social inclusion and community cohesion by promoting active citizenship – that is, empowering citizens to provide their own answers to their communities' social problems (Coalter 2007). Government direction was provided by the Policy Action Working Group 10 (PAT 10), which argued:

> Participation in the arts and sport has a beneficial social impact. Arts and sport are inclusive and can contribute to neighbourhood renewal. They can build confidence and encourage strong community groups. However, these benefits are frequently overlooked both by some providers of arts and sports facilities and programs and by those involved in area regeneration programs.
>
> (DCMS 1999: 5)

In the first national sport policy introduced under New Labour in 2000, *A Sporting Future for All*, the government argues that 'sport can make a positive contribution not only to tackling social exclusion in our society ... We fully recognize that this is not something that sport can tackle alone but by working with other agencies we believe it can make a significant contribution' (DCMS 2000: 39). This belief was reiterated in New Labour's joined-up approach to tackling social exclusion. Further feathering the social inclusion nest, the DCMS (2002) strategy document *Game Plan* lists participation benefits for groups deemed 'at risk' of social exclusion, including people with disabilities and minority ethnic groups, but especially at-risk young people. The latter category has been the principal target of many sport-related interventions where proactive responses to varied social problems and the achievement of broader social goals are emphasized (Bloyce and Smith 2010). The public value of sport thus became prioritized and utilized as part of wider social inclusion strategies.

Given the UK government's focus since 1997 on the role of sport in its social inclusion agenda, it is necessary to consider how this focus impacted on those involved in sport development work, as organizations were now expected to deliver outcomes beyond sport. Sport developers were increasingly required to demonstrate the efficacy of sport-based programs in achieving both traditional objectives of increased participation and broader social policy objectives. Indeed, several aspects of sport policy delivery were now characterized by 'a desire for developing people and their communities *through* sport alongside a correlative decline in the commitment to simply developing sport amongst people *in* their communities' (Bloyce and Smith 2010: 83). In this context, Coalter (2007) contends that two approaches to sport-based programs focusing on social inclusion emerged: 'sport plus' and 'plus sport'. The former are programs in which traditional sport development objectives of increased participation and development of sporting skills are emphasized, even though these objectives are 'rarely the sole rationale and very rarely the basis for external investment and subsequent evaluation' (Coalter 2007: 71). 'Plus sport' programs, however, give primacy to social, educational and health objectives. Within such programs, sport, especially its perceived ability to unite and engage disaffected or 'at-risk' young people, is part of a broader and more complex set of processes (Coalter 2007). This distinction (further illustrated in Chapters 5, 6 and 7) is important to recognize, as the UK sports programs that feature in this book are located within this changing dynamic of sport development work and the social inclusion agenda.

Returning to *A Sporting Future for All*, using sport and physical activity to improve the health and wellbeing of the nation was a central component, with the Department of Culture, Media and Sport (DCMS) arguing that 'the strategy provides the context for local authorities to link the value of sport to the wider benefits of health' (DCMS 2000: 39). According to Bloyce and Smith (2010: 115), the policy exemplified the government view; hence:

> ... sports development work has diversified to include broader notions of what such work should entail because the government seems to be encouraging this broadening of horizons ... it is important to note that emphasis came increasingly to be placed on the contribution that physical activity could make to public health strategies at the time.

Game Plan further reinforced the government view of the relationship between sport, physical activity and health by advocating a doubling of regularly physically active people by 2020 (DCMS and Strategy Unit 2002). The strategy received both praise (Bloyce and Smith 2010) and criticism (Coalter 2007; Collins 2008), but there is little doubt that it was a further expression of New Labour's attempt to enhance 'joined-up' thinking between disparate policy areas and government departments (Bloyce and Smith 2010).

The focus on sport, physical activity and healthy lifestyles was maintained throughout the mid-2000s, with Sport England aligning itself with the physical activity and health agenda of New Labour, mainly because of the increased funding available to organizations with objectives and targets linked to physical activity and health (Coalter 2007; Houlihan 2011). Its shift in strategic focus towards combating obesity and promoting active travel further exemplifies Sport England's broadened activities in response to the wider sport, physical activity and health strategic alliance. Houlihan (2011: 21), however, notes that UK government policy and strategic direction through *Game Plan* was confusing with regard to sport participation:

> The underlying tensions between the government's (and consequently Sport England's) concern with the promotion of physical activity/ exercise for health reasons, the use of sport to generate social welfare benefits and social capital, the utilization of participation as a necessary prerequisite for talent development and the promotion of participation for intrinsic reasons came to a head, though were not resolved, between 2005 and 2009.

Also muddying the waters was Gordon Brown's uncontested election as Prime Minister in June 2007. This brought a change of sport policy direction through a new strategy to 'build a world class community sport infrastructure to sustain and increase participation in sport and allow everyone the chance to develop their sporting talents' (DH/DCSF 2008: 19). The awarding of the 2012 Olympic and Paralympic Games to London had a significant influence on this policy shift (Houlihan 2011).

The first key policy declaration on health focused on obesity through the promotion of community sport. In 2008, Labour demonstrated a major policy shift from its previous focus on promoting physical activity to emphasizing 'sport for sport's sake' (Collins 2010: 370). Henceforth, physical activity was to be the Department of Health's responsibility rather than that of Sport England, which rapidly shifted its strategic focus towards hosting the 2012 Olympic and Paralympic Games in London. Further, DCMS (*Playing to Win*, 2008) shifted its policy strategy away from 'sport for social good' towards performance and excellence. Some scholars have expressed grave doubts about the efficacy of the UK government's strategy (e.g. Collins 2010), with Houlihan (2011: 22) contending that its core problem is the inconsistency within government policy about the rationale for supporting increased participation in sport:

> In the last ten years the primary rationale has shifted from contributing to tackling social problems associated with community fragmentation, educational under-achievement and anti-social behaviour, to improving

the nation's health and in particular tackling the problem of overweight and obesity, and most recently to providing support for the pursuit of Olympic medals.

A new era looms?

Following 13 years of New Labour, the Conservative-Liberal Democrat Coalition government was elected in 2010 with the immediate task of reducing the significant public debt to set the UK on the path to economic recovery. The social policy agenda of the current Conservative-Liberal Democrat government is interesting because it arguably represents the most far-reaching attempt to fundamentally restructure an established welfare state in a larger Western economy in recent years (Taylor-Goodby 2012). In October 2010, the newly appointed Chancellor of the Exchequer George Osborne outlined in the Comprehensive Spending Review in the House of Commons that there would be GBP83 billion public spending cuts over the next five years, starting with an initial budget cut in 2011 of GBP23 billion. The welfare reform targets several key areas of social welfare provision, including social security benefits, education, healthcare and housing. There are concerns about the scale and pace of the reforms but also a political fissure has been opened as the lower classes are predominantly targeted for budget reform. Of the situation ahead for the UK, Taylor-Goodby (2012: 78) offers a rather pessimistic outlook:

> The likely outcome is an increase in poverty and inequalities in the next few years, but whether more far-reaching changes leading to systemic restructuring will follow is at present unclear. This matters, because, if such changes are achieved, they will demonstrate the feasibility of policies which achieve a permanent retrenchment in state welfare by damaging the living standards for the poor in an established welfare state.

The position of sport has not been immune to government spending cutbacks, although the Coalition did protect the GBP9.3 billion allocated to the London 2012 Olympic Games and its legacy. However, the DCMS's annual budget of GBP1.6 billion, of which approximately GBP160 million is directed at sport, has been cut by 25 per cent, while Sport England (33 per cent) and UK Sport (28 per cent) have also had their budgets reduced (Sports Development 2011). For the focus of this book, the 28 per cent cut to the Department for Communities and Local Government between 2011 and 2015 holds the greatest significance, as there will be a reduction of GBP500 million in funding for sport that will affect the types of programs highlighted here.

In the first step towards providing future policy direction, the Coalition government in 2012 launched Creating a Sporting Habit for Life: A New Youth Sport Strategy, which seeks to capitalize on the feel-good factor of the 2012 London Olympic and Paralympic Games in terms of engaging young people.

It remains to be seen how this policy develops and also what other sport-related policies will emerge from the government. However, it seems that New Labour's social exclusion mantra is becoming a distant memory in policy terms.

Zambia: local, national and transnational vectors of sport and social exclusion policy

Social inclusion policies within Zambia generally fall within a broader rhetoric of development, which portrays the country as a peripheral nation in the world system and, as such, excluded from the core of the global political economy. The current National Development Plan outlines the government's ambition to make Zambia 'a prosperous middle income country by 2013' via 'sustained economic growth and poverty reduction' (Republic of Zambia 2011: i). National Development Plans have provided an ongoing framework for public policy in Zambia since 1964. While all six plans lack specific mention of the term 'social exclusion', each plan outlines measures to improve core structures seen to contribute to social inclusion, including economic, housing, employment, health and education. The social policies inspired by the plans recognize that certain groups experience more acute forms of social exclusion than others. The first two development plans, for example, highlighted the greater disadvantages that rural communities face compared to urban communities, and focused on bridging the rural/urban divide. The nationalization of the mining industry in 1968 also created some semblance of social welfare for impoverished Zambians, with the government redistributing income from this industry and investing heavily in education and health infrastructure. This allowed cheaper access to these resources for those living in low socio-economic areas (Noyoo 2007). However, from 1974 onwards Zambia's economic downturn began to erode the welfare system. Hence, while the National Development Plans continued to focus on establishing structures to improve the quality of life for impoverished Zambians, a more neo-liberal philosophy began to dominate that meant tangible actions from these policies were limited (Noyoo 2008). The impact of this became evident in the sports sector, as outlined below.

Policies relating to sport appeared in several of the early plans but initially focused on developing sport provision more broadly within Zambia. The first National Development Plan (1966–70) prioritized the building of infrastructure to support elite sport (including a 30,000 seater capacity stadium), while the second plan (1972–76) identified football as a key priority sport (Banda 2011). The third plan (1979–83) resulted in the establishment of the Ministry for Youth and Sport (now Ministry for Sport, Youth and Child Development). While this was a considerable advance by the government in recognizing sport as an important aspect of society, the ministry focused mainly on supporting elite sport, particularly football (Banda 2010). The fourth plan (1989–93) contained the first National Sports Policy (1994) that in part sought to address issues of access in sport (Banda 2011). At a general level, this policy aimed to encourage the development of facilities and a sport structure to encourage participation across all groups under a broader banner of sport for all. However, specific references to disadvantaged groups were lacking, and the government was unable to implement the policy due to limited resources within national sports associations, and limited funding within the government sector because of continued economic hardship.

In 2005, the late Zambian President Levy Mwanawasa opened the 'Next Steps' sport for development conference held in Livingstone with a speech that acknowledged the role sport could potentially play in addressing critical issues facing Zambian society, as well as the importance of access to sport and games for young people (Sport for Development and Peace International Working Group 2006). From this, the fifth National Development Plan (2006–11) became the first plan to explicitly link sport to addressing disadvantage among impoverished Zambians. This plan and the subsequent National Sports Policy (2009) that emanated from it both suggested that sport could be a useful tool for addressing exclusion affecting young people, particularly young women, HIV/AIDS orphans and those living in impoverished conditions in compound communities. The National Sports Policy suggested that sport could be used to address health and gender inequalities as well as mobilize young people within compound communities to undertake community development activity. However, while the Ministry for Sport, Youth and Child Development acknowledged the potential role of sport in addressing social exclusion, this was not reflected in other ministries traditionally responsible for addressing aspects of social exclusion. Policies within health, community development, social services and education ministries did not mention sport within their development plans. The focus on sport as a means to address youth exclusion not only reflects the connections of sport and youth within the ministry that developed the policy, but is also indicative of the position of sport within Zambian culture. While football remains the only sport that adults (mostly males) participate in in large numbers, participation tends to dwindle in adulthood unless an individual is talented and participates at an elite level. Zambians generally see sport as a youth pastime, something played for fun that ceases in adulthood. Hence, within the 2009 National Sports Policy the value of sport was singularly focused on addressing issues affecting young people.

The 2009 Policy also acknowledges the potential exclusion from sport that many Zambians experience and states a commitment to address this. The document outlined an intention to improve resources in highly impoverished and rural areas, to increase the number of girls and women participating, and to encourage participation among people with disabilities. The latter policy focus led to the creation of the Zambian National Paralympics Committee (Banda 2010). In 2010, the National Organization for Women in Sport, Physical Activity and Recreation (NOWSPAR), which plays an advocacy role to promote improved gender equality both within and through sport, held the first policy consultative meeting on women and sport in Zambia. NOWSPAR executive director Matilda Mwaba convened the meeting, which brought together officials from the ministries of Sport, Education and Gender, as well as sporting bodies, the National Sports Council, National Paralympics Committee and National Olympic Committee. The meeting aimed to encourage policy-makers to 'recognize their pivotal role in meeting the challenge of gender inequality in sport which manifests itself in the limited participation of women' (NOWSPAR 2010).

Although the 2009 National Sports Policy led to a greater focus on issues of social exclusion both within and beyond sport, limited tangible activity emanated due to economic constraints (Banda 2011). While recognized in policy rhetoric, sport was still a very minor aspect of government develop-ment policy and as such received little funding. In 2009, funding provided by the government for sport and recreation activities formed only 1.2 per cent of overall government expenditure. Of this, the Department for Sports Development (which sits below the Ministry for Youth, Sport and Child Development) allocated resources disproportionately towards football, with the Football Association of Zambia receiving 70 per cent of the budget in 2009 and only 2 per cent allocated to 'sport for all' initiatives (Banda 2010). The Zambian national football team's recent success in the 2012 African Cup of Nations tournament suggests that this investment is likely to be prioritized. While the Football Association of Zambia outlined in their development policies a commitment to increase provision and opportunities for women to play, it has not invested significant resources in this area (Magee and Jeanes 2009). As discussed below, the growth of the women's game in Zambia has largely emerged from sport for development policy rather than specific poli-cies developed at a national level to address gender inequity within sport.

Sport for development in Zambia: transnational policy, local practice

Because of limited funding, government or national sport association programs funded via government that seek to use sport to address aspects of exclusion are rare. However, there has been a proliferation of activities in this area over the last decade that have emerged as a result of local non-governmental organ-izations (NGOs) connecting with international and transnational development policies and agencies, and effectively bypassing the Zambian government's lack of financial commitment in this area (Banda 2011). Key policies informing such work have been the United National Millennium Development Goals (MDGs) (2000) and the UN Convention on the Rights of the Child (1989). NGOs have particularly focused on using sport to work towards the MDGs of gender equality, combating HIV/AIDS, and ending poverty and hunger.

The use of sport within international development work emerged with fervour in the early 1990s and gathered significant momentum during the 2000s, with an estimated 250 NGOs in Lusaka alone using sport to work with disadvantaged communities (Kay and Jeanes 2010). The Norwegian Agency for Development Cooperation (NORAD) provided initial funding in this area to the indigenous NGOs Sport in Action and EduSport. As indicated, other NGOs emerged that included transnational sporting agencies such as Right to Play and the Global South driven NGO SCORE, while Sport in Action and EduSport continued to be central in driving the on-the-ground translation of international development policy into practice (Banda 2011). The UK Department for International Development (via UK Sport) and Commonwealth Games Canada provided subsequent funding. The funding provided by external agencies has generally been double or more than that allocated by the government for all sport activities; for example, in 2006, the Department for Sports Development allocated USD100,000 to the National Sports Council while NORAD provided USD550,000 to EduSport and Sport in Action (Banda 2011). This continued investment in sport for development activities by external agencies was largely responsible for pressing the government to recognize the potential of sport to contribute to other areas in the 2009 National Sports Policy. The 2009 budget for 'sport for all' activities was motivated by the International Inspiration program (discussed below) funded by UK Sport, UNICEF and the British Council (Banda 2011), with agencies pressuring the government to provide partnership funding. Thus, the international context has largely driven the role of sport in addressing social exclusion within Zambian national policy.

Numerous initiatives have emerged from global sport and international development policy discourses. EduSport manages the Go Sisters program that has been running for over a decade. The program aligns with the Millennium Development Goal of gender equality and seeks to empower females by raising their profile and status within Zambian communities, supporting access to general and HIV/AIDS education, and developing key life skills to enable positive behaviour choices. The program adopts a peer leader model where NGO staff members recruit and train female peer leaders to work in their local community and deliver sports activities and life skills training. The program now has a thriving base of several hundred trained peer leaders in regular sports activities in local communities, including in competitive leagues for young women across several sports (Kay and Jeanes 2011). Further examples include Sport in Action's Young Farmers' Club, an initiative specifically target-ing rural deprivation and its impact on young people. This program again utilizes a peer-leader approach and works with young people outside of the school system. Here, sports activities provide a focus and a platform for health and skills education. The Club also provides support to the target group to develop self-sustaining, income-generating activities, as well as livestock, farm-ing tools and various crop seeds (Sport in Action 2010).

The interconnection between social exclusion policy and practice in and through sport

While the policies that have driven such programs perceive sport as a useful 'hook' to address broader issues such as poverty and gender inequality, they have also resulted in the increase of sports provision for those groups who were previously unable to access regular sport participation opportunities. As the outline of Go Sisters suggests, young women in many impoverished compound communities now regularly participate in competitive leagues and games in basketball, netball, volleyball and football (Kay and Jeanes 2011), despite limited input from national sport governing bodies to address exclusion in this area. More broadly, both young males and females with limited access to sports equipment or resources to participate in sport are now able to do so because of the multitude of opportunities that have sprung up from external investment in sport for development.

The International Inspiration initiative in Zambia (2008–11) provides a further example of the intersection between promoting inclusion within sport and using sport to address exclusion in other spheres. Funded by UNICEF, the British Council and UK Sport, the program has several facets including a focus on broadening sports participation for disadvantaged young people. As part of the program, UK Sport works with the Zambian Volleyball Association and the Zambian Athletics Association to support the development of activity for young people with disabilities (Kay and Jeanes 2010). This includes funding for coach education and to purchase adapted equipment and activities for young people with disabilities within local communities. Addressing social exclusion within sport and using sport as a tool to address wider exclusion is interwoven in Zambia. The development of more equitable sports provision (addressing social exclusion in sport) is often overshadowed by a desire from NGOs to demonstrate how sport contributes to wider international development agendas (addressing broader social exclusion through sport). The UNICEF component of the International Inspirations initiative also contained a safe sporting spaces component. This focused on addressing structural issues of safety with regard to sports facilities in impoverished compound communities, such as providing level playing surfaces and goalposts and basketball rings that would not break and cause injury when used. However, this initiative also promoted the development of more inclusive sporting environments, including training peer leaders on how to establish sports activities that were inclusive, particularly for young women, and how to discourage violence in a sports setting. NOWSPAR sought to develop similar policies, with a meeting held in 2010 to discuss women and sport funded via the Norwegian Olympic and Paralympic Committee and supported by the Ministry of Sport, Youth and Child Development and the National Sports Council. At this meeting, NOWSPAR established a code of conduct to address violence against women within sport. The meeting also explored possible strategies to encourage uptake of these policies among sporting bodies within Zambia and Southern Africa more broadly (NOWSPAR 2010).

As indicated, the driving force for much of this activity has largely occurred outside Zambia and permeated local communities via international agencies working with grassroots NGOs. Importantly, there is a localized desire to address social exclusion within communities that is not connected to formal policy from either the Zambian government or International Development agencies. Lindsey and Gratton's (2012) ethnographic research work in Zambia highlights how impoverished compound communities have sought to broaden access to sport, and also use sport to address issues within their community independent of wider agendas and policies prompting them to do so.

The connections between sport and social exclusion within policy are therefore complex within Zambia. There is somewhat of a commitment by the Ministry of Sport, Youth and Child Development to tackle social exclusion within sport and to use sport as a means to engage with disadvantaged groups. However, limited tangible activities have emanated from this, and there is a general lack of connection with other ministerial departments responsible for addressing social exclusion across health, education and employment more broadly (Lindsey and Banda 2011). This is understandable given the severe economic constraints faced by governmental departments, and the fact that although sport is recognized as a possible player in the social exclusion field it is not generally seen as a serious contributor at a ministerial level. Policies stemming from an international development agenda have, however, led to extensive on-the-ground work. This bypassing of state-led structures has catalysed intense activity that sees sport being used to address social exclusion among a range of disadvantaged groups, particularly young people within materially deprived communities in Zambia. As indicated, while this work has by default gone some way to address inequity within the sports setting, it has not been a policy priority and how sustainable it will be in the longer term is questionable (Banda 2011). Some Zambian Sports Associations recognize the need to improve access to their sports and, as discussed, particularly prioritize females and individuals with disabilities. For organizations such as athletics and volleyball, connecting with international agencies has provided some funding to develop provision for these groups. However, despite the rhetoric of other organizations such as Football Association Zambia to address inequity within their particular sport, they remain relatively disengaged in practice (Magee and Jeanes 2009). While the lack of funding available to make serious inroads into social exclusion in sport within Zambia clearly presents a considerable constraint, broader cultural norms surrounding sport as an exclusively masculine, able-bodied activity also play a significant role in restricting the translation of policy into practice in this area. Hence, social inclusion is not prioritized in many sports associations that focus on developing existing male provision and, in particular, enhancing elite performance (Banda 2011).

The People's Republic of China: rapid growth and enduring inequalities

China is a developing country that from the late 1970s rapidly accelerated through significant economic reform and social change to become a major global economic force (Chan 2001; Chan *et al.* 2008; Li 2004, 2005).

Established in 1949 by the Communist Party of China following the flight of the then ruling Nationalist party (Kuomintang) to neighbouring Taiwan, China is a nation of staggering enormity and proportions – a geographic land size of almost 10 million square kilometres (the second largest in the world), a population of over 1.37 billion (the most populated country in the world), and a Gross Domestic Product (GDP) of USD8.2 trillion. China is traditionally a rural farming nation but has experienced rapid urbanization and industrialization (Chan *et al.* 2008), with nearly half of the Chinese population now living in urban areas (Shan 2011).

China is governed by the Central Communist Party (CCP) as an authoritarian single-party state, a type of governmental rule relatively distinct in global politics. In 1949, China established a pyramid hierarchy organizational structure based on the Leninist principle of democratic centralism (Chan *et al.* 2008) that still exists today. In this system, the CCP 'is the paramount source of power and its members hold almost all of the top government, police and military positions' (Chan *et al.* 2008: 6). With the CCP at its organizational heart, government administration extends outwards through an extensive network of party cells across 2,100 counties and 400 county-status cities.

China's economy and GDP rapidly expanded following the introduction of economic reforms in 1978, and has been fundamentally transformed from an exclusively communist to a mixed economy. Yet, China's economic success has been inequitably shared among its citizens. Indeed, the transformation of its economy to a more market-oriented economy initially has entailed a marked rise in inequality (OECD 2012). Hence, socio-economic inequalities have widened between social classes, rich and poor provinces, and urban and rural areas, with significant consequences for social exclusion (Chan *et al.* 2008; Li 2005). However, recent figures published by the OECD (2012) suggest that socio-economic disparities in China may have eased in recent years; for example, income inequality has fallen, the urban–rural income gap has narrowed, the number of people living below the poverty line has fallen to 6 per cent, and the lower-income provinces have started to grow more rapidly than higher-income regions. In addition, the coverage of social protection systems has widened and total spending on social protection has increased as part of the Chinese government's 11th Five Year Plan (2006–10) that focused greater policy attention on the creation of a more harmonious society and the reduction of rural poverty (OECD 2012; Information Office of the State Council 2011a). Nevertheless, major policy challenges remain. While the social protection system may have widened, it is far from universal. There is still a large and persistent informal sector with limited rights and, as discussed below, rural–urban migrants are often prevented from acquiring the same rights as people with local urban registration status in the area in which they live. Further, rural areas continue to have less access to basic services such as medical insurance and education (Herd 2010).

Although the issues of unequal rights and socio-economic disparities closely reflect the types of social exclusion discussed in Chapter 2, social exclusion as a concept is relatively uncommon in Chinese policy and academic research. A major reason for this is the political connotation of the term. Writing in 2004, Li (2004) has contended that the Chinese government neither accepts the notion of social exclusion nor sanctions social policy research unless such research is considered non-political and non-confrontational *vis-à-vis* government interests. However, despite the limited uptake of the concept in Chinese policy and research, at a practical level there is strong evidence of the prolonged existence of social exclusion within this society which has included the systematic denial of basic human rights to citizens by the ruling authority of the CCP (Li 2004, 2005; Li and Piachaud 2004; Chan *et al.* 2008). Li (2004, 2005), Li and Piachaud (2004) and Chan *et al.* (2008) agree that the denial of basic human rights to members of Chinese society has been endemic and resulted in various forms of social exclusion. Li (2004) conclusively argues that social exclusion has existed throughout the history of China and offers four dimensions through which it has been experienced:

- Rural residents have been denied equitable access to urban areas, with urban residents enjoying far superior rights and benefits.
- Those labelled as subversive or politically dissident have been denied basic human rights.
- Employment and welfare allocation has been selective on an 'insider/outsider basis', regulated by the government (as discussed further on in this chapter).
- Strict control over the employment system has allowed the Chinese government to exclude (and even remove) people from it at will.

These mechanisms of social exclusion, Li (2004, 2005) contends, have generated social vulnerabilities that make it difficult for people at the 'bottom' of Chinese society to share the dividends of economic and social reform. In a similar vein, Chan *et al.* (2008: 41) argue that China has failed to respond effectively to the welfare needs of its citizens, and that the 'path of welfare reform is still a long one for the Chinese Government'.

Government responses to welfare needs and social disparities should be understood within the context of China's distinct welfare regime, which is diversified and in which social welfare arrangements vary greatly according to locality. One reason for this diversified welfare regime is that the Chinese state lacked the resources required to develop a unified national welfare system (Chan *et al.* 2008). Therefore two welfare systems exist within China: an urban system that is prioritized by urban-centric policy-makers but critically excludes rural migrants to urban cities; and a rural system that receives far less financial assistance from central sources and is highly variable across different regions (Li 2004, 2005; Li and Piachaud 2004; Chan *et al.* 2008). Thus, social policy within the Chinese context is uniquely different from the majority of other nations, including the other countries examined in this chapter.

Chinese social policy in historical context

The development of social policy in China can be divided into three broad periods: the Central Planning Era (1949–78) (also known as the 'pre-reform period'); the Pro-urban Growth Model (1979–99) (also known as the 'post-reform period'); and the policy changes from 2000 onwards (Li 2004, 2005). The social and economic policies of each period reflect the overarching political and developmental strategies at these times. In this section, attention will be drawn to those policies that are most closely aligned with social exclusion.

The Central Planning Era (1949–78) can be summarized as a planned socio-economic system in which individuals were treated unequally, with major consequences for social inclusion/exclusion. During this period, a political system based on class struggle was quickly established, citizens' basic rights were suppressed, and millions were tortured or killed. A key element in this class system was the labels that separated individuals and groups, with everyone having a label in his or her personal archives that were kept by employers, employer organizations, or the local government (Li 2004). The labels were used to clamp down on 'bad' classes in a series of political campaigns from the early 1950s to the late 1970s, with these labels crucial in terms of access to employment, education and welfare provision (Li 2004). The labels contained political, educational and employment histories, and were archived by employer organizations should an employee move to a new employer. The authorities used these labels to track citizens, and removed labels from those they considered troublesome, hereby excluding them from access to mainstream society (Li 2004). This system created boundaries between insiders and outsiders, effectively excluding an 'underclass' that was voiceless in the political system (Li 2005).

Economic development from the 1950s onwards commenced with the Great Leap Forward, which centred on a dual strategy of the redistribution of rural land to 300 million farmers and the nationalization of large businesses (Fan and Lu 2011). Hence, all private enterprises and most free market activity were eliminated during this period (Chan *et al.* 2008). The Resolution on the Establishment of the People's Communes in Rural Areas (1958) created 26,000 communes by 1958 whereby central government promoted town and village enterprises through a central economic resourcing socialist welfare system that distributed daily ration necessities to members. However 'this collective welfare system suffered low productivity and only provided a low public standard of living ... [and] left the nation backward and impoverished' (Chan *et al.* 2008: 29). A further factor in this growing rural–urban divide was the establishment of an urban social security system with the 1951 Regulations of Labour Security for the People's Republic of China, a social security system that provided pension, healthcare and injury protection to workers in an employment enterprise of more than 50 people, but critically only in urban areas. Hence, rural workers were excluded (Li and Piachaud 2004).

Another key government policy in this period centred on the restriction of labour mobility through the Hukou system of residential registration that gave the government power over people's geographical mobility (Chan *et al.* 2008; Li 2005). In effect, it functioned as a *de facto* internal passport mechanism as people needed to apply to the authorities to move residency (Chan *et al.* 1999). As heavy industry grew, rural workers were needed in major urban cities to maintain high levels of productivity, but were required to obtain a temporary residency (*zanzhuzheng*) permit, a work permit (*dagiongzheng*) and an identification card (*shenfenzheng*) from the government to be allowed to migrate.

Despite low productivity in rural areas and meagre livings, these measures were introduced to ensure official urban employment and prevent begging, vagrancy and homelessness. However, this further excluded rural workers by creating two types of migrants: those with local resident rights (Hukou migration); and those without residency rights (non-Hukou migration). The latter were 'treated as a floating population or temporary migrants … working in low-paid, dangerous and dirty jobs' and excluded from access to basic public services (Chan *et al.* 2008: 9). This 'floating population' of migrant workers is a key example of social exclusion within China both historically and at present. It reportedly reached a high of 221 million in 2011 (Xinhua 2011a).

The result was such that, through Hukou, the government was able to control labour mobility by excluding outsiders from employment (Chan *et al.* 2008). As such, 'rural residents were treated differently from urban residents in social welfare provision', reinforcing the insider/outsider divide and exacerbating social exclusion (Li 2005: 56). Social exclusion also occurred through the political system, as people with unfavourable political backgrounds were deprived of many of the rights enjoyed by their fellow citizens (Li 2005), further affecting the wellbeing of some of the poorest members of society (Li 2004; Li and Piachaud 2004).

The Cultural Revolution (1966–76) was subsequently a watershed era for China, with the education sector in particular being vilified as capitalist education. A large number of students and teachers were sent to factories, the countryside and military camps for re-education, and some schools and universities closed (Chan *et al.* 2008). The Cultural Revolution left China in social and political chaos, with many citizens 'struggling to eke out a bare subsistence lifestyle' (Chan *et al.* 2008: 3). At the end of the Cultural Revolution, the focus of the CCP shifted from previously non-stop political campaigns and class struggle to economic development in order to transform China into a prosperous country and hereby to enhance the political legitimacy of the CCP and the country's global image (Chan *et al.* 2008).

In the post-reform period of 1979–99, the government developed a pro-urban growth model that liberalized trade markets by aiding growth in heavy industries in urban areas and relaxing previous labour mobility restrictions (Li and Piachaud 2004). This model entailed a fundamental change to the economic base of China's socialism by introducing private economic activities as an essential supplement to state-owned enterprises (SOEs). Private property and market forces were expected to create more employment and business opportunities (Chan *et al.* 2008). Hence, the new model focused on industrial achievement with state provision of advanced education for the urban population, housing and transport systems for urban expansion, and social security for urban industrial workers (Li and Piachaud 2004).

By the late 1980s, the government permitted full private ownership of SOEs. Non-publicly owned enterprises emerged as profit-making organizations that benefited individuals, instigating 'a major ideological breakthrough because it legalized the status of the private sector, providing legal protection for private property' (Chan *et al.* 2008: 31). In effect, this change created a labour market where previously one had not existed because labour regulations had been centrally controlled. This new private sector, however, also had negative consequences in terms of social exclusion. First, as SOEs became private enterprises, many individuals were not retained and became unemployed. Second, those who were retained were required to sign an employment contract, but these were short-term, low-paid contracts with immediate termination a possibility. Last, many rural SOEs went bankrupt as private investors saw insufficient value in investing in rural areas as agricultural productivity had limited profitability. Hence, unemployment further threatened social stability, leaving many rural and urban households too poor to meet basic needs, and often deprived of financial, medical, education and housing protection (Chan *et al.* 2008).

Fundamental changes in social provision were also made to healthcare, housing and education (Li and Piachaud 2004). The privatization of healthcare was most acutely felt in rural areas and among rural–urban migrants, with many poor families denied the basic healthcare previously provided by SOEs (Chan *et al.* 2008). Further, private housing reform allowed individuals to purchase property, further boosting the central economy by making housing a commodity, but again excluding those that could not afford to purchase property. Central government used various macro-strategies to regulate housing prices and to prevent quick selling on the now private market (Chan *et al.* 2008). Elite education was further strengthened, with a move towards tuition fees and increased higher education opportunities within urban universities. However, as the government did not prioritize rural education, these changes negatively affected the rural–urban divide (Chan *et al.* 2008). Li (2004) argues that the limited educational attainment of rural inhabitants placed migrants to urban areas at a disadvantage in the labour market when compared to their relatively educated urban counterparts. This restricted education often resulted in migrants being employed in low-skilled, menial work that was among the lowest paid. As a result, rural workers were easily identifiable by urban residents, considered to be lower class, segregated into lower-quality houses, and even prevented from using certain public transport (Li 2004).

The new economic system appears to have primarily benefited those who already possessed economic capital, whereas those who did not were largely excluded from access to private services and goods (Li 2005). While benefiting urban conditions, the pro-urban model did not similarly affect rural areas, especially in relation to housing conditions, employment, education and social welfare support (Li and Piachaud 2004). Thus, Knight (2000) identifies an emergence in the 1990s of the 'new poor', who survived around the poverty level. These included the unemployed, rural migrant workers, people with disabilities, the long-term ill, and the elderly who were not supported by family members.

The growth of private enterprise in China has continued steadily into the twenty-first century (Chan *et al.* 2008). However, rising unemployment and a dated welfare system reliant on SOEs are still considerable problems. With the withdrawal of SOEs creating significant pressure on welfare provision, new market-oriented welfare measures were introduced. The Chinese government established a welfare model based on three security lines: a basic living guarantee system, unemployment insurance, and the Minimum Standard of Living Scheme (Chan *et al.* 2008). A feature of these measures is that they typically reward those who make contributions to economic productivity, while those who are non-participants are unable to have a decent standard of living (Chan *et al.* 2008). According to the OECD (2012), these measures have had some effect on easing socio-economic disparities between the rich and poor in China; nevertheless, as noted earlier, economic disparity is still marked.

Rural–urban migrants continue to be denied many of the political, social and economic rights afforded to urban residents. As such, they experience an enforced lack of participation in mainstream urban society (Li 2004, 2005). Chinese official data estimated that the country's migrant worker population was 253 million by the end of 2011 (Xinhua 2013a). However, significant change may be on the way. In early 2013, the Chinese government highlighted as an important national task the transition of rural migrant workers to urban residents. The central policy document stated that the country would ease requirements for obtaining residency permits in small and medium-sized cities and small townships. China also vowed to protect migrant workers' social security and rights, alongside its efforts to extend basic public services to all permanent residents in the cities (Xinhua 2013b).

Linkages between sport and social exclusion in Chinese government policy

China's emerging status as a global economic superpower is also reflected in the realm of elite sport. In the London 2012 Olympic Games, China was second placed, winning 88 medals that included 38 gold. The 2012 Paralympic Games were even more successful for China with a landslide win of 231 medals (95 gold). However, it is not merely elite sport that has witnessed significant investment by the Chinese government. As outlined below, China is also concerned with growing its mass sport participation and has introduced a flurry of policies to promote sport participation among disadvantaged population groups.

Chinese sport policy has long focused on using sport as a vehicle to facilitate strong national and self-strengthening sentiments, with training healthy and strong bodies for national defence and building the socialist state major themes in its early sport policy (Fan and Lu 2011; Stone 2001). For example, the semi-governmental All-China Sports Federation (1952) focused on mass sport as a way to promote the health of the nation, a focus that increased during the 1950–53 Korean War. The 1952 Helsinki Olympic Games provided further impetus to sport policy, as it stimulated the government's determination to use sport as a vehicle to promote the new China in international politics (Fan and Lu 2011). Fan and Lu (2012: 21) label this early stage of sport development in China as 'the Sovietisation of Chinese sport'.

The Great Leap Forward of Sport was initiated in 1956 with a ten-year plan dedicated to mass sport and competitive sport dominance, which sought to simultaneously develop sport in urban and rural areas (Lu and Henry 2011: 1060). This strategy was underpinned by Mao Zedong's belief that sport and physical exercise were the backbone of the nation, and that the development of sport and physical education was crucial for national development (Fan and Lu 2011; Stone 2001). In 1956, the State Physical Culture and Sports Commission (SPCSC) also introduced a formal competitive sports system with regional and national championships to promote sport both in rural and urban areas. While the Great Leap Forward ended in 1958, sport policy continued to focus on simultaneously developing mass sport and competitive sport, with further emphasis on war-type sporting activities in the 1960s following threats from the Soviet Union and India.

The power struggles of the Cultural Revolution also extended to sport. In particular, the relationship between mass sport and competitive sport altered significantly during this period. Competitive sport was now considered representative of bourgeois and capitalist ideology, while mass sport was regarded as communist and proletarian (Fan and Lu 2011). As a consequence, the entire sport performance training system in China was dismantled. Athletes and coaches were 're-educated', while some were executed, national squads were not allowed to participate in the international forum, and sports schools, stadiums and training venues were closed down (Fan and Lu 2011). In contrast, mass sport regained popularity as government attention on physical exercise moved from its earlier focus on material concerns (e.g. defence and production) to more abstract concerns of spiritual and moral development (Lu and Henry 2011). During this period sport policy remained very much aligned with wider Maoist policy, especially in rural areas where sport and physical activity were central elements of government policy (Fan and Lu 2011).

With the ending of the Cultural Revolution, a shift in sport policy occurred with elite sport prioritized over mass sport. In the 1980s elite sport was used for political purposes and to promote China's new image on the international stage, even though it was still an underdeveloped country with limited finance to invest in sport (Fan and Lu 2012). The rapid growth of elite sport was reflected in improved performance at the Olympic Games, which reportedly 'exhilarated the Chinese people and was linked to nationalism, patriotism, collectivism and heroism' (Fan and Lu 2012: 82).

As the market economy grew throughout the 1980s and 1990s, so too did the role of sport. The sport and leisure industry boomed, with China becoming the world's largest sporting goods market (Fan and Lu 2011). The success of the sports industry was influenced by private ownership and economic prosperity that allowed wealthier people to spend money and time on sports goods, equipment and facilities. The sports lottery was established in 1994, and has also been a key factor in the development and success of the sports industry. Hosting the 1990 Asian Games and the 2008 Olympic Games not only promoted China's international image, but arguably also stimulated a transformation of Chinese society (Fan and Lu 2012). The country's elite sport success culminated in China finishing first on the gold medal table at the 2008 Beijing Olympic Games, ahead of the United States.

This overview demonstrates how the Chinese government has used sport for varying political purposes. However, the use of sport to address the social exclusion of disadvantaged members of society is still in its infancy. Three main areas of sport-related policy focus can be identified: the rural population, minority ethnic groups, and people with disabilities. These target areas should be understood in relation to historically experienced disadvantage in China, as well as contemporary regulations and policies such as the National Human Rights Action Plan that stipulates a range of measures to protect the rights and interests of ethnic minorities, women, children, elderly people and people with disabilities (Information Office of the State Council 2011b). As shown below, however, they should also be understood more critically within the context of market competition and a moral emphasis on individual responsibility and self-help (e.g. Stone 2001).

The need to improve access to sport for disadvantaged groups is articulated in China's national sports policies such as the National Fitness for All Program (2011–15), which aims to improve the population's physical fitness. This program is partly funded from the proceeds of China's sports lottery. One program objective is to grow the development of sports in rural, poor and 'ethnic' areas through investment in sports infrastructure (e.g. indoor and outdoor sports and fitness centres), the establishment of ethnic, rural and disability sports associations, and the organization of sports festivals (State Council General Office 2011). The Chinese government invests in sport in these areas to achieve its policy goal of enhancing mass sport participation, and improving public health and living standards. Mass sport participation is also seen as a foundation for elite sports success that in turn is deemed important for national development. For example, China's Olympic Strategy for 2011–20 stresses the importance of enhancing mass sports participation in ethnic and rural areas for the identification and recruitment of high-quality athletes. Government investment in elite sports in poor and ethnic areas is also seen to contribute to the development of mass sports and wellbeing in these areas (General Administration of Sport 2011).

The Chinese government's attempt to stimulate sport participation in rural areas is particularly interesting within the wider context of rural exclusion and disadvantage. As noted earlier, despite rapid urbanization, rural residents remained the largest social group in China, and traditionally vulnerable to social exclusion (Li 2004; Chan *et al.* 2008). Sport has been used at different times to assist China's rural population (Fan and Lu 2011, 2012; Lu and Henry 2011), but there is no literature to suggest that these efforts were sparked by a commitment to social inclusion. Yet, current government policies on the promotion of sports in rural areas refer to the development of rural sports as 'a crucial step to construct a new socialist rural China', where sport can serve to improve people's life quality and contribute to the development of rural areas (General Administration of Sport 2007). The Chinese government views the lack of sports activities in rural areas as a major factor contributing to the lower health status of the rural population (General Administration of Sport 2007).

The causes of the relatively limited access to sport in rural communities, sometimes referred to within the Chinese context as 'rural sports poverty' (Fu and Dong 2008; Shen *et al.* 2009), are multifaceted. A key factor is economic poverty. Lower incomes mean that spending money on sport is generally lower in rural households than in their urban counterparts (Shen *et al.* 2009). However, research also points to other factors that affect rural residents' sport participation opportunities. In addition to specific cultural attitudes that may afford low priority to sport as a form of physical exercise, there is often a lack of opportunity to participate in sports in rural areas due to the shortage of sports spaces, resources and administration (Fu and Dong 2008). Simply put, rural residents have long been disadvantaged by Chinese sports develop-ment policy. There is a discrepancy in government funding allocations for sport, with investment in urban sport systematically prioritized at the expense of rural communities. Herein lies a significant form of social exclusion that underpins rural sports poverty (Shen *et al.* 2009).

There are important parallels between Chinese policy aimed at increasing sport participation in rural areas and government-led programs that target minority ethnic, non-Han groups. China officially recognizes 56 distinct ethnic groups, the largest of which is Han that constitutes more than 91 per cent of the total population. Ethnic minorities are estimated to constitute 8.5 per cent or 113.8 million of China's population in 2010, with many of these non-urban residents (People's Republic of China 2012).

The development of sport in areas inhabited predominantly by minority ethnic groups is constrained by a number of factors (Yao 2004; Rao *et al.* 2007). First, as with rural areas in general, economic resources are a major contributing factor with several minority ethnic groups, especially those in rural areas, facing economic hardship and poverty and often lacking access to a reliable social security system (with the exception of informal welfare such as family support). Ethnic minorities are also perceived to have a more limited understanding of the importance of sport participation, and this is compounded by the shortage of culturally appropriate sports organizations and facilities in the areas where they live (Yao 2004).

The Chinese government recognizes that limited access to sport among minority ethnic groups is a policy concern. The Regulations on Ethnic Autonomous Regions of PRC (2005) frame the importance of promoting sports among minority ethnic groups in terms of their potential to increase their 'physical qualities' (Rao *et al.* 2007). A major objective in China's mass sports policy, then, is to address this problem by propagating sports-related information in minority ethnic areas and by increasing the number and quality of sports facilities. The Chinese government has undertaken a range of initiatives in this policy area, such as the introduction of sports with 'ethnic characteristics' among minority groups and the promotion of sports in schools by incorporating 'ethnic characteristics' into physical education programs (State Council General Office 2011). These initiatives are informed by the idea that there should be targeted sports policies that align with the characteristics and culture of the ethnic groups in question (Rao *et al.* 2007).

Another important area of policy focus as it pertains to ethnic minorities has been the celebration of minority ethnic sports games in different parts of the country. The National Traditional Games of Ethnic Minorities of China evolved from a relatively small-scale performance of minority ethnic sports in Tianjin in 1953, when 395 athletes from 13 minority ethnic groups took part (Rao *et al.* 2007). Nowadays, the games are a major event that brings together more than 4,000 athletes representing all 55 minority ethnic groups. The games aim to promote and maintain the sporting cultures of China's minority ethnic groups as well as promote the aforementioned national fitness campaign. Unlike other multi-sports national games, the minority ethnic sports games do not include a single Olympic sport on the program, with most events sourced from the daily life of particular minority ethnic groups, such as broadsword walking, horse racing and stilts running. Nine editions of the games have been held, most recently in Guizhou in 2011 where more than 15,000 participants including over 6,700 athletes competed in 16 title events and 188 demonstration events (Xinhua 2011b).

A third area of the Chinese sport policy focus with important links to social exclusion is the promotion of sport participation among people with disabilities. This policy area is particularly important as people with disabilities in China have historically suffered from social exclusion, particularly during the Cultural Revolution. As potential non-workers, non-soldiers and non-mothers, people with disabilities were perceived to pose a threat to Maoist socialist ideologies (Stone 2001). Based on a narrow definition of productive work, these people were separated and excluded from mainstream Chinese society. However, there now appears to be a greater emphasis in Chinese law and policy on the rights of people with disabilities. Sport can be seen to play a role in this, with Feng Jianzhong, Deputy Director of the General Administration of Sport, stating that 'sport is a way for the disabled to participate in common social lives like the others' (Lu 2011). This national policy interest in disability sport has been driven to a major extent by the China Disabled Persons' Federation (CDPF), a state-controlled quasi-governmental organization established in 1998 under the leadership of Deng Pufang, a wheelchair user and the eldest son of the then CCP leader, Deng Xiaoping (Stone 2001).

The CDPF (2012) estimates that 83 million persons have various categories of disability in China. The rights of people with disabilities are protected by law through the Law of the People's Republic of China on the Protection of Disabled Persons. This legislation aims to protect the equal right of persons with disabilities to participate in social and cultural life and to safeguard their share of the material and cultural wealth of Chinese society. Sport is one area of social life that is specifically addressed in the Law. Article 41 states that 'People's governments at all levels and departments concerned shall encourage and assist persons with disabilities to participate in various forms of cultural, sports and recreational activities' (People's Republic of China 2008). Article 42 elaborates on this by noting that sports activities for persons with disabilities 'should be based on communities, integrated into public cultural life and geared to the different characteristics and needs of different categories of persons with disabilities with a view to bringing about extensive participation'. The Law stipulates that government and society adopt a number of specific measures to enrich the spiritual and cultural life of persons with disabilities. These measures include mobilizing and supporting persons with disabilities for sports activities, hosting sports games for persons with disabilities, and providing sports facilities and accommodations suitable for persons with disabilities (People's Republic of China 2008).

The legal underpinning of sport as a social right for people with disabilities is put into practice through policy strategies aimed at promoting 'disabled people's sport' (*canjiren yundong* or *canjiren tiyu*). This policy objective is articulated in the National Fitness Plan (2011–15) that underlines the need to establish low-threshold sporting facilities to help people with disabilities and to invest in the development of sports among students with disabilities. Government investment in this area has primarily targeted cities such as Liaoning, Shanghai, Beijing, Guangdong and Chengdu, among others (Hao 2010).

Similar to the ethnic minority sports games described earlier, China has held National Games for Disabled Persons since its inauguration in Anhui province in 1984. Since its third version in 1992, the games have been held every four years. In 2011, more than 3,000 athletes from 35 delegations attended the eighth edition of the games in Hangzhou. The nine-day games were described in the Chinese media as a 'national gala for the disabled' and a platform to show their strength and dignity (Lu 2011). The games were also considered a warm-up for China's athletes who competed in the 2012 London Paralympic Games in London, thus contributing to the country's Paralympic strategy.

Chinese policy on disability sport development has also focused on the local grassroots level. A range of initiatives has been adopted in localities, including the organization of sports competitions and fitness activities for people with disabilities, the construction of new sports facilities and coaches' education. Examples include the Fitness Week for People with Disabilities, the National Rope Jumping Contest of Blind Students from Special Schools, and the Basketball Competition of Deaf Persons (CDPF 2012). These initiatives closely align with broader efforts to promote physical exercise among people with disabilities as part of the National Fitness for All Program. Similar initiatives can be found at the elite sport level, for example with regard to government investment in international disability sport exchange programs, intensive training programs, and coaches' education. Activities organized in recent years to promote the development of elite-level disability sport in China include the sixth National Special Olympic Day, Special Olympic competitions in athletics, volleyball and basketball, the health program Special Olympic Week of Football, and training courses focused on family support networks (CDPF 2012).

The emergence of disability sport on the Chinese policy agenda can be interpreted as a significant step towards the social inclusion of people with disabilities in Chinese society. It has helped to raise public awareness about disability in China and challenge some stereotypes and social prejudices about people with disabilities. Yet, the promotion of disability sport in China can also be seen to condone or reproduce forms of exclusion, especially within the broader context of a social security system that typically rewards only those who contribute to economic productivity (Chan *et al.* 2008). Disability sport is portrayed by the authorities as a platform for people with disabilities to demonstrate and cultivate their strength and dignity, and in so doing the promotion of athletes with disabilities is also about setting high standards for people with disabilities to follow in the face of material and socio-normative barriers. In other words, while the Chinese state recognizes the disadvantage experienced by many people with disabilities, it tends to place the onus on individuals with disabilities themselves to overcome structural and socio-normative barriers to social inclusion (Stone 2001), rather than to proactively reduce or remove such barriers through public policy.

Conclusion

The discussion of public policy in the UK, Zambia and China in this chapter highlights how policy approaches to sport and social exclusion differ markedly across time and space. It further shows that important intersections between sport and social exclusion in public policy reveal three broad themes: access to sport, inclusive sporting environments, and the use of sport as a vehicle for social policy objectives. The Chinese and Zambian experiences, however, indicate that in reality the boundaries between these three main areas of intersection are often blurred.

Access to sport involves policies that centre on mass sport participation – sport and recreation activities and pursuits undertaken by the wider population – accentuating, in Coalter's view (2007), the wider social and health benefits presumed to be associated with participation in sport that are central to the idea of the good citizen. Examples of policies and programs designed to increase participation on a mass or generic scale within each of the case nations should be viewed in this light, as should those policy initiatives targeting specific underrepresented or marginalized population groups.

Policies and programs designed to create inclusive sporting environments aim to improve the quality of experiences gained through sporting activity and participation by providing safe, inclusive and welcoming sporting cultures. Of key importance here are the twin issues of barriers and discrimination, in that individuals or groups should not feel denied a sporting experience nor discriminated against within that experience. While there is a correlation here with policies relating to access, the policies in this second theme differ in that they are not actually focused on raising participation rates or increasing membership numbers but on enhancing the quality of the sporting experience through inclusiveness; for example, they provide policy guidance on safety, injury prevention, child protection, and the prevention of gender-based violence. While such initiatives abound in the UK, they are less well established in Zambia and China.

Lastly, policies and programs focusing on the use of sport as a vehicle for social policy objectives are those engineered to tackle issues that create social exclusion within society more broadly, or at least to alleviate some of their symptoms. From this perspective, sport is a malleable policy tool that can be used to achieve particular government objectives (Bloyce and Smith 2010). Hence, sports programs in this area are designed with an ulterior purpose in mind. They typically focus on a particular target group such as the homeless, people with disabilities, ethnic minorities and the elderly, with the overall aim geared towards increasing their capabilities, and resources to stimulate participation in key societal domains and reduce feelings of social exclusion. Providing access to key resources such as education, employment, health literacy or human rights knowledge through a sports program would be typical. While abundant examples of this can be found in Zambia and the UK, this policy approach is less prominent in China. This area of public policy will be examined further in Chapters 5 and 6. In the next chapter, we shift our attention to mechanisms of social exclusion in sport.

4 Mechanisms of social exclusion in sport

Introduction

The previous chapter outlined the connections between policy, sport and social exclusion. In this chapter, we consider in more detail the ways in which sport produces or perpetuates aspects of social exclusion. Extensive literature has examined how involvement in sport is restricted for particular groups and individuals in society (e.g. Sawrikar and Muir 2010; Bailey 2005), and a cursory glance at participation statistics across a range of countries illustrates that, despite the different societal contexts, under-representation most often occurs among females, those with CALD backgrounds, individuals with disabilities, and those with lower socio-economic status (Sport and Recreation South Africa 2005; Statistics Norway 2011; ERASS 2010; Sport England 2012).[1] While the actual total figures are very different (and non-comparable due to differences in survey methodology), and in some countries the gap is closing (e.g. Van Bottenburg 2011), these wider trends exist in both the Global North and Global South. Certain groups of people therefore continue to participate less in sport than others.

Nowadays, absolute and complete social exclusion from sport, such as that experienced by black athletes seeking entrance to white sporting spaces during South Africa's apartheid era, is rare (Elling and Claringbould 2005). However, particular social, cultural and material factors continue to shape (non-) involvement in sport. Most analyses focus on the social exclusion experienced by particular social groups in isolation, notably on the basis of disability, gender, class and so on, while some studies have begun to examine the inter-sectionalities between these axes of differentiation. The purpose of this chapter is not to provide an exhaustive account of the different ways in which sport excludes particular groups or individuals; rather, it outlines at a more general level the key mechanisms of exclusion, before turning to a more detailed analysis of how these play out in practice via a case study that explores the mediating influence of gender on the participation of women in Zambia.

As discussed in Chapter 2, there are numerous, interrelated factors and social processes that contribute to the social exclusion of groups and individuals, both in sport and other societal domains. These factors and processes influence individuals in different ways through a complex constellation of inclusionary and exclusionary mechanisms (Elling and Claringbould 2005). Exclusion from sport is more prevalent in particular types of sporting spaces. Increasingly neo-liberal attitudes within Global North society have seen a shift in sporting trends away from regular, structured, club-based activity towards more individualized, fluid and unregulated lifestyle sports opportunities (Wheaton 2012). This has made sport available to different audiences and, as we discuss below, particularly encouraged participation among women (Thorpe 2005). However, even more diverse forms of participation are exclusionary to some, for instance those who do not have the financial resources to access individualized lifestyle activities (Coalter 2000; Hylton and Totten 2013). The more traditional forms of sporting provision, particularly voluntary sports clubs, continue to attract socially dominant groups (Elling and Claringbould 2005). The broad array of mechanisms discussed below appears to manifest more intensely within the context of structured, organized sport to create powerful forces contributing to social exclusion.

It is also important to note that while it is possible to identify particular practices that contribute to exclusion, these will affect individuals and groups differently according to context, time and space. As noted in Chapter 2, it is essential to understand social exclusion as something that individuals may move in and out of during particular times and in particular contexts. Thus, in relation to sport, Elling and Claringbould (2005: 501) note that 'mechanisms of exclusion cannot always be identified clearly ... because people have multiple social identities, they might often simultaneously experience inclusion and exclusion according to specific social power relations'. Practices of social exclusion within a sports context can largely be broken down into key domains – that is, structural, cultural and social, all of which interlink and overlap. Demographic factors such as social class, gender, age and ethnicity intersect across all these domains. The following section provides a brief overview of how social exclusion manifests across these areas.

Structural mechanisms of social exclusion in sport

In general, groups that dominate sports participation also control its organization and management (Anderson 2009a; Numerato and Baglioni 2011). Middle-class males with majority ethnic backgrounds control organized sport in most countries in the Global North and Global South. Much of the research in this area has focused on the gender discrimination that occurs in senior management positions in sport (e.g. Shaw and Hoeber 2003; Shaw and Slack 2002; Aitchison 2005). A recent report produced by the Australian Sports Commission (2012) highlights that in Australia almost a fifth of national sporting organizations have no women on their boards, an issue we return to further on in the chapter. Other studies show the lack of ethnic diversity within sport governance around the world (Long *et al.* 2005; Massao and Fasting 2010). Similarly, people with disabilities are virtually non-existent in management positions other than for disability-specific sport (DePauw and Gavron 2005).

This exclusionary trend goes beyond higher-level governance organizations and permeates leadership and management at all levels of sport. Various studies highlight how opportunities are often limited within management and coaching roles for individuals from minority ethnic backgrounds. Cashmore and Cleland (2011) discuss the persistent challenges that black managers face in professional football in the UK, while Hallinan and Judd's (2009b) examination of Indigenous players' experiences in the Australian Football League (AFL) shows the low transference rates of Indigenous players into coaching and management positions. At a more local level, studies of voluntary clubs, including our own research of community sports clubs in Victoria, Australia, suggest that the majority of club committees are composed of individuals that reflect the majority rather than the minority of sports participants (Spaaij *et al.* in press).

The capacity of dominant groups to maintain control over the organization and management of sport is significant for understanding social exclusion. It is via this control that institutional discrimination can continue to occur, making it difficult for marginalized groups to feel that they will ever be in a position to make significant change to encourage greater inclusivity. For example, Hallinan and Judd's (2009b) study illustrates how those in power use racialized discourse to portray Indigenous players as not having the necessary skills to be effective AFL managers or coaches. Such discursive positioning enables the perpetuation and reinforcement of certain norms, values and systems that provide the best opportunities for socially dominant groups and restrict the access of outsiders. The scheduling of the 2012 London Olympic Games during the Islamic holy month of Ramadan is one example of the exclusionary practices that can occur when sport governance does not contain adequate representation of minority groups. From a gender perspective, the regulation of female volleyball players' uniforms at the Olympic Games further illustrates how power holders in sport use their position to enforce particular norms and values (Russell 2011): in this particular case, that sexualization of female athletes should take precedence over an appreciation of their athletic performance.

Examining this domain also requires consideration of how physical sporting structures create social exclusion. Environmental perspectives have been utilized to demonstrate how location and, in particular, access to resources can lead to exclusion from particular sporting opportunities (Ravenscroft and Markwell 2000; Van Ingen 2003). This can manifest in various forms, from tangible exclusion due to a lack of adequate facilities within an individual's local area through to a perception of exclusion created from not feeling welcomed within a particular sporting space. Lack of access to particular sporting infrastructure tends to be problematic for some minority groups compared to others. Disability studies highlight how access to sport and recreation facilities can be limited for individuals with physical disabilities

(DePauw 2009; Wedgwood 2011). While disability legislation has begun to regulate and improve access within public and private sector provision, this remains an issue within the voluntary sector. Our own research with junior voluntary sports clubs highlights that many do not have the funds to make structural adjustments to clubhouses and facilities that would be necessary to allow full access for individuals with physical disabilities (Jeanes *et al.* 2012).

Income and socio-economic status also influence access to particular sports opportunities. Those with a low income are less likely to fully participate in organized sport than those with a higher income, as the former may not be able, or willing, to afford the costs of sports club membership, equipment and travel necessary to engage in sport even at a grassroots level (Collins 2007). Indeed, in the Global North, financial restrictions prevent a small proportion of the population from participating in organized sport, joining a sports club, or attending professional sporting events (De Haan 2010; Collins 2012). Considering the restrictions that poverty and low income impose on sport participation, Collins with Kay (2003) suggest that poverty is at the heart of social exclusion in sport, an argument we discussed in some detail in Chapter 2. However, the influence of socio-economic status on sport involvement does not merely work through material barriers or facilitators. Rather, social class also tends to structure to a significant extent variations in the perception and appreciation of, and access to, different sporting practices (Bourdieu 1978). For example, British tennis clubs have traditionally functioned to bond socially compatible members together and exclude 'undesirables'. This social exclusivity still persists today, albeit in a diluted and more hidden form (Lake 2013).

Socio-cultural mechanisms of exclusion in sport

Cultural factors mediate sports participation in two overarching ways. The culture of organized competitive sport itself can be exclusionary and unwelcoming to particular groups; connected to this, particular broader cultural customs prevalent in some communities can construct sport as undesirable and unattractive for members of those communities. Sport continues to be one of the few domains within the Global North to celebrate and actively encourage hyper-masculinity by normalizing aggressive and misogynistic practices, and through valuing strength, muscularity, whiteness and physical ability (Anderson 2009b; Hickey 2008). The privileging of these discourses can create powerful feelings of exclusion for those who cannot, or refuse to, display such qualities. Various studies illustrate how physical education teachers in the Global North privilege young people who display physical competence, resulting in the disengagement of lower ability young people from an early age (Fitzgerald 2005; Wellard 2006; Evans and Penney 2008). In this context, Elling and Claringbould (2005: 509) contend that 'irrespective of social background, people who are talented as regards sporting abilities are more included than those who are not'.

Disability sport literature points to the exclusionary capacity of negative attitudes communicated by those who are able to sit comfortably within dominant sport cultures. Although a lack of physical access can restrict participation (as highlighted above), several studies point to attitudinal discrimination as discouraging many people with disabilities (Le Clair 2011). Our own research highlights how parents with children with disabilities experienced open discrimination in the form of name-calling, staring, and more discrete practices such as other children and parents ignoring their children and refusing to involve them in activities in various recreation contexts (Jeanes and Magee 2011b).

In a similar vein, recent research demonstrates how overt and covert racism manifest within many sport settings (Hylton 2010; Adair and Stronach 2011; Long and Spracklen 2011; Burdsey 2011a). Although overt racism is generally no longer tolerated, there continue to be grassroots examples of participants experiencing racism (Burdsey 2011b) as well as high-profile cases of elite athletes being taunted by racist comments (Doidge 2013), such as Indigenous AFL player Adam Goodes being called an 'ape' by a spectator during a game in 2013 (Crawford 2013). While not necessarily condoned in contemporary society, racism in sport is still very much evident (Carrington 2010; Rowe and Garland 2012). During our research that examined junior sports clubs in Australia, one development officer (male, early 30s) describes some club committee members and coaches as ignorant of contemporary non-racist expectations. He claims that some coaches still refer to children from CALD backgrounds as 'darkies' and consider doing so to be acceptable behaviour: that is, 'they just wouldn't see that as racist' (Spaaij *et al.* in press).

Other aspects of sporting culture can also be off-putting for particular groups and individuals. The connections between sport, violence, alcohol and the demeaning of women, as well as being discouraging for females, can also reduce the willingness of certain men to become involved (Fletcher and Spracklen 2013; Palmer 2013). Males with particular cultural, religious or personal beliefs that discourage alcohol consumption or promote respect for women may well be able to participate on the pitch but cannot engage in the rituals and bonding that occur away from the game (Fletcher and Spracklen 2013). As Fletcher and Spracklen (2013) outline in their analysis of Muslim cricketers in the UK, putting aside personal values to be able to engage in dominant bonding rituals is not an option and compromises players' ethnic and cultural identities. This provides a useful example of how those in the dominant group may construct certain communities as 'choosing' to be excluded from sport (Coalter 2000). Those that see the dominant sporting culture as normal and appealing assume that individuals or communities who reject it are making a personal choice, rather than understanding how participation requires individuals to deny values and beliefs that are central to their identity construction. This reflects the point made in Chapter 2 that not wanting to participate (i.e. self-exclusion) is often a response to a perceived lack of opportunity, acceptance or recognition, rather than simply free choice.

Socialization into sport at a young age affects ongoing participation into adulthood, with several studies showing the particular importance of family support in this sport socialization process (Coakley 2011; Kay and Spaaij 2012; Wheeler 2012). However, demographic factors heavily influence the type of socialization processes available to individuals. As discussed earlier, low-income families are less likely to be able to provide the financial and practical support needed to support ongoing sport participation among their children, especially in relation to relatively exclusive and costly sports. A lack of financial resources is frequently coupled with a lack of time, due to low-income parents often having to work long hours in poorly paid work or to hold down multiple jobs to ensure family survival (Collins with Kay 2003). In this situation, it is unlikely that children will be substantially encouraged to participate in sport because parents recognize that this will use valuable income needed for other essentials. Family experiences also shape the sport participation of young people with disabilities (Shields *et al.* 2012). In terms of disability, and depending on its nature and severity, young people with disabilities may need parental support to participate in sport in a way that is far more intense than for able-bodied young people. Parents have to source appropriate activities, provide transport, and often need to stay and support these activities. Young people with disabilities also tend to receive less encouragement to participate in sport from key socializing agents compared to 'able-bodied' participants (Kirk 2005).

Socialization research further highlights the importance of school experiences in shaping involvement and attitudes towards sport into adulthood. Much of this research illustrates how social exclusion generally occurs early, with teachers struggling to integrate those of diverse abilities and cultures (Bailey 2005; Azzarito 2009). Rich (2004) demonstrates how physical education teachers embrace dominant sport discourses and perpetuate them in the ways they organize and deliver physical education and school sport. This inevitably leads to the exclusion of those young people who are not able to ascribe to the dominant sporting norm. Social exclusion also occurs for young people within the informal structure of the school, where boys tend to occupy central spaces in playgrounds to engage in sporting activities while girls might be pushed to the fringes and forced to engage in more sedentary activities (Renold 2002; Clark and Paechter 2007).

This brief overview indicates how exclusionary mechanisms at all levels of sport are often implicit, subtle and complex, and therefore difficult to identify, deconstruct and transform (Elling and Claringbould 2005). These mechanisms influence individuals and communities differently in different situations and contexts. An analysis of the various dimensions of social exclusion is useful to highlight that it may be possible to participate in sport and therefore appear included, but still experience feelings of isolation and exclusion that emanate from not fitting in with or accepting practices and/or beliefs that prevail in this environment. This perspective is in line with social exclusion theory which posits that individuals can experience elements of inclusion and exclusion simultaneously (Chapter 2), and that 'superficially inclusionary moments cannot be taken as evidence of a deep-seated inclusionary tendency' (Parr *et al.* 2004: 47). The following section provides a prelude to the case study presented in this chapter, and offers a more detailed analysis of how these mechanisms intersect with gender and the impact that this has on the participation of some women in sport.

Gender, sport and social exclusion

The relationship between sport, gender and social exclusion is an interesting one to explore considering the large increases in participation by women in sports that are traditionally male-dominated (Lafferty and McKay 2004). Football, for example, is now the most popular participation sport for women and young girls in a number of European countries (Jeanes 2011b; Welford 2011). Broader participation statistics suggest that female sport participation is rising, and in countries such as Australia and Finland is on a par with male participation (Collins 2011; ERASS 2010). We can explain such changes as emerging from challenges to culturally rooted exclusionary mechanisms, which have shifted notions of acceptable femininity and normalized the societal participation of women (Knoppers and Elling 2001; Pfister 2010). Over recent years there has been increasing focus on the ways in which women's participation in sport may contribute to the contestation of particular repressive gendered assumptions, and offer a space where alternative femininities can be constructed (Howe 2003; Pfister 2010).

Nonetheless, recent studies of the gender/sport/exclusion relationship demonstrate the continuing influence that hegemonic gender discourses have on the (non-)participation of some men and some women (Anderson 2008; Palmer 2009; Mennesson 2009). A more detailed examination of participation statistics illustrates, for example, that while women's participation on the surface appears to be growing we can more readily explain this by acknowledging the wider definition of sport, which now includes activities such as walking and fitness exercise, than the significant increases of female participants in traditional sporting spaces (Knoppers and Elling 2001). In the area of club-based sport, there is still a disparity between male and female participants in surveys conducted in Australia, the Netherlands and the UK (ERASS 2010; Sport England 2012; Collard and Hoekman 2013). Hence, despite promising changes, sport 'remains dominated by masculine values that disadvantage women by pitting their performances against (hegemonic) masculine standards' (Light and Wedgwood 2012: 181). The case study documented further on in this chapter highlights in particular the profound impact of gender relations on the sport participation and engagement of women in the Global South.

Women's exclusion from sport has been a focus for academic attention since the 1970s, reflecting the development of the women's rights movement in Global North countries during this era. Using a liberal feminist perspective, early studies stressed the structural inequalities women faced with regard to participation in sport, including a lack of opportunities to play, disproportionate responsibilities in the home, and economic dependence (Greendorfer 1993; Hargreaves 1994). Academic research also identifies the cultural or symbolic exclusion women face as a result of dominant notions of masculinity and femininity that operate in organized competitive sport, for example, the difficulty of reconciling sport participation with gender norms that position them as inactive, weak and vulnerable (Cockburn and Clarke 2002; Mean and Kassing 2008). This stream of research led to a proliferation of studies on how women who do participate in sport reconcile their participation alongside broader gender norms and expectations (Howe 2003; Hills 2006; Azzarito 2009). In the Global North, women negotiate a fine balance between participation and maintaining appropriate feminine ideals (Markula 2004; Jeanes 2011b). The threat of being labelled 'butch', 'masculine' and 'lesbian' can be a constant one for young women choosing to participate in sport and, as studies of adolescent girls demonstrate, can discourage participation as girls become more cognizant with the cultural requirements of adult femininity (Clark and Paechter 2007). In a similar vein, some studies explore how female sports fans negotiate masculine sporting environments. Those female fans who choose to adopt masculine norms and perspectives can come to be accepted as 'authentic fans' by their male peers. However, some female fans instead respond to men's domination in the football stadium by founding women-only fan groups that allow them to construct their own identities and practices as female fans (Pfister *et al.* 2013). Further analysis in this area highlights the lack of profile experienced by elite female athletes within the media, and the tendency to sexualize and trivialize women's sport performances when they are given media attention (Bernstein 2002; Messner 2002; Lumby *et al.* 2010).

At a structural level, women are still heavily under-represented in the governance and management of sport (Claringbould and Knoppers 2008; Anderson 2009b). As discussed, relatively few women hold senior management positions within sport organizations, and those who are employed tend to be given positions that focus on either specifically dealing with women's sport or development and education roles that are perceived to be more 'nurturing' and therefore suitable for women's skill sets (Shaw and Slack 2002). There are fewer women's coaches, particularly at elite level and even within traditional female sports, due to multiple barriers that restrict their entry and continued involvement in the coaching profession (LaVoi and Dutove 2012). The control of organized sport remains firmly in the hands of men, a situation that is frequently viewed as unproblematic by those in positions of power (Hoeber 2007; Claringbould and Knoppers 2008).

While in general more women and girls are now participating in sport, this expansion has tended to occur across particular types of women. Most noticeably, participation in Global North countries is increasing among white able-bodied women with mid to high socio-economic status (Elling and Claringbould 2005). In other words, it is inadequate to consider 'women' as an homogeneous category, with certain mechanisms of social exclusion being more problematic for some groups of women than for others (Palmer 2009;

Ratna 2011). For example, several studies examine how gender, ethnicity and religion intersect to create particular barriers to sport participation for young Muslim women (Kay 2006; Walseth 2006; Palmer 2011). Muslim women living in the Global North encounter multiple barriers to sport participation, including stereotyping and ignorance of their needs by sport providers, feelings of not belonging and otherness in sporting environments, informal institutional practices such as uniform requirements that may be considered culturally inappropriate, and a lack of family support (Taylor and Toohey 2001; Sawrikar and Muir 2010). These mechanisms can combine to create powerful exclusionary forces that discourage Muslim women's participation. Particular stereotypes can prevent sport providers from identifying genuine mechanisms of social exclusion as opposed to the ones that they perceive (Walseth 2006). For example, Muslim women report that while it is often perceived that religious traditions discourage female participation, this is not always the case, as such constraints affect Muslim women in different ways depending on their interpretation of Islam and their particular family contexts (Walseth and Fasting 2003). This suggests the fluidity of gender and feminine ideals, the potential for women to both comply and contest these within different contexts in their lives and, in turn, the shifting nature of exclusionary mechanisms. Hence, what creates social exclusion for an individual may not remain constant and will inevitably differ across women.

Historically, early analyses of gender within sport tended to focus on women's exclusion and the dominance of certain types of masculinities. Since the 1990s, a detailed body of research has emerged that considers how hegemonic masculinities in sport are also exclusionary to particular types of men who do not reflect the sporting ideal (e.g. Connell 1995; Anderson 2005; Wellard 2009). While women may have taken considerable strides in participating in traditionally male-dominated spaces, the reverse cannot be said for males' involvement in traditionally female sporting arenas (Elling and Knoppers 2005; Anderson 2008). The dominance of heteronormative masculinities has meant that gay men in particular continue to experience considerable social exclusion within traditional sporting environments, generally preferring not to reveal their sexuality to team-mates in that environment (Caudwell 2011). Thus, Elling *et al.* (2003: 443) argue that 'male gay athletes in the dominant (media) sports are even more closeted than lesbians'. There has instead been a growth of both gay and lesbian sports teams, which are felt to provide a safe space for alternative sexualities that these athletes do not believe are readily available within traditional sporting spaces (Symons *et al.* 2010; Caudwell 2011). Elling *et al.* (2003: 443) further explain that the often 'hostile, homophobic environment of most masculine defined sports may mean that gay men trade their initial choice for these sport environments for a less homophobic or gay friendly sport environment'. The perceived need of marginalized population groups to create their own sporting spaces to feel included is indicative of the strength of exclusive mechanisms in sport, and an aspect we discuss further in Chapter 8.

The broader literature on how gender intersects with other factors to exclude particular men and women provides a useful context for the following case study. The majority of literature examining gender, exclusion and sport tends to focus on the experiences of women in the Global North, and portrays sport as one of the last bastions of hegemonic masculinity in societies that continue to forge towards gender equality. However, within Global South countries, gender disparities, particularly those associated with women's rights, tend to be much more prominent within broader society and culture (Pelak 2005; Saavedra 2009). As noted, in recent times the mechanisms restricting or constraining men and women's involvement in sport in the Global North have been increasingly subtle and symbolic, rather than consisting of overt discriminatory practices. However, in at least some Global South countries, women continue to experience more overt repression that excludes them from engaging in sport. Women's participation in sport in Saudi Arabia, for example, is highly restricted: women are unable to openly participate in sport, no provision for sport is available for girls in public schools, and the attendance of women as spectators at sporting events is discouraged (Dorsey 2013). In Zimbabwe, gender-based violence is endemic in football (soccer) stadia across the country, and many Zimbabwean women refrain from attending football matches for this reason (Daimon 2010). With the provision of sport infrastructure in Zimbabwe being heavily biased towards male football, this leaves women with very few viable sport participation opportunities. As a consequence, women and girls remain grossly under-represented in Zimbabwean sport (Daimon 2010).

Zambian women and social exclusion in sport: a case study

This case study examines the experiences of young women playing football in compound communities in Lusaka, Zambia, and builds on the discussion of sport and social inclusion policy in Zambia in Chapter 3. Chapter 6 also returns to Zambia to examine how health education is delivered via sport. As illustrated in Chapter 3, while there has been a focus on promoting female sport participation in policy rhetoric, this has not necessarily translated into tangible practice. Many females do participate in sport in Zambia but, as we show below, dominant gender relations that exist in wider society have considerable influence on their involvement. Gender and sport has been considered within a Global South context using an SFD framework that highlights the potential value of sport as a vehicle through which gender repression is challenged and contested. This premise often fails to acknowledge that sport is an arena from which women are excluded and, rather than being a site of contestation, can actually reinforce the marginalization of women that occurs within the broader society (Saavedra 2009). This case study provides a critical examination of the ways in which women's participation in football is restricted and discouraged in Zambia.

The position of women in Zambian society

To ascertain the constraints that women experience in the sporting arena, it is important to understand their position within wider society. Zambia is a patriarchal society, but the subordinate position of women in Zambia is a legacy of the British colonial era (see Chapter 3). While male dominance existed pre-colonization in Zambia, women were highly respected as producers and social agents (Ogbomo 2005). European rule resulted in the establishment of new economic relationships and social norms, including increasing subordination of women. Gender norms were transformed into a hybrid of traditional customs and new European expectations that reinforced 'indigenous patriarchy and introduced new forms of sexism' (Ogbomo 2005: 51). Victorian values imposed via British colonial officers reduced the position of women in Zambian society, rendering females with little power or voice, particularly in the public sphere. While Zambian liberation in 1964 resulted in some changes to various repressive social structures, gender liberation was not prioritized (Nfah Abbenyi 1997).

In contemporary Zambian society, women from low socio-economic backgrounds are largely confined to roles within the home (Hansen 1997). The young women involved in this research are all from impoverished compound communities (we provide a more detailed description of these communities and their impact on health in Chapter 6). While females in these communities face considerable difficulties entering the labour market in a significant way, they do have considerable responsibilities within the home. Economically, lower-class women in particular have limited claim to financial resources. As Hansen (1997: 9) explains, 'a husband's earnings are not household income in the sense that they go into a common purse to which wives have equal access ... but while wives have no claims on husbands' earning, husbands make culturally legitimated claims on their wives' time'. Hegemonic beliefs of male superiority and female complicity have led compound communities to tolerate and to an extent normalize violent relations between men and women (Nshindano and Maharaj 2008). Further, due to the challenges of surviving financially without attachment to a male, women find it extremely difficult to navigate their way out of abusive relationships (Hallman 2005). Young Zambian women therefore face considerable difficulties within their everyday lives.

Sport in Zambian society

Meier and Saavedra (2009: 1159) describe the contemporary Zambian sporting landscape as one 'dominated by men's football, with perennial hopes for World Cup advancement despite significant deficits in infrastructure and programme resources at all levels'. Football is heavily connected to dominant masculinities and commands a central place in Zambian culture. Other sports generally struggle for status among the adult population, and sport more broadly is seen as a hobby or pastime, something for youths to casually participate in. Adult teams and leagues exist across a range of sports including boxing, netball, handball, athletics and basketball (Saavedra 2003), but, beyond football, sport does not command a significant audience or interest. However, for young people, and particularly young men, sport is an important aspect of everyday life and the establishment of masculinity that supports the transition to manhood. For young women, opportunities to participate in sport are available even in impoverished communities; nevertheless, as we discuss below, these opportunities are not always prioritized or encouraged within the wider family. Thus, female football in Zambia is something of a contradiction, with dominant masculine values considerably restricting women's involvement in football. While organized football for women did emerge in the 1970s with a national team established in 1976 (Meier and Saavedra 2009), Saavedra (2003: 225) illustrates the difficulties of establishing female football in African countries more broadly:

> ... the immense popularity and weighty social meaning of the men's game in Africa, has made it that much harder for a women's game to develop. Even where other sports for women, such as netball, handball, athletics and basketball, have flourished, women's football has been met with scepticism, neglect and sometimes, outright hostility. Yet, women's football has nonetheless emerged.

This development has been fragmented, with various teams that were established during the early 1980s disappearing towards the end of the decade (Liwena 2006). The emergence of the SFD movement in the 1990s, however, provided significant financial resources to establish gender empowerment initiatives that indirectly supported the expansion of female football in Lusaka (Meier and Saavedra 2009). Teams began to emerge within compound communities with a women's league established that consisted of teams attached to NGOs, and a small number of teams attached to local businesses. Players in the latter group of teams were mostly drawn from the wealthier, middle to upper classes in Lusaka. The development of women's football in Zambia is illustrative of the shifting, fluid nature of social exclusion. In this context, social exclusion as a result of gendered discourses and practices has never been absolute, but continues to permeate participation experiences on a daily basis. However, some women do challenge and negotiate various mechanisms of social exclusion to enable participation in sport.

Young women's experiences of social-normative mechanisms of exclusion

As noted, female participation in football in Zambia contradicts the dominant gender norms that permeate impoverished communities. Football is seen as a man's sport and all the young women we interviewed recognize that their participation conflicts with accepted gender norms. They comment that although they are prepared to challenge restrictive gender stereotypes, many of their friends will not consider doing so. As one player (late teens) points out: 'Yes, many young women would not play at all because they see it as a sport for men. They do not think they can play because it is just for men.' As this comment indicates, for the majority of females participating in football is rarely a consideration, because they unquestioningly accept its position as a masculine activity and a space that they are unable to occupy. Even though the players who were interviewed have negotiated this initial barrier, they discuss how their participation creates problems for them in their local communities. Several talk about enduring verbal abuse and threats from other community members who feel that their behaviour is inappropriate and shameful. A number of players have been told by community elders that their participation is disrespectful of conventional values and traditions. One player (20s) describes this experience as follows: 'I have had men say to me I should be ashamed, I don't behave like a woman should. They say I am trying to be like a man and it is wrong ... they say these things as I walk down the street.'

Here, community members reference their traditional culture's understanding of masculinity and femininity that constructs female players as deviant. Again, while these particular girls are willing to endure abusive comments and antagonism towards them, they recognize that this will discourage many young women from considering playing. Another player (20s) notes:

> I am strong and I love to play so these people, they say these things but I can ignore them. Others they are not like that, they think I am not going to play football, everyone will say these things to me and I will be made to be an outcast.

The last part of this comment is particularly powerful, and illustrates the consequences for young women who contest gender expectations in an overt and public way. Reflecting on the experience of black female South African footballers, Pelak (2005: 58) documents how this process reinforces dominant gender expectations:

> The cumulative effect of treating women footballers with hostility not only constructs women as outsiders and discourages their participation, but reinforces dominant gender ideologies that demand clearly marked differences between women and men.

While the young women do not necessarily feel they are excluded completely from their community, they express being constantly challenged about their participation and having to justify their transgression from traditional Zambian gender ideals. Walseth's (2006) study of young Muslim women's involvement in sport reports similar findings. The study acknowledges that sport participation for young Muslim women 'seems to challenge the boundaries of their ethnic identities because their participation is in conflict with hegemonic notions of femininity' (Walseth 2006: 91). Similar to the situation for Zambian women, Walseth's (2006: 91) study suggests that some women are unwilling to push the boundaries of their ethnic identities and therefore do not participate in sport, while 'others challenge it; and some create alternative ideals of femininity'.

As with women in the Global North, Zambian women find that their participation continually leads to questions about their sexuality, which are heightened if the players are not married or at least in a relationship with a man. Several players are regularly accused of being lesbian, and with the undertaking of homosexual acts being a criminal offence in Zambia this understandably makes them extremely nervous. One player (late teens) discusses how the connection between participation and homosexuality is likely to prompt her to cease playing:

> When you play a man's sport, people say these things that you are not a woman, that you are butch and that you do not like men. This is dangerous, if people here think you are a lesbian then you can get people attacking you and your home. I do not want this to happen to me, if things are said about me then I will stop playing.

The women's responses to this threat are similar to those noted in research in the Global North (Caudwell 1999; Shakib 2003; Jeanes 2011b). They seek to emphasize their femininity in other ways, particularly in their dress and appearance away from football. Several players talk about wearing braids and keeping their hair long, and it seems particularly important to them not to participate in other perceived 'masculine' behaviours. One player (20s) comments about needing to dissociate herself from some young women players that she knows:

> [They] just let themselves go, they wear their hair short and they do not care what they look like. They play football and then they want to do other things that men do so they go drinking in bars and they smoke, they are loud ... this is not good behaviour, this is not how a girl should be behaving. It makes others think that if we play football we will become badly behaved ... it is important for us to show we are not like that. We still know how to behave as a woman.

This comment illustrates the fine balance many of the young women feel they have to navigate as both Zambian women and footballers, and the potentially dire consequences of being perceived to be 'too butch' or masculinized (Jeanes *et al.* 2013). Meier and Saavedra (2009) outline some of the dangers faced by African women who openly contest gender regimes via their participation in sport. The authors draw on the experiences of Hassiba Boulmerka and Eudy Simelane to illustrate this. Boulemerka, an Algerian middle-distance Olympic athlete, received death threats from Islamist militants in the lead-up to the 1992 Olympic Games as they believed her participation was inappropriate. In the year preceding the Olympics, Boulmerka had to train and race outside of Algeria for fear of her own life. Simelane was a talented South African female football player. In 2008 she was brutally beaten, gang-raped and stabbed to death on her way home in a crime described by her attackers as 'corrective rape' to punish for her living openly as a lesbian in her community. Being labelled 'deviant', therefore, could potentially have far more broad-reaching consequences for Zambian young women, something that they are acutely aware of.

Several of the young women feel that their participation is not condoned by either the broader community or their family members (as we discuss further on) and, at best, is tolerated as long as they do not continue playing into adulthood. Concepts of youth and adulthood are fairly fluid in Zambia. Generally a female is considered to have moved from girlhood to adulthood when she marries, rather than at a chronological age point. However, there is an expectation that young women will marry relatively young. Several of the players in their mid-20s discuss how they feel under pressure from family and friends to cease their participation because they are becoming 'too old'. Relatives express concern that the young women's participation may discourage potential husbands and in doing so jeopardize her future security. One player (20s) describes this pressure as follows:

> My auntie and my friends, they say to me, 'you are too old for this football now; when are you going to stop doing this?' They didn't mind me playing when I was younger but they say now I should be acting like a woman. They tell me I will never find a husband when I am running around acting like a man.

Similarly, while these young women tend to ignore such pressures, they acknowledge that many young women are unwilling to risk their future financial stability and position in the community by participating in an unsanctioned sports activity.

The role of the family in regulating participation

The family plays a central role in shaping female participation in sport (Kay and Spaaij 2012). Some of the parents of the Zambian girls, particularly mothers, are very supportive of their involvement. These girls discuss the importance of parental and family support for encouraging their ongoing participation, particularly in light of the other constraints highlighted above. As one girl (late teens) suggests:

> If my mother had not told me to ignore others I would have stopped playing. When people were saying bad things to me in the street I would have stopped but my mother said no, I should ignore them, and if I wanted to play a man's sport then I should do this.

Family responses and reactions to women's participation are contrasting. Other young women speak of their families' disapproval of their participation and how challenging this is to their playing regularly. Again, a lack of approval is connected to feminine cultural expectations and the belief by family members that players shame the family by not complying with these expectations. One player (late teens) comments how her father is concerned that others will believe he has not raised his daughter appropriately:

> My father he says that young women should not play football, it is for boys and that if I play it brings shame on him. People will think he has not raised me well … he thinks no one will want to marry me if I play football.

As discussed earlier, families constantly use the idea that women will not be able to pursue their expected path into marriage as a way of discouraging women's participation. This allows those that do play to be constructed as abnormal or deviant. Some women speak of friends whose families (usually senior male family members) have completely banned them from participating. Two of the players involved in the research are in this situation. They attempt to navigate this by joining teams in neighbouring communities and lying to their families about where they are when they are attending training and matches. Both players recognize that this situation is not viable in the long term, and that they will eventually have to cease participation.

The young women also talk about their families being unsupportive of their participation because they are concerned that it will lead them to neglect other expected roles within their homes. None of the young women have secure paid employment and senior family members expect them to perform domestic chores and care-giving duties within the home as their contribution to the family. Several young women discuss how parents raise concerns that not only will playing football mean they have less time to undertake these roles, but that they will also start to question the validity of these roles. The latter concern emerges from parents' recognition that by playing football young women are challenging appropriate norms of masculinity and femininity, and they want to ensure this does not spill over into other social contexts. One female (20s) reports:

> My father he tells me that I may be doing what boys do at the ground but that does not mean I can behave like a boy in the home. I still have to help my mother and if I don't want to do this then he will stop me from playing.

Similar to the way the young women negotiate tensions between their feminine identity and participation, many of them speak of having to navigate a fine balance between fulfilling requirements as homemakers and caregivers and negotiating space to play. Most young women offer compromises to be allowed to play, as this player (late teens) explains:

> My father, he did not want me to play, he said I should be at home and helping my mother with my sisters … I told him that I would do my jobs in the morning before I went to the ground and once we had finished I would come straight home … in the end he let me play but sometimes I can't because my mother needs me to do work for her.

As this player suggests, participation is not always possible. The young women have to prioritize family commitments but they see such compromises as a way to ensure they are able to continue playing.

Structural inequalities and social exclusion

A lack of resources also constrains women's participation experiences. While the growth of the SFD movement ensures that there is a reasonably regular supply of footballs (they generally played in bare feet with no shin-guards), the women discuss how they never have enough balls to train effectively. Similar to Global North analyses (Welford 2011), they also outline how male teams and even casual male players are given priority to use the limited recreational space available. Players talk about having to train early in the afternoon to be able to access pitches, or play games early on a Saturday morning. They also mention that if they are playing and males want to use the space they will be 'driven away', as it is accepted that the male game will take precedence.

Several of the girls had played or were currently playing for Zambia at elite level and they further highlight how limited the resources were that they could access. For those playing in international teams, the Football Association of Zambia (FAZ) would usually organize one training camp prior to an international game. Although FAZ paid for this, the girls were expected to stay in low-grade accommodation and have limited food compared to their male counterparts who would come together for several training camps and be placed in high-quality accommodation. Due to financial constraints, women's international fixtures were limited to a small number each year, with none played in some years. As discussed in Chapter 3, while FAZ undoubtedly has limited resources compared to Global North football governing bodies, it secures a significant amount of government funding compared to other national sporting organizations in Zambia. However, it uses very little of this to support the development and growth of the women's game. The lack of support and establishment of a clear playing pathway can further discourage women's and girls' involvement, particularly those who want to take participation seriously. Several of the elite players voice their frustrations at the lack of support they receive. As one player (20s) comments:

> I get angry. They call us for training and they say we will play this match but then it does not happen. I want to get better and I want to be good

but I don't have a chance. If I was a male I could be earning a lot of money now; I would play in Europe, but for me playing for Zambia makes no difference.

Although these constraints are more pronounced in the Zambian context, they do reflect the structural constraints many female participants experience in the Global North, particularly those involved in male-dominated sports (Scraton *et al.* 1999). The lack of resources sends a clear message about the limited significance and value of women's participation.

Conclusion

The initial part of this chapter examined the multifaceted processes that create social exclusion in/from sport for some population groups and individuals. The relationship between sport and sport exclusion is a fluid one, and cannot be understood simply in binary terms of participation and non-participation. Non-participation may be indicative of acute exclusion but, as illustrated, it is possible for individuals to participate in ways that are constricted or produce feelings of isolation and being 'on the outside' because they do not ascribe to the dominant sporting ideal, even though they are present within sporting spaces.

The case study highlights a range of exclusionary processes that affect Zambian young women's participation in football. While this particular group of young women attempt to navigate these processes, for many others they present barriers that they are unwilling to challenge and therefore preclude them from participating in sport. The case study emphasizes how multiple mechanisms of social exclusion co-exist and intersect, and affect women in different ways. While playing sport regularly, these young women still have to contend with and resist various exclusionary discourses and practices. The case study exemplifies the problems of viewing social exclusion and inclusion as dichotomous, instead demonstrating that even when 'included' in sport (i.e. actually playing), various constraints continue to shape and affect the participation experience. Hence, sport may enhance processes of social inclusion and exclusion/differentiation simultaneously, which might both contradict and reflect dominant meanings and power relations (Elling *et al.* 2003). The young Zambian women continually had to contest various discourses that sought to prevent or devalue their participation. The experiences of these young women also highlight how social inclusion in particular spaces (such as the football pitch) has consequences for feelings of exclusion elsewhere (within their community). These women were prepared to essentially sacrifice some of their community connections to pursue sport participation. They also adopted strategies to attempt to lessen their disconnection with broader community values, continuing to undertake stereotypical roles within the home and ensuring they displayed other aspects of culturally appropriate femininity at all times away from the football pitch.

In the introduction to this chapter we touched on how, despite some significant cross-national variations, sport participation trends are generally replicated across the Global North and Global South. From the case study we are able to identify socio-normative mechanisms that constrain the involvement of young Zambian women in ways that are readily identifiable with those described in Global North gender and sport research. However, as Pelak (2005: 67) notes, while Global North and Global South countries are far from monoliths, 'women footballers who live in nations that dominate the global economy have different material experiences than women footballers of "poor" nations'. Indeed, the Zambian young women experienced socio-cultural and structural constraints far more intensely than those we have worked with in the Global North (Jeanes 2013), and potentially face more severe repercussions when they challenge or resist exclusionary mechanisms. This is particularly relevant when considering the influence of cultural expectations on participation. While any minority group that challenges dominant power relations is likely to experience negative consequences, for these young women there were very real possibilities of vilification, physical abuse and social exclusion within their own communities. Broader gender relations are significant here. For impoverished women such as those we interviewed, long-term financial security will likely be dependent on marriage to a male who can provide this. The potential of football to jeopardize this presents a very real threat for Zambian young women, while this situation would potentially be less problematic for more financially independent women, even those with low income, in the Global North. In this particular example, we see how gender and poverty intersect intensely for impoverished women in the Global South to create conditions that severely restrict their capacity to engage in sport in an equitable way.

This chapter did not intend to give an extensive account of how various groups and individuals experience social exclusion in sport; instead, it has highlighted the common mechanisms via which this can occur and explored these in detail through the lens of gender. Establishing how sport is a site of social exclusion for some individuals and communities allows us to adopt a more critical view when considering how it can also be used as a site to promote broader social inclusion. The following chapter seeks to develop our analysis further and consider how sport itself can be simultaneously exclusionary but also positioned as a cultural space that can contribute to equitable participation in broader societal domains.

Note

1 Finland and Sweden are partial exceptions to this trend. In both countries, overall female participation in sport is higher than, or on a par with, male participation, which suggests that gender disparity with regard to participation in sport is not as great in these countries (Collins 2011).

5 Using sport to tackle social exclusion in the Global North

Introduction

The preceding chapters show how sport is a setting where social exclusion is (re)produced, challenged or subverted. One particular dimension of this is how sport is used to combat social exclusion in other life domains. This theme features centrally in this chapter, and is informed by the assertion that the 'power of sport' to deliver wider social benefits has rarely been so strongly advocated as it is at this point in the twenty-first century (Crabbe 2008; Coakley 2011). Indeed, numerous policy-makers and practitioners in the Global North advocate sport as a vehicle for a range of broader social objectives such as public health, urban regeneration, social cohesion and community safety (Hartmann 2001; Long and Sanderson 2001; Gasparini and Vieille-Marchiset 2008; Spaaij 2013b).

This chapter broadly centres on sport as a policy tool for addressing social exclusion in the Global North. It examines two specific areas of policy and practice – mental health and worklessness – to highlight the rich diversity of programs and approaches that target social exclusion using sport. Drawing on our own empirical research, we present case study analysis of a sports program for individuals with mental illness in the United Kingdom, and a sport-based education program for workless young people in the Netherlands. We purposefully selected these case studies to provide a voice to experiences in two areas that have not until this juncture been as central to the research agenda into sport and social exclusion as others have been. In so doing, the chapter aims to provide a critical examination of the nature, benefits and limitations of the use of sport in these two different contexts.

In line with the broader range of programs and policies discussed in Chapters 3 and 6, the two programs that we examine in this chapter use sport as a 'hook' to engage persons experiencing social exclusion in one or more aspects of their lives. However, both programs move beyond mere participation in sport by embedding sport activities within a mental health treatment strategy and an employability training scheme, respectively. As will be seen, the programs' objectives lie outside of sport; that is, they align with broader policy agendas and political concerns regarding the adverse social and economic consequences of mental illness and worklessness. Their approach is informed by the belief that it is not the practice of sport *per se* that is responsible for particular outcomes, but rather its adoption within a personal and social development model (Crabbe *et al.* 2006). In other words, what is significant is not sport as such, but the context in which it occurs and the ways in which it is implemented (Green 2008).

Mental health, social exclusion and sport

Definitions of mental health and illness reflect a continuum from the broad definition of mental health problems to narrower clinical definitions. In a broad sense of the term, mental health refers to a state of mental and social wellbeing that goes beyond merely the absence of disease. The relationship between mental health and social exclusion can be gleaned from the World Health Organization's (WHO 2013a) description of mental health as 'a state of well-being in which every individual realizes his or her own potential, can cope with the normal stresses of life, can work productively and fruitfully, and is able to make a contribution to her or his community'. From this perspective, mental health is key to unlocking the potential of individuals to lead purposeful and fruitful lives as contributors to the community and wider society while coping effectively with life's stresses. However, this potential is often not realized. It is estimated that more than 450 million people suffer from medically diagnosed mental disorders worldwide (WHO 2010). Statistics have yet to be updated on a global scale, but we do know that in Europe one in four individuals experiences some form of mental health problem at some time in life, with poor mental health accounting for almost 20 per cent of the burden of disease in the European region (WHO European Regional Office 2013).

The WHO (2005) expresses concern that people with mental illness are 'some of the most neglected people in the world' and excluded from mainstream society as 'denied citizens'. This concern resonates with academic thinking about social exclusion as a process of being 'shut out' from social, economic, political or cultural systems, as discussed in Chapter 2. Specifically, it highlights the importance of understanding the lived experiences of those with mental health problems as they seek to navigate access to and participation in differing societal domains. Research shows that social exclusion of individuals with mental illness involves the 'enforced lack' of social, cultural and political participation (Morgan *et al.* 2007: 482). While access to core institutions such as education, housing and employment should be available to individuals with mental illness, in effect it is often restricted. The exclusion of individuals from participation in particular social spheres or institutions does not necessarily stem from material disadvantage, but rather from a range of barriers, including sociocultural. This is a pertinent point to recognize for the case studies at hand, as it underlines the argument advanced in Chapter 2 that gaining a comprehensive understanding of social exclusion involves moving beyond the narrow association of social exclusion with poverty and material deprivation, an association that has dominated the literature on sport and social exclusion.

A significant factor underpinning the social exclusion of individuals with mental illness is public ignorance of mental health problems, which can result in stigmatization and human rights violations. According to the WHO (2005), in many communities around the world mental illness is viewed as a weakness of character or a punishment for immoral behaviour rather than a genuine medical condition. Consequently, individuals with mental health problems are likely to be exposed to a range of human rights violations. Hence, the 'stigma they face means they are often ostracized from society and fail to receive the care they require. [They] also face discrimination on a daily basis including in the fields of education, employment and housing' (WHO 2013b). The stigma associated with mental illness can not only create a barrier to social, economic and cultural participation (Morgan *et al.* 2007), it can also be the main obstacle to the provision of adequate care and lead to discrimination in the provision of services for physical wellbeing (Sartorius 2007).

Chapter 2 identifies stigma as a major aspect of the moral dimension of social exclusion. The issue of stigma is also a significant factor within mental health literature. Stigmatizing processes can affect multiple domains of people's lives and have a significant bearing on the distribution of life chances in areas such as employment, education, housing, health and life itself (Link and Phelan 2001). Corrigan (2004: 616) asserts that 'stereotype, prejudice, and discrimination can rob people labelled mentally ill of important life opportunities that are essential for achieving life goals', including access to good jobs or suitable housing. These are significant factors that can contribute to the potential social exclusion of individuals with mental illness. In addition to public stigma (i.e. the public perception or attitude towards those with mental' illness), Corrigan (2004) emphasizes the role of self-stigma, that is, the self-perception or attitude of the individuals towards social exclusion. Self-stigma often prevents those with mental illness from seeking or fully participating in medical services, with the perceived threat of social disapproval and diminished self-esteem being key factors in this regard (Corrigan 2004).

Engaging with recovery is pivotal to the improvement of mental health regardless of the type of mental illness that is being experienced (Corrigan 2004; Roberts and Wolfson 2004; Andreasen *et al.* 2005; Kelly and Gamble 2005; Liberman and Kopelowicz 2005; Resnick *et al.* 2005). 'Recovery' refers to the process whereby individuals can be helped to understand and come to terms with their illness (Repper and Perkins 2003). However, stigma and public ignorance of mental health problems can skew the view of what a successful recovery comprises. There is more to recovery from mental illness than the alleviation of symptoms or deficits; rather, it involves people moving beyond their problems to embrace their abilities, possibilities, interests and dreams, and to rebuild their sense of self, identity and sense of purpose within meaningful social roles and relationships (Carless and Douglas 2008). Put differently, the recovery process involves addressing the 'loss of valued social roles and identity, isolation, loss of sense of self and purpose in life' (Davidson and Roe 2007: 462).

This raises the question of what (if any) role sport can play within the mental health treatment and recovery process. There is a growing volume of research that shows that sport and physical activity can assist the recovery path across several diseases and diverse sub-populations through increased engagement with the treatment process, with the longer-term aim being one of participation in meaningful social, economic or cultural activities (Taylor *et al.* 1985; Faulkner and Sparkes 1999; Beebe *et al.* 2005; Fogarty and Happell 2005; Penedo and Dahn 2005; Carless 2007; Carless and Sparkes 2008). For example, a recent study into the therapeutic potential of sport and physical activity for men with severe mental illness identifies a number of benefits, including opportunities for social interaction, increased personal meaning, hope and optimism, and a boost to self-esteem and self-identity (Carless and Douglas 2008). This research establishes that sport activities benefit participants through providing an 'action narrative' (a sense of purpose, routine, meaningful activity and mind occupation), 'achievement narrative' (accomplishment, sense of achievement, self-identity recognition and learning new skills), and 'relationship narrative' (commonality, friendship bonds and shared experiences).

The perceived therapeutic potential of sport for individuals with mental health problems has led to the proliferation of sport-based intervention programs targeting individuals with mental illness. The following case study critically examines this therapeutic potential of sport through an analysis of a sports program in the UK that was designed to engage individuals with mental health problems in the treatment and recovery process. We will focus particularly on the ways in which the program used football to engage participants in the recovery process and to deconstruct the stigma associated with mental illness.

Mental health care and de-stigmatization through football: a case study

The football program examined here was part of a mental health rehabilitative treatment service offered by a Mental Health Unit (MHU) of a NHS Mental Health Trust in London, UK, between 2007 and 2010. The program was located at a sports and leisure facility within the premises of an NHS hospital and close to the MHU. As such, the program was embedded within the formal mental health system and not operated by a sport organization. This strategy was based on the program's objective to offer a 'joined-up' strategy to mental health treatment by involving mental health specialists and related multi-service agencies in a structured environment that incorporated football into medical treatment. Funding for the program was provided through public sector funds as well as some sporting funding channels for those whom the UK Social Exclusion Unit deemed to be 'among the most excluded in society' (Morgan *et al.* 2007: 477).

Participants were referred to the program from a variety of agencies such as youth and probation services, a women's refuge centre, drug and alcohol services, police, self-referrals through networking with existing participants, and in-patient and out-patient departments within the NHS hospital. Once referred to the program, each participant was placed in the care of an MHU staff member with knowledge of the individual's mental health condition. As part of the treatment plan, both participant and staff member attended the program that ran two afternoons a week for a period of ten weeks.

Once at the program, participants were involved in three main activities. First, the program coordinator and head coach delivered a football-related activity, that is, a skills drill, a series of fun activities or something game-like. This coordinator/coach was a former client of the MHU who had been recruited to the program following his successful treatment program after the premature ending of his professional football career. Second, educational or counselling workshops run by various external partners and agencies were provided for all participants in a group session. Issues covered were specific to the needs of individuals with mental illness in terms of their re-engagement with mainstream society after the program. These issues included alcohol and drug use, gun and knife crime, self-care, accommodation and independent living, social networking, financial planning and budget management, and nutritional advice and healthy living. Last, at the end of each session participants met with their MHU staff member for a consultation about their mental health and treatment needs. As the consultation was private and confidential, it provided the opportunity for formal medical treatment to take place. The consultation usually took place in a meeting room at the facility, and allowed for this more formal engagement to take place either immediately or at a later time if necessary, especially for those with more severe mental health problems. The program design had enough flexibility for the consultation to take place at any point across the afternoon, although in the majority of cases it occurred after the workshop.

Program design, implementation and experiences

The program was deliberately designed to engage patients with medical treatment as part of their recovery process. Staff members in the MHU expressed the view that they had found it increasingly difficult to engage with clients in the unit as they were:

> ... very isolated and marginalized and vulnerable, dislocated from society really, so when treating them in an individual situation [in the unit] it was often hard to get a bond and also to encourage the patient to engage with others, including ourselves, and this reinforced their illness as isolating.
>
> (Clinical Psychiatrist)

The Clinical Psychologist agrees that 'there are some clients we get referred that just do not engage with us or the treatment and a key part of that is the whole formality of the treatment, which can put a lot of clients off who remain in a state of negativity and decline'. These concerns about client disengagement are well established in the literature on mental health treatment, which shows that establishing and maintaining client engagement are a considerable challenge for mental health service providers, and that clients are unlikely to improve their condition unless they fully engage in care (Baydar *et al.* 2003; Kim *et al.* 2012). As noted earlier, public stigma and self-stigma can act as powerful barriers to engaging with mental health care.

With this in mind, staff members in the MHU sought to establish an alternative approach to client engagement. The Clinical Nurse Specialist expressed this as follows:

> We were keen to establish a place for people with similar ailments to meet in a more informal and relaxed atmosphere in an effort to promote a more proactive recovery process than the one more formally available in the unit.

There was a professional view within the MHU that engagement with the recovery process was problematic to achieve; hence, they sought a model that could help to stimulate the recovery process, with an emphasis on group therapy as the impetus for individual recovery. They decided that football was suitable to be used as an intervention to stimulate the recovery process. The Clinical Nurse Specialist explains the role of football within the program:

> It offered the group dynamic, and we felt that group therapy was a way of engaging individuals in the value of the group ... Football thus is a key element of the recovery process to stimulate and engage the participant on the path to mental recovery, which is our overall aim ... With [the program] we use a model where football is an intervention to stimulate recovery.

The Clinical Psychologist concurs with this use of football as a stimulant to recovery, arguing:

> ... the way this program is developed, with football and medical elements and support workshops together, the staff can develop therapeutic alliances and client-patient trust, and this is essential in individual mental health treatment.

The NHS Borough Assistant Operation Director offers further support for the model:

> The therapy through football is not possible to recreate in the classroom. A classroom cannot recreate the group dynamics the way this program can through football. The program works as it prevents the condition from getting worse and someone going into relapse. This engages users in a way other forms of treatment cannot.

The fact that football is a team sport and one that requires vigorous and strenuous activity also aided the intended recovery process. The NHS Borough Assistant Operation Director observed that the program allowed for 'anger management control in a football setting that a classroom cannot do and that is important for mental recovery as there is much anger in patients'. Indeed, the expression of emotions in the football activities was seen to provide important therapeutic opportunities. As a key program staff member tasked with the delivery of the football activity, the program coordinator advocates creating an environment through football 'where we get the lads to have fun, make sure they enjoy it but also they respect each other in the group, a group that is positive'. This positive environment is critical as a stimulant for group therapy as 'it creates a positive, open and supportive environment where we can deal with the core illness each individual has and work together on it' (Clinical Psychiatrist). The underlying approach is to 'set little goals for achievement so we can build self-confidence, self-worth, that sort of thing, through doing something well in football, like scoring a goal, as we feel that can help beyond the pitch' (Program Coordinator/Head Coach).

The focus of MHU and coaching staff on the use of football as a stimulant or catalyst for engaging individuals with mental illness was supported by many of the participants. For example, one participant states:

> I was sent here [MHU] and had my psychiatrist but we would just sit in the room and he would ask things but I did not want to answer. He suggested I came here and he came with me and I found it more relaxing and easier to talk to him when I did.

Another comments:

> I was quite shy and withdrawn and did not like the sessions, then I came here, found there were others like me; I was able to talk to my psychologist more casually and that really helped rather than the stuff in the unit.

Engaging with professional staff members in this alternative, relatively informal setting was a particular social benefit associated with the program, as the following two participants' excerpts indicate:

> Even though [the Clinical Nurse Specialist] treats us, we see her here, she is always coming up, asking how things are, what do I need, how is it going? She is almost like a mate rather than someone helping me with my depression and we can talk about things here I would not talk back at the unit. If we need though, and there is stuff we want to talk about in private, or I am struggling with something, we can go back to the unit and talk there. It really works for me.

> It's funny really as I come here twice a week and see [the Clinical Nurse Therapist] and don't think of her as someone helping me but more of a friend. She always asks how I am, takes an interest in me, asks me if I want

to talk about anything, that sort of thing. Some days I do and we go off and sit and talk about my problems but other days we just have banter.

These self-reports strongly resonate with the experiences of MHU and program staff. For example, the Clinical Psychologist notes that the program's treatment relationship with participants was 'more informal, and we find that the patients are much more relaxed in the program and more open with us about their treatment, what they need and what they are struggling with'. Therefore, in the opinion of staff members and participants a critical benefit of the program was its organization in an alternative setting. This facilitated the engagement of individuals with mental illness in their recovery process in ways that the more traditional mental health unit setting were unable to do, or at least not as effectively as it could have in comparison.

A further theme that emerged from the research was the removal or the reduction of participants' feelings of isolation. Here again, football was seen to play a significant role: 'football is a family thing where you are part of team and make friends, and for me medically that gives structure to the recovery process as participants are in a better frame of mind to work with me to recover' (Clinical Psychologist). The sense of isolation through medical treatment was a common theme among the participants, as exemplified by one who comments:

> Before I got referred here, I felt very alone. I felt lost and abandoned. I was working with [Psychologist] but was not getting anywhere. I came here [program] and the first thing was that the people here were like me. We had all the same issues, the same things, and that said to me I was not alone. This is a normal situation for us where we can be mates. It gives us a friendship network where we all support each other and make sure no one slips back into the bad ways of drinking or smoking or drugs and pull each other through; we are all the same really.

This sense of friendship, common fate and sameness was considered a critical part of the mental health recovery process. According to the Clinical Nurse Specialist:

> One of the bigger battles is getting the client to understand they are not alone. We are here to support but bringing them to the program and showing them people like themselves, being around similar people, being able to discuss their problems together, that is a real benefit of the way the program is.

In a similar vein, one participant remarks:

> I had been used to being treated alone and felt lonely but here we have group sessions and as we know each other from the football we feel comfortable in the sessions. I do not mind sharing with others as they do that with me.

Another indicates:

> ... before I was shy and did not speak much to my therapist so was sent here and seeing the group work and hearing people I felt better to share my things. At the start I did not speak in front of my group but spoke much more to my psychiatrist and really opened up and after a while I talked to the group.

A related factor critical to the program design concerned the negative stigma of mental health. Reflecting the broader literature, the Clinical Nurse Specialist expresses that stigma is often the 'biggest thing we face'. Removing the stigma associated with mental health problems was central to the program's approach as, according to this practitioner,

> ... often and first of all we seek participants to accept they have a mental illness and not feel it is a stigma. Accepting their illness is not a stigma is the first thing we do and we bring a human element by being around the program to that so we can begin the recovery process.

The program coordinator and head coach, himself a former client of the MHU, agrees:

> [The] key thing we do is get participants accepting they have an ailment, that is why they are at [the program] though that is something we always fight with as participants feel stigmatized before they get to us but we have been successful at changing their mindset ... One thing about mental illness is, it is very courageous admitting you have it. I can relate to the lads I get here that way and respect them for their courage [in admitting to their illness].

A number of participants indicate the difficulties of having a stigma attached to them by having a mental illness. One participant expresses how 'that really hurt and made me feel ashamed. I was really ashamed too about what my family thought of me for having a problem.' Other participants offer similar feelings about the stigma attached to their mental health problems and what they perceive the views of others to be. For one participant 'this was a real problem about coming to the program as getting over that is really hard and admitting I have a problem but one others will think badly about me over'. One way in which the program tackled this was by providing the football setting as an opportunity for individuals with mental illness. As the Clinical Psychologist observes:

> ... in the company of each other, where they see that actually they are not alone and what they are experiencing is in fact normal here and nothing to feel shame about ... This program is normalizing the issue of mental health in a group setting which are both very important issues

and everyone then is placed together and is willing to talk about their illness. A key strength of this intervention is the program is a big family; it is normalizing the issue of mental health so that it is not an issue and everyone is willing to talk about the issue or issues they have.

Involvement in the program as part of the mental health recovery process was, according to one participant, 'not the black mark on me the way previous [medical] treatment has been. I have had times before where I have felt a stigma by being treated for my depression, but here with this program it is different.' Another participant comments:

> Having a mental illness is something really hard to accept, and before this program I had not accepted mine. I just thought I had issues, but when I came here, I saw other people like myself, we sort of were the same and I felt normal, and my psychologist said that I was just normal in the group. That made me feel better.

Another participant comments that he

> ... was able to accept my illness, not class it as a stigma, get into football which I love, it helped me to do other things, look after myself, get responsibility into my life and I see that with others too on [the program] and the program brings happiness and achievement.

Normalizing the mental illness that each participant had was pivotal to removing the associated stigma, with one participant suggesting:

> Before I had been getting treatment but felt very alone, but here you have your mates. We do the football, we have the sessions after it on things like looking after yourself, managing money, and after that we hang around together. I have met some good mates through this and no longer feel alone with a problem as we are just normal around here. I don't feel the shame I used to.

A further benefit of how the program was successful in removing the stigma of mental health was its location on the hospital premises. As one participant points out:

> Before if people had seen me come up to the hospital they would be like, 'yeah there he goes again, in for more treatment'. But now, I come up with my football bag, I say I am off to football and they think I have joined a club. I come here, play football, but get my treatment at the same time, and nobody knows and that makes it feel normal to me to do. I don't feel like people are staring at me as I am getting treatment and I have got a lot of confidence from that.

Therefore, many participants perceive that the program offers both a setting and a location that negate the stigma of mental health by normalizing it to aid the recovery process.

Participant and staff narratives reveal some of the program's successes in terms of engagement and the removal of stigma from individuals with mental health problems. Our data also shed some light on the perceived association between mental health and physical fitness, as reflected in the following comment by the Clinical Nurse Specialist:

> The improvement of physical fitness to aid mental recovery is a success factor of the program as it improves the mental state of our participants by making them feel physically better about themselves through football activity. The positive effect of physical activity on mental health wellbeing and improvement cannot be ignored and is central to our ethos and was so right from the start.

Similarly, other program staff members argue that there are both physical and mental health benefits that stem from the football activities in the program. Overall, the participants discuss some positives related to the generic improvement in their mental health state through the physical aspects of the football component, as the following comment from a male participant attests:

> The program gets you fit as football needs you to be fit, but this then makes you feel better about yourself. It makes you tired after the session, but also makes you look forward to the next one, and my mind does not wander like it used to, and I have football to think about now. I used to be a 60-a-day man but now my smoking is reduced and I can carry on for much longer in the games than before.

As an overall conclusion regarding the program, the NHS Borough Director offers significant praise, viewing the program as a method of intervention that 'greatly assists us with engaging referrals back into society and improves mental and physical health to the point we do not see them again'. The General Manager of the facility, a retired social worker and psychiatric nurse with an intense personal interest in the program, concludes that 'with my medical hat on, this program is one of the best psychiatric programs I have seen in the last 30 years as the group dynamic setting through football is crucial as it offers vital structure to the treatment'. This participant summarizes the success of the program for him:

> I was happy to stay [as a permanent resident] in the unit and be looked after, but I came on the program and saw other players had got themselves into their own places. After a while I thought I'd fancy that so I worked with the staff to set that in place. The program has helped me

to be able to look after myself and without it I do not know what I would have done or where I would be.

This is a pertinent concluding point regarding the program's ability to engage individuals with mental illness on the path to recovery – a path they can follow without stigmatization – and their eventual (re-)engagement with key social, economic and cultural activities.

Challenges and limitations

The mental health case study provides insights into how the program is experienced by participants and staff members. These insights raise the question of how specifically sport can assist mental health treatment and the recovery process. The reduction or removal of previously felt stigmatization is a key issue in this regard. The stigma attached to mental illness is arguably the main barrier to the provision of adequate care as it often prevents mental health patients' engagement with medical treatment and rehabilitation (Corrigan 2004; Sartorius 2007). The football program was aimed neither at widening sport participation opportunities for marginalized and excluded groups, nor at providing a vehicle to extend sports club membership. Rather, the program was designed by healthcare professionals who sought a model that used sport, in this case football, to provide a setting for group therapy with the purpose of improving engagement with treatment and removing the stigma attached to mental illness. Placing similar individuals together in a group setting where football acted as a catalyst was seen to help reduce the barrier of public stigma as well as negate self-stigma on the road to mental health recovery (Corrigan 2004).

However, a more critical reading would suggest that there is a tension within targeted programs such as these, a tension that can be called 'exclusive inclusion'. By bringing together only people with similar experiences of mental illness in a football setting that is confined to a mental health unit, the program did not encourage interaction between mental health clients and others who do not have mental illness, nor did it provide participants with access to mainstream football clubs or facilities. This deliberate isolation, program staff members believe, assisted the recovery process; however, it may also have reproduced stigmatization and isolation from mainstream settings. Indeed, social integration is considered to be a key component of recovery from mental health problems (Repper and Perkins 2003). In a similar vein, recent research on sport participation among young people with learning disabilities suggests that sharing inclusive sport settings with non-learning disabled young people can result in a destigmatization of impairments and increased inclusion for young people with learning disabilities (Devine and Parr 2008). However, these benefits occur only where integration is the specific aim of the sporting activity and the continuing challenges faced by young people with learning disabilities, such as stigmatization and tacit exclusion, are actively addressed (Southby 2011).

Further, the qualities of a competitive sport such as football that can be harnessed to stimulate mental health recovery can be criticized on the grounds that they can also exacerbate it. Stress and performance anxiety, confidence reduction for the low skilled, and aggressive bodily contact are known to affect the quality of the football experience (Rookwood and Palmer 2011), and may be particularly damaging for those with mental health problems. In these terms, Magee and Jeanes (2013) consider the negative experiences of the competitive environment on participants at the Homeless World Cup, and question its appropriateness and suitability as a social inclusion intervention. This critique also applies to the second program to be discussed in this chapter, which uses sport to address labour market exclusion among young people in the Netherlands. It is to this case study that we now turn.

Worklessness, social exclusion and sport

Labour market participation is without exception a key dimension in Global North theorizations of social exclusion. Indeed, it was within the context of rising unemployment and economic downturn that the term 'social exclusion' first gained prominence in 1970s France. Many contemporary analysts interpret social exclusion first and foremost as precariousness of work and employment (Vobruba 1999; Bhalla and Lapeyre 2004; Byrne 2005). In Chapter 2 we discussed how restricted access to the labour market can shape experiences of social exclusion and how it often intersects with other aspects of social exclusion, such as the capacity to purchase goods and services and establish meaningful relationships. In the policy arena, it is also the dimension of social exclusion that has received the most attention. In European social policy, for example, labour market attachment is considered key to breaking the cycle of social exclusion and welfare dependency (Levitas 2005; European Commission 2010). From this policy perspective, paid work has an important integrative function and is the fastest and most effective exit from social exclusion.

Yet the challenge of raising employment levels has proven formidable, especially during periods of economic downturn, with significant consequences for experienced exclusion from the labour market. Economic and social changes over the past two decades have disproportionately affected young people, making their transitions into work more fragile and more insecure (Kemp 2005; Colley *et al.* 2007; MacDonald 2011). Youth unemployment rates are significantly higher than those for adults, with the youth unemployment rate in the European Union (EU) around twice as high as the unemployment rate for the total population throughout the last decade.[1] In 2012, the youth unemployment rate in the EU was more than double the overall unemployment rate. At 22.8 per cent, this meant that more than one out of every five young persons in the labour force was unemployed although available for and seeking work (Eurostat 2013). In some European countries the youth unemployment rate was considerably higher; in Spain and Greece, it exceeded 50 per cent in 2012 (Eurostat 2013).

Policy-makers face the challenge of reducing labour market exclusion by designing ways to increase employment opportunities for various population segments, those working in particular economic activities, or living in specific regions. Public policy in this area often concentrates on supply-side measures aimed at raising employability based on the assumption that worklessness is primarily related to a lack of skills, aptitude or motivation rather than to a lack of jobs (Peck and Theodore 2000; Crisp *et al.* 2009). For local labour market attachment programs such as those discussed below, the focus on the supply side of work also derives from pragmatism. Thus, it is at the level of individual attributes and skills that potentially effective interventions can be made within the scope of a program, while broader labour market forces remain largely beyond program control.

Within this vast policy terrain, sport plays but a peripheral role; however, its role in the promotion of labour market attachment, in particular, is an area of growing interest among policy-makers and practitioners (Spaaij *et al.* 2013). Programs using sport to this end are under way in several countries across different world regions (see also Chapter 6). Indeed, sport-focused employment initiatives have been a pervasive yet under-explored feature of the delivery of social policy through sport (Glyptis 1989; Mason and Geddes 2010). Given the continuing rise in youth unemployment across many European countries in recent years, a more detailed analysis of how sport is used in this policy field is both timely and appropriate. Drawing upon our own qualitative research in this area (Spaaij 2009a, 2011; Spaaij *et al.* 2013), we discuss below a Dutch case study to critically examine the nature, impact and limitations of programs that use sport as a vehicle for labour market attachment.

Labour market attachment through sport: a case study

The Sport Steward Program (SSP) examined here commenced in 2007 as a partnership model led by the City Steward Rotterdam Foundation (previously Sport Steward Promotion) in Rotterdam, the second largest city of the Netherlands with a population of approximately 600,000. SSP was initially funded through the European Fund for Regional Development and two regional colleges, but since 2008 has been financed by the Department of Social Affairs of the Municipality of Rotterdam. SSP is one of a range of initiatives developed as part of a local and national government policy aimed at combating socio-economic inactivity among young people who are not in employment, education or training (Ministry of Social Affairs and Work 2009; Municipality of Rotterdam 2011).

SSP reflects a broader trend of engagement mentoring that seeks to re-engage socially excluded youth with the formal labour market by altering their attitudes, values and beliefs (Colley 2003). The focus of SSP is on the supply side of work: that is, on raising an individual's employability through skills training and practical work experience. SSP staff members believe that many unemployed youth in Rotterdam want to work, but lack the opportunities and qualifications to obtain secure employment. Their objective, then, is to better equip these young people for the labour market or to guide them back into education. Specifically, the program provides an educational platform where youth gain knowledge of and experience in the profession of sport steward. The program is delivered by youth workers, teachers and counsellors from a range of backgrounds, including local government, education, sport and police. As the program is a certified educational institution, it allows participants to obtain formal educational qualifications in the areas of stewarding and crowd control, first aid, traffic control and security management. SSP training also involves practical work experience at major sporting events in Rotterdam, which often continues on a (paid) casual, part-time basis after completion of the program. It also offers intensive individual counselling and guidance through regular meetings among participants, teachers, mentors and prospective employers both during and after completion of the program. Program staff members endeavour to assist participants with any issues or concerns that may arise and afford access to job-seeking services and networks.

SSP attracts participants through a variety of routes, including both formal and informal referrals from social service personnel, youth workers, community police, friends, as well as personal initiative. From its inception, SSP has sought to use outreach approaches and loose informal referrals as a means of positive engagement with local youth, for example through distributing flyers and working with community residents. Participants are young males and females aged 16 to 31. Most participants are aged in their 20s and approximately half are female. Participants experience high levels of job insecurity, their educational attainment is typically limited (often with incomplete secondary education), and their prior work experience consists mostly of temporary work through job agencies. Financially, many participants rely on public welfare or the informal economy (Spaaij 2009a).

Although the program objectives go well beyond sport, it is nonetheless a significant activity in the Sport Steward Program. SSP staff members demonstrate a deep belief in the value of sport as a tool for engaging young people and enhancing their motivation to participate in educational activities. In other words, sport participation is considered a means to an end, rather than an end in its own right. This view of sport as a motivator is articulated by SSP's physical education teacher (male, 50s):

> There are a number of people who are really motivated. But there are also several people who are not, and you try to get those on board. I think that's the most important thing about sport [in SSP]. They get their classroom activities and are continuously studying. Then including a bit of sport is very good. And you get to know them in a very different way. They can express themselves differently. And you notice that certain people feel more comfortable with that.

In practice, however, playing sport is a relatively minor aspect of the learning activities in SSP, even though three two-hour sessions per week are devoted to sport and physical activity. Rather, the main emphasis in SSP is on the prospect of these young people working in a sports environment. Nevertheless, for the majority of young people in the program, the sport focus and the prospect of working at major sporting events are important incentives for engagement with the program. One participant (male, 20s) comments how he 'had to attend a program and through social services found out about this program'. He says: 'I really liked the fact that the program had to do with sport because I love football. That's why I chose this program.' In a similar vein, another male participant (20s) reports: 'I don't like books or classes. I only like sport. That's why I chose this program. I read that it was sport-based education. I would love to work in a sporting environment.' We see further evidence here of how sport can serve as a 'hook' to engage young people, in this case young males, in educational activities.

SSP is primarily concerned with the development of knowledge and skills specific to the profession of sport steward. Training also focuses on more generic and transferable skills such as communication, computer, language and job search skills. Young people in the program recognize the significance of these skills for enhancing their employability. They report that they feel better equipped to enter the labour market through the acquisition of both task-specific skills and social skills. For instance, a female former participant in her 30s who now works as a security officer observes that her communication skills improved markedly as a result of her participation in the program. She describes how she used to be 'very angry' and easily agitated, but now believes she has learned to reflect on and manage her temper. This, she argues, also helps her performance in the workplace:

> I notice that I've become more and more relaxed, and people react to me differently now. A lot of my colleagues say 'You are really becoming more relaxed' … It has helped me to get ahead in my work in the security business. And it's also useful outside of my work. You need to be able to understand other people. During the education [at SSP and subsequently in her training as event security officer] you learn to look at people's body language. If you don't pay attention to that, you can easily get in trouble.

This participant also appreciates the formal qualifications in stewarding, first aid, traffic control and crowd management that she obtained through the program, and that these qualifications afford her a competitive advantage in the labour market:

> I'm glad I've got those certificates. It puts you a step ahead of others who haven't done the program, and of course the vast knowledge you acquire in those six months [of participation in SSP]. Many stewards lack that knowledge … the quality of stewards is often poor. They only get two evenings of training. The program has given me a lot of confidence

in how to do my job. You work in a more self-confident manner. I notice that my boss also observes this. When he needs to leave he asks me whether I can keep an eye on things.

This experience reflects SSP program staff members' belief that formal qualifications are mandatory nowadays for young people to be able to enter the labour market. As noted, a complementary approach taken by the program to encourage labour market attachment is to provide practical work experience such as internships and casual paid employment. This provides participants with a foot in the door as well as a better understanding of what is required of them in the workplace. The female participant cited above is a case in point. Her practical work experience at a professional football club initially continued on a casual basis after she graduated from the program, and subsequently helped her gain permanent employment as a sport steward and later as a security officer.

Challenges and limitations

The Sport Steward Program is generally well received by local young people, who recognize the personal and professional skills development and employment opportunities that the program offers. However, our research also points to some important limitations that profoundly affect the program's capacity to facilitate participants' labour market attachment in the long term. First, a program like SSP can play only a limited role in supporting participants in accessing and retaining secure jobs. The short-term nature of program participation, which spans approximately four months, and the limited availability of post-program assistance and job opportunities are important factors in this regard. We know that young people with low educational attainment are more likely to experience a mix of training programs, temporary and part-time jobs, and periods of unemployment (Kemp 2005). Since completing the program, several participants have found part-time jobs in the sport or event security industry. While for some of them this constitutes an important change to their social and financial situation, they also know that their employment is typically of a temporary, fixed-term nature and that their future remains uncertain. For many participants, then, their employment situation is still fragile and in constant flux.

Program staff members believe that post-program engagement mentoring is a key factor in breaking the vicious cycle in which young people repeatedly move between unemployment, employability programs, low-paid work, and back again, a cycle that can deepen job insecurity rather than lead to sustainable employment that provides some element of progression (Kemp 2005). This is particularly pivotal, they argue, for young people with complex needs:

[E]very young person from this type of program should basically have someone who keeps in touch with them and kind of monitors how they are going, or who can help them if they regress. Because with these target groups you often see that they start a new program, but for one reason or another they end up in a downward spiral again. And then you lose them again. Sometimes the program seems successful, but six months later they are back at square one. That's what you have to prevent.

(Program worker, male, 30s)

Program workers thus regard labour market attachment as a longer-term process that, for this target group at least, is likely to involve ups and downs. The impact of program activities on participants' labour market attachment is also strongly affected by events or situations outside the realm of the program's influence. The program manager (male, mid-40s) argues:

You notice that if they get a job or an apprenticeship that they really enjoy upon completion [of SSP], that's a huge gain and a major step forward. Because it's theirs, they achieve this. And for a large number of youth that's all they need, the rest will follow from that. But some problems can resurface along the way. If they lose their job the chance of falling back is very high. That's why post-program support is very important, so they can come to you for support and reassurance.

Participants also recognize the importance of their ongoing engagement in work beyond the life of the program. A former participant (male, 20s) expresses this as follows:

I was worried that after the program I would fall back, but because I kept working as a steward at Sparta [a professional football club in Rotterdam] and stayed associated with the program and its staff it has actually brought me to a higher level. Probably if I had slipped back into unemployment things would have been different. I would have fallen back into my old situation, sitting at home doing nothing. In our group perhaps one or two persons have remained in that situation, but the majority have made some progress.

Critically, however, SSP staff members realize that not every participant is able to benefit from the program to the same extent. This is particularly the case for those who are not intrinsically motivated to move out of worklessness, and for those with multiple problems and needs. With regard to the latter, young people with learning difficulties or mental health issues often require far more intensive support than the program is able to offer. Some program staff members question whether the program is suitable for these individuals: 'We teach them a little bit, but you cannot make up for years of non-education [or other complex needs] within the space of four months. That's impossible.' (Program worker, 30s).

A second major challenge that SSP faces is its focus on the supply side of labour market attachment, with little acknowledgement of institutional or structural fields of power that shape youth worklessness and social exclusion. Research shows that the decisive determinant of successful labour market inclusion programming remains the underlying nature of labour demand (Peck and Theodore 2000). Skills development and employability training by no means provide an automatic passport to better employment opportunities (Crisp *et al.* 2009). Rather, more attention ought to be paid to demand-side factors. A key concern is that programs aggressively mobilize workers for low-waged work by 'churning' them back into the bottom of the labour market, or holding them deliberately close to the labour market in a permanent job-ready state (Byrne 2005). Without an adequate supply of decent work, this strategy can have deep and adverse effects not only on the self-formation of workless young people, but also on the structure of labour markets where it serves to erode pay and conditions (Peck and Theodore 2000). One former participant (male, 20s), who has attended several state-funded employability programs, expresses this concern: 'It gave you a temporary job, but after a couple of months you were out on the streets again. It didn't give you any lasting improvements.' In the same vein, a female participant (30s) comments:

> I want job security now. My previous jobs were always temporary, for a period of six months or so, and then I had to leave again. So then you're back in that black hole and dependent on welfare payments again. I simply don't want that any more.

Demand-side factors clearly constrain the effectiveness of programs like SSP. For example, there is some evidence of employers' reluctance to recruit the long-term unemployed, especially those with relatively complex needs (e.g. language difficulties and mental illness) and criminal records. Program staff members recognize this issue and seek to build positive relationships with prospective employers in order to reduce any prejudices and biases among employers (Spaaij 2009a).

In the next section, we draw together and reflect on the insights that can be gleaned from the two case studies presented in this chapter with regard to the use of sport to tackle social exclusion.

Critical reflections

The two case studies outlined above offer a number of critically relevant points regarding the use of sport for individuals who experience mental illness or worklessness. As noted, these case studies highlight two different ways in which sport has been utilized to address social exclusion in the Global North. The mental health case study draws attention to how marginalized individuals are able to find a 'home' and share a sense of space in which to feel 'included' and 'normal'. The narratives of program participants portray the program as an inclusionary space for the marginalized and vulnerable to come together, share their own experiences of mental illness and establish friendships and camaraderie, while at the same time engage with the recovery process through the rehabilitative program offered by the program. This subjective experience of social inclusion cannot be overestimated or devalued in the lives of individuals who beyond the football program report high levels of social exclusion. Indeed, this experience can be seen as a significant factor in stimulating their engagement in the recovery process against the backdrop of the difficulties individuals often encounter during the recovery process (Morgan *et al.* 2007; Sartorius 2007). In this regard, there are significant parallels between the subjective experiences of participants in the mental health program and those of the young people who participate in SSP. While the latter program principally focuses on creating pathways to work through sport-based education, the narratives of participants similarly indicate how they tend to experience the program environment to be inclusive, respectful and supportive, which they believe positively affects their engagement with the program and its overall objectives.

However, the case studies also raise critical notes regarding the use of sport interventions to address social exclusion. A first conclusion that can be gleaned from the two case studies is that structural exclusion processes remain largely unaltered. The SSP program's focus on the supply side of labour market attachment is a case in point. As noted, we know that the decisive determinant of successful labour market inclusion programming remains the underlying nature of labour demand (Peck and Theodore 2000). However, small-scale programs such as SSP have very little, if any, effect on the broader labour demand. This raises the question of whether programs such as these can have a deep, long-term impact on participants' ability to navigate job insecurity and the precariousness of work (Spaaij *et al.* 2013). In other words, can such programs move beyond a narrow focus on 'fixing' individuals to address the broader causes of social exclusion?

Any positive social impact that the two programs have produced is at least to some extent associated with their role as cultural intermediaries (Crabbe 2008, 2009; Spaaij 2011). This role enables the programs to (partly) bridge the gap or alleviate tensions between marginalized individuals and dominant social groups and institutions, which in turn allows them to provide access to social worlds and opportunities not currently accessible to the individuals with whom they work (Crabbe *et al.* 2006). The constituencies they target tend to value their work because it is perceived and experienced as non-interfering and non-threatening, and is carried out in a way that is respectful and understanding of their conditions. In the mental health program, the role of the program coordinator and head coach is a case in point. Having previously experienced mental health treatment as a client of the mental health unit where the program was housed, he was subsequently recruited as a coach to assist with the program. Because of his personal experience he was able to connect with participants in terms of their biographies and social outlook. In a similar vein, the SSP program employs staff members whose social backgrounds are broadly similar to those of the target group (Spaaij 2011).

While it may not always be possible or necessary for programs to recruit a cultural intermediary in the way these programs have (consider, for example, the aforementioned positive experiences of participants in the mental health program with their Clinical Nurse Specialist), the value of the experiences and empathy such individuals bring to the programs should not be underestimated.

The data presented here are directly relevant to the ongoing scholarly debate on the need for robust empirical evidence when it comes to policies or programs that use sport for wider social objectives (Long and Sanderson 2001; Bailey 2005; Coalter 2007). Specifically, one cannot ignore the inherent limitations of programs of the type discussed here. For example, despite the positive perceptions of staff members and participants from whom qualitative data were collected, the mental health program was unable to provide evidence of the numbers of participants who had not (fully) benefited from the program by disassociating from it as non-attendees, remaining with the mental health unit upon exit, or exiting the program only to return as re-referrals to the mental health unit at a later date. The absence of strong supporting data was due in large part to client–patient confidentiality; however, it provides further ammunition for the 'lack of hard evidence' argument in academic research (Coalter 2007, 2013).

Further, the case studies problematize this argument by highlighting the complexity of the social processes that the programs seek to generate. For individuals with complex needs, personal and professional development is inevitably a long-term, non-linear process that is profoundly affected by events outside the realm of program influence. As the mental health case study shows, this process can involve the rebuilding or recovering of one's sense of self within meaningful social roles and relationships. As Crabbe *et al.* (2006: 15) rightly note, the fractured progression stories that often result from this process 'should not be seen as a "failure" but rather as the inevitable context in which work with participants occurs'. In such conditions, the continued engagement of participants represents an important positive outcome in and of itself. An appreciation of this social complexity and the influence of broader contextual factors, however, is often absent in calls for 'hard evidence'. As such, any attempt to establish a 'hard' (i.e. statistical) causal relationship between sport and singular outcomes may well be 'a rather crass effort to bang square pegs into round holes' (Crabbe 2008: 31). We concur with Crabbe that such efforts ultimately represent 'a staged attempt to validate the benefits of sporting programmes rather than providing a more valid and complete account of what is actually involved in the process' (2008: 31). The challenge, then, is to recognize and capture the inherent complexities of initiatives aimed at ameliorating experiences of social exclusion among people whose needs are strongly affected by forces beyond the control of the program.

Beyond the scholarly debate on what constitutes 'evidence' looms the spectre of public sector budget cuts and their potential implications for the future of programs such as those we have discussed in this chapter. The politics of sport and social exclusion are evident in both programs. Despite its documented accomplishments, the mental health program was brought to an end after its original three-year funding had run out, with its closure due to budget cuts foreshadowed by the NHS Borough Director during our research. Although the SSP program continues to operate because of local government funding, it faces significant financial pressures. These pressures have led the program to target young people with less complex needs who it is felt are more likely to respond to the support available (Spaaij *et al.* 2013). These experiences question the commitment directed towards the use of sport to address social exclusion within the mainstream public sector. One can only speculate the impact this will have on future participants who are denied access to what have been heralded as relatively successful programs. More generally, it remains to be seen whether support for and investment in sport as a viable policy tool in the Global North will remain strong, or wane within the changing social policy context.

Note

1 Based on the International Labour Organization (1982) standard definition, youth unemployment refers to persons aged 15–24 who are without paid work, available for work and seeking work.

6 Sport for development in the Global South

Introduction

The previous chapter examined how sport is utilized to address social exclusion in the Global North. In this chapter, we shift our attention to the ways in which social exclusion has been addressed in the Global South as part of the 'sport for development' (SFD) movement. SFD programs in the Global South are usually couched in international development language rather than in social exclusion discourse, due in part to the influence of external, Northern-based development agencies on local SFD policy and praxis. Nevertheless, there are parallels between the ways in which sport is used to address social exclusion in the Global North and SFD in the Global South. Several SFD programs that have been initiated in the Global South specifically address issues of rights, recognition and resources that are central to our understanding of social exclusion. Further, they often focus on user groups' opportunities to participate in educational, economic or social activities; as such they align with the academic and policy thinking on social exclusion that we address in Chapter 2.

This present chapter first discusses the development objectives of SFD initiatives as well as their increased diversification in terms of the actors involved and approaches adopted. We then explore how the aims and expectations of SFD work are delivered in practice within particular communities by drawing upon our research in Brazil and Zambia. We show that despite the different intended outcomes of the programs, how sport works within the programs and the issues and challenges they encounter are broadly similar. Finally, the chapter reflects on some of the key issues facing SFD praxis in relation to ameliorating social exclusion at different levels.

The SFD sector: aspirations and diversification

'Sport for development' is a key buzz phrase at this point in the twenty-first century (Coakley 2011). Sport is increasingly used to assist development strategies and initiatives in the Global South, to the point where it can be seen to constitute a significant element within global civil society (Giulianotti 2011) or 'a new engine of development' (Levermore 2008a). The potential of sport as a tool for development is being harnessed by various international, national and local organizations that have begun to translate this idea into hundreds of programs across the developing world. These organizations range from governmental and intergovernmental agencies to sports associations, transnational corporations to NGOs and other community-based organizations.

Intergovernmental institutions and international sports federations have played an important role in this diffusion process. In 2005, Jacques Rogge, the President of the International Olympic Committee (IOC), and UN Secretary-General Kofi Annan issued a joint message in which they state that sports entities are working together to 'harness the great power of sport to change people's lives for the better', noting that well-designed sports programs can be cost-effective catalysts for social change (UNOSDP 2005). The rationale for this partnership is articulated in terms of how sport allows individuals to 'experience equality, freedom and a dignifying means for empowerment, particularly for girls and women, for people with a disability, for those living in conflict areas and for people recovering from trauma' (Beutler 2008: 365). The UN General Assembly (2006) has gone as far as to call for sport participation to be enshrined as a human right. From this standpoint, then, any enforced lack of participation in sport constitutes a significant form of social exclusion.

The UN Inter-Agency Taskforce on Sport for Development and Peace and other UN agencies are major proponents of this vision. The UN (2008) argues that sport can play an important role in achieving the Millennium Development Goals by addressing education, health and development issues, and by increasing understanding and tolerance among communities. The UN (2008: 11) emphasizes the role of sport in social inclusion by arguing that 'sport contributes to combating discrimination and marginalization, enabling the full and equal participation of all in societal life'. Young people, especially those deemed vulnerable or 'at risk', are believed to be among the main beneficiaries of the positive effects of sport, which contributes to improved health, education and employment skills and opportunities (UN 2008). In other words, sport is regarded as a potentially powerful solution to the problem of social exclusion. This belief is evident, for example, in UNICEF's (2006: 5) statement:

> [Sport] teaches core values such as cooperation and respect. It improves health and reduces the likelihood of disease. And it brings individuals and communities together, bridging cultural or ethnic divides. Sport is also an effective way to reach children and adolescents who are excluded and discriminated against, offering them companionship, support, and a sense of belonging.

The growing interest in and support for SFD have resulted in the sector's diversification. A wide variety of SFD applications now exist that demonstrate tremendous diversity in purposes, methodologies, actual activities, levels of intervention and social contexts (Burnett 2010; Kidd 2011). Key development areas addressed in SFD include community development, personal development, public health, children's education, employment creation and entrepreneurship, women's rights, conflict resolution and intercultural understanding. Several of these objectives directly relate to the different dimensions of social exclusion that we discussed in Chapter 2, such as economic, social and political exclusion. However, an unintended consequence of the burgeoning of SFD programs (and attendant competition for funding and status) is that while programs are taking on ambitious development objectives, they often lack a clear change theory and methodology linking sport with specific development objectives and specific causal mechanisms (Coalter 2013). As Bartlett and Straume (2008) point out, effective programs with a clear and focused agenda do appear to link sport activities to specific development objectives, processes and outcomes.

The pluriformity of the SFD sector is reflected not only in the diversity of development objectives, but also in the range of program models that are under way throughout the Global South. Programs vary on a range of variables such as organizational development, social relations (with donors, sector and recipients), scale (transnational, national, local), pedagogical approach, monitoring and evaluation model, and the types of sport used in the program. Giulianotti (2011) identifies three ideal-typical models of an SFD program that capture much of this diversity: technical, dialogical and critical. However, the philosophical paradigms, pedagogical methods, institutional forms and social relationships of these three models differ markedly. The majority of contemporary SFD programs feature different mixtures of the first two models, while the critical model has been less apparent.

The technical SFD model was particularly evident during the late 1990s and early 2000s among NGOs and sports federations that had limited contextual knowledge or sensitivity (Giulianotti 2011). This model centres on utilitarian and hierarchical intervention, with a commitment to the resolution of social problems such as community division and conflict. The technical model favours externally imposed agendas and program content and a directive pedagogical method, all of which are largely determined and controlled by Northern-based agencies. This type of SFD work typically features intervention activities with specified social units that are differentiated by age, gender and residence. Technical SFD programs often work within particular time-space contexts with established sports in which competitive aspects are retained. Further, SFD agencies operating within this model tend to accept regulation by donors who seek to influence program objectives and methods of evaluation (Giulianotti 2011).

According to Giulianotti (2011), the dialogical SFD model aims to facilitate the positive reconstruction of social relations among and within communities. SFD agencies working within this model use a dialogical pedagogy that engages and teaches user groups, often through formal peer education (Spaaij and Jeanes 2013). The paradigmatic method is the 'training the trainers' technique, wherein the SFD agency trains local volunteers to become SFD teachers and practitioners and they then return to their host communities to train more volunteers and to implement programs. Participation is more open-ended than in the technical model, allowing recipients to drop in and out of programs. Further, the dialogical model is willing to modify existing sports to accommodate the SFD program's inclusive goals (Giulianotti 2011).

Finally, the critical SFD model pursues bottom-up transformations in relationships among communities and in how SFD work is conducted, with the purpose of forging thriving, fully inclusive communities and programs (Giulianotti 2011). It does so by enabling user groups to identify their own needs, ascertain the nature and sources of social problems and conflicts, and choose appropriate strategies and responses. The critical SFD model also seeks to instil strong principles of local program ownership through full user-group participation in formulating, implementing and evaluating programs. The pedagogical paradigm underpinning this SFD model centres on the importance of sustained learning experiences among self-directed learners who assume decision-making and leadership responsibilities. The critical SFD model engages with diverse community groups – not just young people, but also parents, families, friends, community leaders and other local stakeholders who all contribute to the success of programs. The critical SFD model typically develops new activities with distinctive community-building properties that lack the cultural baggage of established sports and as such may be approached equally by all participants (Giulianotti 2011).

Giulianotti's (2011) typology of SFD programs is instructive for mapping the terrain and critically examining current policy and practice within the SFD sector. For the present purpose, however, we specifically examine SFD in relation to the issue of social exclusion as it is constructed in academic research (Chapter 2) and in public policy (Chapter 3). Within these particular contexts, SFD programs can be categorized using two basic axes of differentiation. The first axis refers to the *longevity* of a program. This scale ranges from discontinuous, one-off events to sustained, longer-term programs that are often community-based and institutionally embedded. The assumption here is that programs must be sustained to have a lasting impact (Kidd 2011). The second axis refers to the degree to which SFD programs are *targeted* to specific population subsets that experience one or multiple forms of social exclusion within particular social contexts. In practice, this area of differentiation tends to distinguish programs that focus primarily on the development of sport ('sport for sport's sake') from those that focus primarily on ulterior development objectives (see Chapter 3 for the related, but not identical, distinction between 'sport plus' and 'plus sport'). The former focus is often driven by the desire of the sports community, particularly international sport organizations, to expand the global reach of particular sports. This typically involves what Levermore (2008b: 57) terms 'sport first', where organizations 'primarily stimulate participation in sport, and developmental consequences are an unintentional or poorly articulated by-product'. As shown in Figure 6.1, a partial exception is special needs programs that aim to increase access to sport among people with disabilities, ethnic minorities, people living in remote areas, and others who are under-represented in sport participation. Examples of such programs can be found in Chapter 3, where we compare sport and social exclusion policies in the UK, China and Zambia. Special needs programs have potentially important albeit often poorly articulated consequences for social exclusion within and possibly also beyond the realm of sport.

Figure 6.1 shows how the combination of the two axes produces a basic taxonomy of SFD programs. We indicate where common SFD program types may be found on this taxonomy, although we recognize that the char- acteristics of individual SFD programs may deviate from this indicative structure as well as change over time. The figure is far more rudimentary and partial than the comprehensive typology developed by Giulianotti (2011), yet it is particularly well suited to exploring the opportunities and challenges associated with different types of SFD work in terms of how they address and affect social exclusion as it is experienced by program user groups. For example, the literature shows that the most ubiquitous form of SFD programs – one-off events – presents particular challenges with respect to

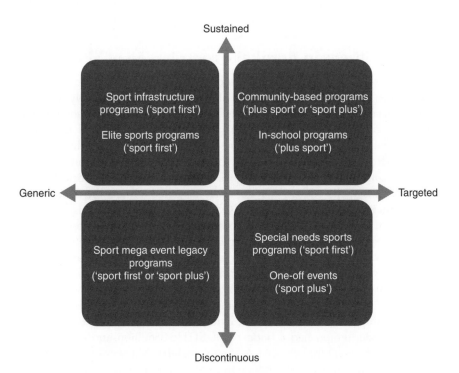

Figure 6.1 Sport for development program categories.

sustainability and raised expectations (Bartlett and Straume 2008). Elite sport programs, on the other hand, raise serious concerns regarding equity and inclusiveness, and can be taken to involve the further exploitation of peripheral countries in the Global South by sports federations and corporations based in the Global North (Levermore 2008b). Hence, there are a number of key questions for the analysis and evaluation of the relationship between SFD programs and social exclusion. To what extent and in what ways does the program aim to address different forms and degrees of social exclusion? What are the intended and unanticipated effects of SFD programs in terms of ameliorating, preventing or perpetuating social exclusion, and whose interests do they serve? What processes produce these effects for which participants and in what circumstances, and what are their limitations?

In the remainder of this chapter, we explore these questions for selected SFD programs where we have conducted intensive research fieldwork to illustrate some of the ways in which sport has been used to address social exclusion in the Global South. The programs examined here can be understood as relatively targeted and sustained approaches, yet with significant variations in specific content, process and context. The two countries that are the sites for these programs are Brazil and Zambia. In Brazil, a program (Vencer) aims at improving the skills and employability prospects of disadvantaged young people, while in Zambia several initiatives focus on using sport as a context in which to educate young people about HIV/AIDS.

Making citizens in Brazil: the contribution of SFD

Efforts to use sport as a development tool are under way in a variety of forms and settings in Brazil. The best known of these programs is probably Segundo Tempo (Second Half), a national sports education program established by the Ministries of Sport and Education in partnership with state and municipal governments and NGOs. The Brazilian government recognizes that it has a duty to act to universalize access to sport, a right that is enshrined in the Brazilian constitution. A key challenge is to provide sports for all Brazilians in a context of a public education system that has failed to meet the demand for sport participation opportunities (UNOSDP 2010). To address this, Segundo Tempo provides regular after-school sports activities for public school children during the second half of the day when lessons are not held. While enhancing sports knowledge and motor skills is a program objective, the primary concern is to achieve a wider range of educational and social inclusion outcomes (Ministry of Sports 2011), namely 'to foster the social development of children, adolescents and young people, encourage their integration as citizens of the State, and improve their standard of living' (Ministry of Sports 2010: 13). In 2010, Segundo Tempo had a budget of USD146.3 million and reached one million Brazilian children across 1,366 municipalities (Ministry of Sports 2010).

Unlike the nationwide Segundo Tempo program, most programs in Brazil that use sport to address social exclusion are relatively confined in terms of their scale and scope, operating at grassroots level within local communities and being driven by local or transnational NGOs or other community-based organizations. These programs usually target certain population groups such as young people living in areas characterized by high levels of unemployment, violence and crime. Local contextual and institutional factors play a key role in such programs. Programs are often driven by organizations that rely heavily on volunteer and other forms of in-kind support, which means that capacity building is a critical determinant of program success and sustainability (Bartlett and Straume 2008). Yet the confined nature of these programs also has potential advantages, such as the opportunity they provide to forge a more reflexive, locally owned approach that resembles Giulianotti's (2011) critical SFD model.

Luta Pela Paz (Fight for Peace), a non-profit organization established in 2000 by the local NGO Viva Rio and former English amateur boxer Luke Dowdney, serves as an illustration of community-based SFD programs in Brazil. The critically acclaimed Luta Pela Paz program operates in one of Rio de Janeiro's largest complex of *favelas* (shantytowns), the Complexo da Maré, which has a high firearm-related death rate; it provides alternatives for local children and young people to crime, drug-dealing and organized armed violence. Informed by a theoretically grounded approach to the fight against armed violence, the program centres on a social inclusion strategy that combines boxing and martial arts, citizenship education, access to the labour market, the promotion of a culture of peace and youth leadership development (Souza and Constantino 2006; Luta Pela Paz 2012). This integrated approach to social inclusion is considered essential to the program's success, with the different components designed to act in combination in mutually reinforcing ways to promote both social inclusion outcomes and access to sport participation opportunities. Program officials believe that within this holistic model sport plays an important role, both in terms of promoting healthy lifestyles and as a vehicle for reaching and mobilizing young people within the local community.

Luta Pela Paz provides children and young people with the opportunity to participate in age-appropriate boxing, capoeira and wrestling activities, as well as in education via courses on citizenship, conflict resolution and information technology. In addition to the free activities and facilities for children and youth (which include internet access), Luta Pela Paz operates a private gym that charges minimal fees for community residents, its purpose being to promote social interaction between user groups and the wider community as well as contribute to the financial sustainability of the program. Luta Pela Paz currently works with more than 500 young people each year. Participation in the program is open-ended and flexible, allowing children and young people to drop in and out of sports and education activities (personal interviews with program officials, 2009).

Luta Pela Paz operates in a similar social environment to another SFD program in which we have conducted fieldwork, namely Vencer (Spaaij 2011,

2012a, 2013d; Kay and Spaaij 2012; Spaaij and Jeanes 2013). Vencer (To Win) is built on the assumption that sport is an important tool for personal and professional development. The program uses team sports, particularly football, to motivate disadvantaged youth to participate in vocational training, and to teach employability skills that enlarge young people's prospect of gaining secure and rewarding employment. The intended overall program outcomes are demonstrably improved employability skills for participating youth, practical work experience that builds their credentials, and knowledge about how to pursue job opportunities. Participants are young people aged 16–24 living in low-income communities in Rio de Janeiro. Unemployment and low educational attainment are key concerns for these young people, and their participation in the program tends to be motivated by their desire to get a job, preferably in the formal labour market (Spaaij 2011, 2012a). Vencer officials believe that the majority of program graduates will find a job, start their own business, or return to formal education; yet, as will be seen, they also recognize the significant barriers that need to be overcome if young people are to translate their newly acquired skills into secure work (Spaaij 2013d).

Vencer is part of a wider international SFD program called A Ganar, which commenced as a pilot in Brazil, Uruguay and Ecuador but has subsequently evolved into an 11-country alliance of several organizations and donors. A Ganar has now expanded beyond football to include educational activities based on rugby, baseball, netball, basketball and cricket. Vencer is coordinated by the NGO Instituto Companheiros das Américas (ICA) and implemented through a range of grassroots NGOs that work in local target communities. Sponsored by the Multilateral Investment Fund (MIF) of the Inter-American Development Bank (IDB), A Ganar (Vencer) was originally a USD3.6 million pilot that was designed to train more than 3,100 young people in Brazil, Uruguay and Ecuador. Subsequently, the Nike Foundation invested USD1.99 million in a female-specific version of Vencer in Brazil called Vencedoras. In 2010 the MIF approved a new USD3.6 million scale-up of A Ganar, with an additional USD1.4 million investment by USAID in 2009 enabling the program to expand to four countries in the Caribbean. Nevertheless, Rio de Janeiro continues to be the largest program site, and it is this location that provides the focus of the present analysis. Again we see here the significant influence and investment of external, Northern agencies in SFD work in the Global South, an issue that we discussed in detail in Chapter 3 in relation to the Zambian experience.

The role of sport within Vencer warrants further explanation, particularly because the program objectives reach beyond the realm of sport. Like most SFD programs, Vencer provides more than just opportunities to participate in sport; however, it is difficult to disentangle the effect of sport participation from the other components of the program (Spaaij 2013d). Its strategy can be understood as 'plus sport', where social, educational and occupational components are given primacy, and sport, especially its ability to bring together and engage a large number of young people, is part of a broader and more complex set of processes (see Chapter 3). Members of staff describe Vencer as an holistic youth development program in which the different activities, including sport, act in combination in mutually reinforcing ways akin to those described earlier in relation to Luta Pela Paz. Vencer uses team sports activities to create an active learning environment to support and deliver educational content. During the first phase of the six-month program, participants play approximately 50 hours on the field and spend around 50 hours in the classroom. In the remainder of the program, staff members continue to use sports contexts and provide regular opportunities for games (Spaaij 2012a).

The sports activities are an integral part of the broader program of opening up opportunities for improved educational and economic inclusion outcomes. In Vencer, the sports activities demonstrate three characteristics that make them a suitable vehicle for delivering positive outcomes. First, sport is regarded as an effective 'hook' to engage young people in an educational setting. Program staff members believe that the use of sports makes the learning activities on and off the field more enjoyable and more relevant, and that the qualities of team sports provide experiences that allow participants to develop personal and interpersonal skills that equip them to deal with broader issues in their lives. This viewpoint is articulated by a program assistant (male, 20s) who argues that sport has specific qualities that make it a suitable context for learning, including for those who may be hard to reach through other social institutions:

> There are youth who are not really interested in doing a professionalization course but have a strong interest in football, in playing sport. Thus, if you don't succeed in getting them into the employability part, you can engage them through sport, that is, through sport they begin to attend classes, new activities, so it becomes one package with sport, classes, theory … it comprises all of this. So even those who initially may not be interested in the technical part will end up engaging in the technical part.

Second, sport (especially football) is used to facilitate a fluid, experiential learning environment to support and deliver educational content to young people. Sports activities are seen to generate valuable teaching and learning moments that are carried over to the classroom-based education sessions. The activities are delivered in such a way that they align with and complement the more theoretical aspects of the program, which focus on the development of key competencies such as teamwork, communication, discipline and respect. As such, they facilitate a platform for experiential learning where the practical sports activities constitute a concrete learning activity during which subject knowledge and generic employability skills can be applied and reflected upon. A Vencer coordinator (female, 40s) describes the role of sport in this learning process as follows:

> It's a kind of tool for them to realize through doing something the importance of the competencies we develop in the program, like respect

and discipline … You have to construct the learning of the skill. They have to use the skill in practice in order for them to understand its importance and relevance. Through football we show them the importance of the kinds of things we are talking about in class and of the skills we are trying to develop. That is why I think it is a very important tool. And we can see the difference it makes.

Indeed, several Vencer participants note that it is very important to be able to apply the skills they are being taught to the 'real world', that is, to put them into practice in everyday life situations, for instance in work, family or community settings. Thus, the sports activities are believed to provide a practical setting where these skills can be cultivated and applied (Spaaij 2012a).

A third feature of the sports activities in Vencer is that they contribute towards building social relationships that underpin the outcomes of the program. During sport, participants are able to develop a commitment towards each other and display their willingness to work as a team, resolve conflicts, and provide mutual support both on and off the field. As a program coordinator (male, 30s) explains:

Sport, and football in particular, gave us an opportunity to talk about other things, like work skills. Because everybody knows a little bit about football, and even if they don't like it they would like to go watch it. And so it facilitates negotiation and establishes relationships, institutional relationships, personal relationships.

The social interaction aspects of the sports activities are thus seen to further support the development of personal and professional skills such as cooperation, responsibility, communication, conflict resolution, task orientation and discipline. One way in which this is done within Vencer is through the modification of game rules to create a more inclusive, participatory learning environment in which both males and females, and both talented and less talented players, have the opportunity to develop interpersonal skills and relationships (Spaaij 2012a). Group discussions during and after the games facilitate a collective discussion of and reflection on the experiences and lessons learned. These findings on the role of sport in fostering personal and professional skill development are consistent with those found in some other SFD programs such as Segundo Tempo (Kay 2010), Football for Peace (Sugden and Wallis 2007), and the Zambian programs discussed further on in this chapter.

The objectives of the Vencer program and other SFD programs in Brazil need to be understood within the wider context of persistent social exclusion and inequality. Brazil is a country of great wealth and resources and one of the fastest growing economies. However, the level of economic and social inequality remains high in Brazil. Research shows that certain groups face considerable disadvantages, and there is relatively little they can do to overcome these disadvantages over their lifetimes or even the lifetimes of subsequent generations

(Hasenbalg and Silva 2003). Poverty and social exclusion have persisted or even intensified over the decades and are often intergenerational. The poor, especially (but not exclusively) Brazilians of African descent and those living in the rural northeast of Brazil, have been systematically excluded from the growth process, despite general improvements in education levels and broad reductions in poverty (Gacitúa Marió and Woolcock 2008).

A key area of concern is access to high-quality education. Low educational attainment among the poor arguably remains the single most important obstacle to reducing poverty and inequality in Brazil (World Bank 2001; UNICEF 2009). Despite the increased access to primary education for all Brazilians, superior levels of education 'continue to be a privilege enjoyed principally by persons originating from more elevated class positions' (Costa Ribeiro 2003: 146). In the absence of access to high-quality education, many young people struggle to obtain decent work (Abramovay *et al.* 2002; Costanzi 2009). Further, while many young people abandon school in search of employment, they lack the qualifications and skills necessary to obtain steady jobs (Gacitúa Marió and Woolcock 2008). Hence, they commonly end up working in jobs in the informal sector from an early age, where they tend to earn less than the minimum wage and receive far fewer benefits and rights than those in the formal sector.

The citizenship challenge

Although the Vencer program centres on education, employability and access to the labour market as key challenges facing young people living in Rio de Janeiro's *favelas*, it also shares with Luta Pela Paz a concern for other dimensions of social exclusion that are widely felt by these young people. One such dimension that features centrally in the work of the local NGOs that deliver the Vencer program is exclusion from full citizenship rights. In urban areas, where residents of *favelas* and low-income neighbourhoods have long been subject to middle and upper class fears of crime and disorder (Souza 2008; Velho 2008), the poor face a process of silencing that negates their recognition as full citizens (Machado da Silva 2006). Perlman (2006: 167) notes 'the sense of exclusion and stigma that the poor feel as a result of their residence in favelas, a stance expressed in their complaint that they are not seen as people (*gente*) by the middle and upper classes'. In other words, merely by dint of their place of residence, through its association with poverty and crime the place itself has become a factor in their social exclusion from the labour market, education and social life more generally (Castro and Abramovay 2002; Perlman 2006).

Favela residents now tend to feel more excluded, perceiving that they have less political power than in the past (Wheeler 2005; Perlman 2010). Residents' access to public space in their neighbourhoods does appear to have declined due in large part to high levels of public violence, with the level of sociability and the use of public space for leisure and recreation diminishing considerably in recent decades (Perlman 2010). In many communities it can be dangerous to be outside; thus young people are often confined indoors after school, which limits their opportunities to form friendships. As a consequence, young people's mobility tends to be restricted, and they may not be able to exercise their social citizenship rights such as the benefits to be gained from exploring and engaging with their city (Castro and Abramovay 2002).

What Vencer and Luta Pela Paz seek to offer within this particular social context is a safe and inclusive environment where young people can reclaim public sociality and meaningful leisure time. At the most basic level, they provide a space where young people can get to know and learn to trust one another: that is, where supportive peer relationships can be developed. From this perspective, both programs stretch beyond a narrow focus on labour market inclusion to consider the poor's citizenship rights and their ability to participate in public debate and civil society; however, this is a strategy that is more explicitly articulated in Luta Pela Paz than it is in Vencer. In short, the SFD programs seek to promote and contribute to the process of 'making citizens' or, as Vencer coordinator Bianca puts it, 'to transform [marginalized young people] from not being a citizen to being a citizen'. As we demonstrated in Chapter 2, this approach resonates with social exclusion theory that emphasizes human dignity and recognition as key aspects of social inclusion.

Health education through sport in a Global South context

As we discussed in Chapter 3, SFD initiatives began to emerge in Zambia in increasing numbers during the 1990s. Unlike many Global South countries, initial programs were locally developed and implemented by Indigenous NGOs EduSport and Sport in Action. The latter was the first registered 'sporting NGO' in Zambia and formally constituted in 1998 (Banda 2011). Both founding NGOs have achieved considerable success at attracting external funding to devise ongoing SFD initiatives, predominantly targeting young people (Banda 2011). They continue to thrive as successful enterprises delivering SFD activity mainly in the capital Lusaka, but now also in more rural areas including the Copper Belt region and in Livingstone in the South. Over the past decade, numerous other NGOs have emerged that use sport to address various social issues affecting young people within Zambia, including transnational organizations such as Right to Play and SCORE. However, examining particular programs or programs in isolation is problematic, particularly those organized by the original NGOs EduSport and Sport in Action. Programs have often been running in communities for many years, but take on new names or formats depending on the external funding available at that particular time. Programs will often be delivered simultaneously, with those young people who attend being relatively unaware of which particular initiative they are attached to.

Rather than attempting to examine a specific initiative, this case study focuses on a community within Lusaka and examines how SFD programs aimed at providing health education to young people are delivered within this community. This allows for a more realistic exploration of how sport for development is delivered in practice within Zambia. Young people will often attend more than one program, but generally there is commonality in how these are delivered and how health education is incorporated into these programs.

Along with many other countries in sub-Saharan Africa, Zambia has been ravaged by the HIV/AIDS pandemic that has dismantled the country's economic and social fabric (Gough 2008). Most recent statistics suggest infection rates are beginning to decline, but are still high at one in six adults infected (UNICEF 2010). The infection rate is proportionately much higher for women than men. This is the result of several factors: Zambia remains a patriarchal society, making it difficult for women to take steps to protect themselves against health risks. The economic decline since the 1970s, which has been exacerbated by the HIV/AIDS pandemic, has led to prostitution, both forced and voluntary, being the only means of survival for many families. Finally, it is generally culturally acceptable for Zambian males to have multiple female partners, and this means that even within steady relationships the risk of infection for women is considerable.

Socially, HIV/AIDS has been responsible for dismantling family structures, networks and communities. There are an estimated 690,000 AIDS orphans in this country (UNICEF 2010), a group that is often considered to be the most socially excluded in Zambian communities. Unlike in many other African countries, the HIV/AIDS pandemic in Zambia has not only affected the most disadvantaged in society but also impacted on the professional classes. With the loss of many skilled professionals to HIV/AIDS, particularly teachers and government workers, opportunities for recovery continue to be hindered (Hansen 2005).

The compound communities where the majority of NGO-led SFD work is focused continue to suffer immensely from the impacts of HIV/AIDS. As with all health problems, however, HIV/AIDS cannot be divorced from other social issues that exist within compound communities. These areas were initially developed in Lusaka by the British colonial rulers to provide housing for black employees and their families who had migrated from rural communities to work within a rapidly urbanizing colonial Zambia (Hansen 1997). In contemporary Zambia, high-density shantytowns comprise thousands of small breeze-block houses that are often, individually, home to eight to ten family members. Residents of these compound communities regularly experience problems accessing basic resources such as electricity, water and drainage, and have limited community resources beyond schools, churches and waste land that can be used for sport and recreational purposes (Schlyter 1999). Unemployment within compound communities is high, particularly among young people, and this exacerbates an array of social problems including high levels of crime and violence, heavy drinking and drug-taking (Hansen 2005). For a number of reasons, this backdrop provides fertile ground for the spread of HIV/AIDS. In general, young people within these communities receive little formal education; thus, genuine knowledge of HIV/AIDS, how it is caught, and how they can protect themselves can be very limited.

As mentioned earlier, many young women in particular view prostitution as their only source of income and will often be forced by male family members to participate to secure an income (Magnani *et al.* 2002). Beyond formal prostitution, transactional sex is seen by many young women as a 'way out' of the compounds, leading them to take unnecessary risks to secure basic items like soap, clothes and even education (Kaufman and Stavrou 2004; Nshindano and Maharaj 2008). For young men who are unable to secure regular employment and provide for families, promiscuity can be the only way in which they can demonstrate their masculine identities when they have little else to offer (Meekers and Calves 1997). The breakdown of family structures and systems can mean that young people have few role models and limited guidance on how to navigate the health and social challenges they face, while a lack of 'things to do' provides a potent context for young people to experiment in ways that could potentially damage their health (Gough 2008). Several studies suggest that many young people living in compounds have a fatalistic attitude towards HIV/AIDS, believing that infection is inevitable and therefore it is futile to attempt to protect themselves (Kalunde 1997; Nshindano and Maharaj 2008).

Compound communities are built on the periphery of Lusaka away from the central government and financial districts; hence, young people from these communities are excluded economically, socially and geographically from inner-urban opportunities. These young people will rarely travel to the central business districts, and will certainly not have visited the westernized shopping malls that have emerged within the city over the last decade and are frequented by middle and upper class Zambians. While schools do exist within compound communities, these schools are often staffed by voluntary teachers and the standard of education can be very low. Young people who demonstrate academic ability can obtain scholarships to continue their education into high schools (generally compound communities do not include high schools), but many find the gap in expectation considerable and this results in low numbers passing their final Grade 12 examinations (Kay and Jeanes 2011). Access to other resources is also often limited; for instance, while some communities support a police presence, compounds, particularly at night, are generally described as lawless places that the police will not visit (Gough 2008). Hence, the combination of poor education and high unemployment enmeshes many young people in a cycle of poverty that leaves them feeling 'trapped' in the compound (Hansen 2005). It is within this context, then, that HIV/AIDS education programs delivered by sport take place.

HIV/AIDS education in a compound community

This case study focuses on a compound community that has been involved in programs delivered by EduSport since the late 1990s. The community's population is estimated at approximately 16,000 with 1,500 housing units. The compound community is fairly typical of those described above, experiencing continually rising crime rates, inadequate sanitation and overcrowding. The programs delivered by EduSport within this community vary by name and in their target group (some targeting girls only, some mixed, others working with non-school-attending children); however, all seek to use sport as a mechanism to attract young people and then deliver health and life skills education via a peer-led approach.

High numbers of NGOs work within the community and frequently utilize peer-led models to deliver their activities. NGO staff members initially recruit young people from the community who are interested in delivering activities. Volunteering is popular among some young people as it provides a focus and structure to their lives, as well as the opportunity to develop particular skills that might enhance their chances of securing paid employment. NGO staff members tend to recruit peer leaders from recommendations by community leaders: that is, young people known to already participate in community sporting teams and via recommendations from other NGOs from their volunteer cohorts. There is an element of snowball recruitment here: as programs are established more young people are identified, and when new initiatives emerge they become peer leaders.

NGO staff members then train young people to deliver sports opportunities (predominantly based around four sports: football, netball, volleyball and basketball), how to incorporate HIV/AIDS education messages within traditional Zambian games, and how to promote the development of generic life skills such as leadership, negotiation and effective communication. The programs seek to raise awareness of HIV/AIDS among young people, including how it is contracted and spread, to improve their understanding of how they can prevent infection. The educational elements are designed to move beyond simple transference of information and to acknowledge that knowledge of risks is often not sufficient to prevent detrimental health behaviours (Campbell 2004). Hence, beyond simple information transmission, the programs also provide young people with a space to discuss and debate core issues (including HIV/AIDS) within their community and develop strategies to help overcome them. The educational element therefore draws on elements of critical pedagogy (see Chapter 7) to seek to empower young people to make changes within their lives and communities that allow them to engage in positive health behaviours.

An SFD session within the case study community typically comprises traditional games incorporating HIV/AIDS messages, playing sport, and then factoring in some time for debate and discussion among peers afterwards. Debates may have a broad focus and consider key issues within young people's communities such as drug and alcohol problems, or be more personally focused on how to navigate the pressure to have sex or strategies to ensure condom use during sex. The participants and peer leaders generally determine the content of an SFD session. Sport sessions usually take place in the afternoons on most days of the week, with formal competitive games played on Saturdays against other compound community teams. Attendance is generally fluid with young people arriving and leaving at different times and not always participating daily. Alongside the sports sessions, peer leaders are also encouraged to hold parent and stakeholder forums. Within the case study community, peer leaders have developed a community action group which comprises peer leaders delivering sports activities, local teachers, and other stakeholders such as parents or community leaders who are interested in working with young people. This action group is supported by NGO staff members, but largely initiated by the peer leaders, forming an informal committee overseeing the sport for development activity that takes place within the community. The stakeholder forums and action groups acknowledge that for young people to engage in health-enhancing behaviour they must be supported by their broader environment to do so. While young people's attitudes and values toward HIV/AIDS may change, this is unlikely to lead to significant alterations in behaviour unless this change is encouraged and supported by the wider community.

While the education programs seek to address different social issues, there are many similarities between the beliefs of program staff members within Zambian NGOs and those within the Brazilian case study that sport is able to address social exclusion among young people within disadvantaged communities. Sport is again primarily seen as a 'hook' to engage marginalized young people regularly in activity. NGO staff members consider that incorporating sport makes the program far more appealing to young people than attempting to deliver a more formal education program. As one practitioner observes: 'Take a ball into a community and you'll have 50 children come to you straight away. Tell them to come to a talk and no one will come.' Similar to the Vencer and Luta Pela Paz programs, staff members and young people in the Zambian SFD programs also discuss the value of the more experiential approach to learning that sport can offer. Many of the traditional games convey key messages via young people participating in activities which young people suggest tends to make the information resonate more strongly with them compared to just being given information in a classroom setting. As one female participant in her late teens explains: 'If I play games and you tell me things in the games, I will remember. If you just tell me I will not always listen to you. Games are better, you get to see what happens; you understand it.'

Beyond the perceived value of sport to attract young people to an educational context, peer leaders and NGO staff members also believe that many of the skills young people develop in the sports context can support the delivery of critical pedagogies. Staff members outline how the sport context encourages young people to work together, cooperate with each other and help each other. For example, one program worker (male, 40s) observes:

> To do well in sports, you have to help your team-mates. If they are not playing well you have to step in and help them. You have to learn to

work with the person that maybe you don't like to help the team and you learn ways to work with them and listen to their view. You have to always watch out for each other for the team to do well.

All these social skills are required of young people when attempting to work together to develop collective action regarding broader issues within their community (Campbell and MacPhail 2002). Participating in sport, therefore, is considered to develop the types of relationships among young people that are necessary to attempt to engender community change. Peer leaders and participants discuss feeling comfortable addressing health issues that are often sensitive with other young people that they connect with regularly through sport. For example, navigating peer pressure is a key issue for many young people when attempting to engage in safe sexual behaviour. Peer leaders often invite discussions on appropriate ways to resist peer pressure, ask participants to share examples, and the group then discusses a range of possible strategies. A young woman (20s) explains:

> Some of the things we talk about you would not be able to do it with an adult or a stranger ... It is good that through sport I know a lot about this person, she is a team-mate ... I feel it is ok to talk to them about sex or who is trying to force me to do things.

Hence, as we identify in the Brazilian case study, sport is not only a 'hook' but also a platform for the educational process, facilitating the type of interactions and relationships among young people that are essential in mobilizing the type of community action the programs are seeking.

While the educative aspect of the program is essential for fostering change, young people within the community case study highlight that at a more basic level sport is important to help them navigate the ongoing challenges of their daily lives. Among participants the theme of sport as a context for escapism is prevalent. Some see sports sessions as providing a 'safe space' where they can relax and enjoy themselves for a period of time:

> When I play football, I can forget everything. I go to the ground and my friends are there and for a while I just play. I think about how good it feels to make a good pass or to score a goal. I don't think about the bad things in my life when I am at the ground.
>
> (Female participant, late teens)

In some ways, sport makes young people's experiences of social exclusion more bearable rather than actually addressing aspects of exclusion. They discuss how through friendships developed in a sports context they now have a support network that they can turn to. As one young person puts it, 'My team-mates are now like my family ... they are the people I go to when I need help.' This is particularly important for young people who have lost parents or other key family members to HIV/AIDS. One young female discusses how one of her 'team-mates' offered her somewhere to stay when she felt she could no longer tolerate an abusive relationship within her home. In this instance, while the educational aspect of the program is valuable to increase the young woman's awareness that she does not have to tolerate such behaviour, it is the network created through her engagement in sport that provides a practical solution to addressing this. Within the educative element, young people discuss the importance of encouraging respect for women within their communities and consider various ways they could begin to do this; however, in reality such changes will be slow to occur and do not address the immediate problems young people face. Hence the importance of sport in facilitating the relationships that encourage young people to offer this type of immediate support cannot be overplayed.

Theoretically, the programs within the case study community offer the potential to address aspects of social exclusion among young people and, as indicated, contain many of the advocated elements of transformative community development initiatives (Ledwith 2011). While NGOs support these elements, they are largely led by young people and localized to particular communities, with the delivery of critical pedagogy centred on investigating issues that young people feel are most pertinent to them. However, the broader social and cultural context within which the programs occur can place considerable constraints on how effective they are at developing communities that support young people to engage in health-enhancing behaviour. As discussed above, compound communities experience a broad array of social problems largely resulting from the acute levels of poverty experienced by residents. While young people may be more aware of the importance of positive health choices and the fatal consequences of negative health behaviour, the need to economically survive is likely to prevail when making everyday decisions.

Traditionally, young people in Zambia, particularly young women, are excluded from having any visible presence within community leadership (Gough 2008). They have limited involvement in community affairs, no say or influence within any of the structures of power within communities, and are largely disregarded as contributors to community functioning (Hansen 2005). This is despite the huge role young women and men play in the everyday functioning of society, keeping homes running, caring for the elderly or the sick, and in some cases providing economic income for families. All these responsibilities have increasingly been assumed by young people since the loss of much of the middle adult population from HIV/AIDS (Esu-Williams *et al.* 2006). Urban young Zambians therefore face a conundrum: they are central to the functioning of communities and increasingly noted as valuable actors within international development rhetoric, but remain marginalized and disempowered within Zambian culture (Bakilana and de Waal 2002; Ansell 2005). It is this and other wider structural constraints that work against programs such as those delivered within the case study community. While some young people become heavily involved in the programs and are deeply committed to facilitating change among other young people, they are continually restricted by a lack of broader recognition and commitment within the wider community to bring about change. As this peer leader (male, late teens) explains:

> It is hard getting others to listen; we change the behaviour of some young people but others they do not have support in the home. They just don't care and it is difficult to make a difference beyond the ground when this happens.

The EduSport programs discussed above undeniably have considerable value and importance for young people within the community beyond simply educating them about HIV/AIDS and risk. For young people they offer a space to connect with peers, a structure and focus to their day, as well as the opportunity to develop friendships and relationships that support basic survival. The programs also seem to be effective in some cases at fostering a critical awareness among young people to reconsider their lives and acknowledge how they are disempowered and the consequences of this. However, what the programs struggle to do, even those delivered using high-quality critical approaches, is to prompt serious structural changes within the communities in which they are located.

Critical reflections

The case studies presented in this chapter illustrate how sport is used to address different forms of social exclusion in the Global South. Despite the different intended outcomes and the situation-specific nature of the programs, how sport works in the programs and the issues and challenges they encounter are broadly similar. These issues and challenges can be understood through the conceptual frame of social exclusion presented in Chapter 2. A relational approach to social exclusion directs attention to the 'strong' conception of social exclusion that asks who or what is doing the excluding. This focus on the role of excluding agents or institutions is pertinent to SFD work in the Global South. The SFD programs examined here involve supply-side interventions aimed at enhancing recipients' access to economic, social and civic participation through developing their employability skills and attributes or their health knowledge and behaviours. This focus on individual skills, knowledge and attributes corresponds to the 'weak' conception of social exclusion, one that explains social exclusion as first and foremost an outcome of the individual's handicapping characteristics (Veit-Wilson 1998).

However, we know that external factors do have an influence on what is or is not achievable in development work within a local context (Kingsbury 2004). In the Zambian case study, the wider context of structural poverty and the lack of recognition of young people within the wider community are noted. In Brazil, external constraints affect program participants' opportunities for gaining employment as well as their sense of agency and autonomy. Specifically, participants' employment prospects are strongly influenced by structural factors emanating from the labour market and education system, including labour market discrimination and the relatively low quality of public education in many low-income areas (Spaaij 2013d). In both settings, where positive social impacts result from SFD programs they are to be found at the level of individual participants and their families. The programs struggle to affect deeper, structural changes within the communities in which they are located and leave the structural conditions for poverty and social exclusion unchanged. This raises the question of whether, and if so how, community-based SFD programs can realistically address drivers of social exclusion beyond interpersonal, inter-group and neighbourhood levels.

Social exclusion involves the mutual, interdependent shaping of local struggles and global forces. As we noted in Chapter 2, marginalizing or exploitative processes operating in the global political economy graft themselves onto the dynamics of exclusion operating at local and national levels (Beall 2002). The notion of 'adverse incorporation' is instructive in this regard as it focuses attention on how the life conditions of marginalized people are situated within broader social and economic formations of power in ways that exploit and marginalize them, and undermine their ability to control and have a impact on the systems into which they are locked (Du Toit 2004). The influence of extra-local drivers of social exclusion as a structuring context or pretext for local experiences is recognized in the scholarly debate on how power inequalities among various regions of the world are reproduced or subverted in SFD programs. Darnell and Hayhurst (2012) draw on hegemony and postcolonial theory to critique the top-down, Northern-led nature of much SFD work in the Global South. They argue that the local agency that SFD programs seek to build should be viewed as coping or survival strategies within oppressive neo-liberal structures rather than evidence of any structural change. SFD work can thus be seen to reproduce or exacerbate unequal power relations between the Global North and the Global South, especially where the leadership and agendas of SFD schemes are Northern-led and where there is a tension between the needs and expectations of Northern donors on the one hand, and local beneficiaries and stakeholders on the other (Kay 2012a; Levermore 2008b).

The SFD sector has traditionally used volunteers from the Global North to impart their knowledge to marginalized young people in Global South countries. Global North agencies determine the curriculum and translate it into practice via volunteers, many of whom have extensive sport development knowledge but limited experience of youth and international development work (Darnell 2007; Guest 2009). In so far as SFD programs are heavily dominated by external actors and undervalue the local knowledge and lived experience of local recipients, they can be characterized as donor-biased or neo-colonial (Spaaij and Jeanes 2013). SFD programs that are dominated by Northern institutions working in the Global South often involve a (relative) lack of voice, recognition and decision-making power on the part of target communities. In so doing, such programs can actually contribute to the social exclusion processes identified in Chapter 2 instead of ameliorating or subverting them.

While recognizing that SFD efforts initiated in the Global North are aligned with the maintenance of hegemonic power relations between different regions of the world, it is important to consider how global influences take shape within, and interact with, localized processes and experiences. In this regard, Lindsey and Grattan (2012) identify how SFD work can take place in local environments with relatively limited influence from international, Northern institutions. They postulate a 'decentred', actor-centred approach that urges us to take Southern perspectives seriously. Their research in Zambia shows that while the causes of many of the social problems SFD programs seek to address have roots to different degrees in global and national inequalities, the aims and approaches adopted by those programs are commonly aligned with the local cultural context, such as their emphasis on the preservation of communal aspects of local culture. This finding is consistent with the case study data presented in this chapter, which similarly show an important local dimension to SFD programs in Zambia and Brazil. Lindsey and Grattan (2012: 107) further posit that local stakeholders 'may have more scope to exert their own agency than is often implied by portrayals of Northern power' within the SFD movement. Their actor-centred approach underlines the need for the development of more genuine dialogue whereby actors in the Global North ally their efforts with the needs, interests and self-determination of those in the Global South (Darnell and Hayhurst 2012; Kay 2012a).

At a more practical level, the material presented in this chapter raises important questions concerning the role of the development worker in SFD programs. Scholars such as Darnell (2007, 2010) and Guest (2009) problematize the role of external, international 'change agents' in SFD programs, and many scholars argue for the empowerment of local people to build community capacities 'from below' (Kidd 2008; Spaaij 2009b). However, recent research also highlights the importance of international change agents within SFD programs in divided societies as external and impartial mediators of community conflicts (Schulenkorf 2010). Without external involvement, SFD programs with a conflict transformation objective might simply not be feasible due to mistrust, suspicion and a lack of reciprocal engagement between opposed parties. The idea here is that the degree of control over program development is likely to shift over time. Schulenkorf's (2010) model of community empowerment posits that external change agents are largely in control of program planning and management processes in the initial stages of a program. Over time, however, expert knowledge, skills, responsibilities and control are to be transferred from the change agent to local communities, who are expected to guide and lead programs in the long-term (Schulenkorf 2012).

Still, the initial control that the external agent is afforded in this model is questionable, especially in non-conflict settings. Not only do external actors often lack local cultural knowledge and robust community development experience (as opposed to *sport* development experience) (Guest 2009), but outside aid providers can also, sometimes unwittingly or unknowingly, shape local agendas or inappropriately insert themselves into local decision-making processes that may not be sustainable and may destabilize local social relations (Kingsbury 2004). Moreover, from a critical pedagogical perspective, it can be countered that local participants ought to be able to define their own needs and desires and set goals for SFD programs in collaboration with external actors. Thus, participants must feel that programs meet their needs and that they are consulted in their design and delivery. To be effective, then, programs should directly involve the intended beneficiaries in planning, implementing, monitoring and evaluating them (Kidd 2011). From this perspective, critical SFD programs of the kind theorized by Giulianotti (2011) require co-creation and local ownership from the outset rather than a gradual transfer of power and control. This issue is further discussed in the next chapter, which considers how sports coaches can develop approaches and practices that engage socially excluded young people and support them in challenging their exclusion.

7 Engaging socially excluded young people in sports programs

Introduction

This book draws upon more than a decade of empirical research by the authors to critically examine various aspects of the relationship between sport and social exclusion. In Chapters 4, 5 and 6 we presented critical findings from different sports programs that provide a voice to different individuals and groups who experience diverse forms of social exclusion. In this chapter we move beyond participants and program personnel to focus more specifically on sports coaches. This will be done through an in-depth case study of, and personal reflection on, a football program delivered by one of the authors (Magee) for individuals who were homeless. Elsewhere, Magee as sole author (Magee 2010, 2011) and co-author (Magee and Jeanes 2013) details this program with a particular focus on participants' experiences; however, in this chapter the program is analysed from the unique perspective of Magee as a coach aiming to engage homeless individuals. We believe that this analysis is distinct and unique, as not only does the chapter progress our understanding of how sport relates to and affects social exclusion/inclusion, it also extends and informs contemporary debates within the sports coaching literature.

Robyn Jones is a key champion for the sociological study of sports coaching and an advocate for the under-heard voices of sports coaches within sport development literature. This chapter is inspired by his emphasis on 'the personal aspects of coaching through feelings and perceptions of those who deal with its complex dilemmas and ambiguities' (Jones 2009: 378). These 'complex dilemmas and ambiguities' surrounding sports coaching are fuelled in part by the wider social inclusion agenda which has placed significant and diverse demands on community sports coaches that are presently under-researched, under-theorized and rarely considered by coach educators and policy makers (Jeanes 2010). This chapter therefore offers some critical insights into these demands.

It is important at this stage to clarify terminology regarding the coaching setting. The terms 'community coaching', 'grassroots coaching' and 'participation coaching' are interchangeable within the literature to describe coaching conducted in the non-performance competitive setting. Lyle (2002: 54) high-lights that participation coaching is at the opposite end of performance coaching on the coaching spectrum, as there is 'no specific preparation for competition, or alternatively, that participation in competition is not supported by an extensive preparation programme [and] there is no attempt to influence or control the variables that affect performance'. This encapsulates the setting in which the football program under study took place; however, as outlined below, we feel that the term 'community coaching' is more appropriate to use given the particular nature of this football program. To fully understand the coaching context of the case study, it is necessary to first outline the develop-ment of community sports coaching in the UK. We consider this development within the broader context of sport and social exclusion policy in the UK, as covered in detail in Chapter 3.

The sports coach as an agent of the welfare state

The use of sports coaches within a community setting to engage socially excluded individuals can be traced back to the 1980s when, in the UK, programs like Action Sport were devised to equip young sports leaders to engage disaffected youth in inner-city neighbourhoods (Collins 2010). Chapter 3 indicated the significant expansion of sport-focused social inclu-sion programs during the tenure of New Labour, which included the estab-lishment of programs located in a variety of alternative settings that increased opportunities for sports coaches to deliver activities to marginalized and excluded members of society. Within the plethora of interventions associ-ated with the social inclusion agenda, the sports coach is in effect the interface between social policy and young people and acquires the role of translating policy into tangible outcomes (Sandford *et al.* 2006; Crabbe 2008). Indeed, Crabbe (2009: 190) suggests that the main role of coaches in social inclu-sion programs is that of a cultural intermediary to provide 'gateways between what are often seen as alien and mutually intimidating worlds' by acting as both interpreter and go-between. We highlighted this role in Chapter 5 in our discussion of sport-focused intervention programs in the Global North.

   Considering the critical role sport coaches are often afforded in social inclusion programs, it is important for those coaches operating in such envi-ronments to understand their roles as moral and social educators (Cassidy *et al.* 2009). Within sports coaching, according to Taylor and Garratt (2010: 124), the sports coach has duly been redefined as 'an agent of the welfare state' with 'the imperative towards community responsibility, bestowed by the state'. They argue that the result has been that coaches have adopted 'a moral identity, in which core moral purposes are combined with objectives towards widening participation, coupled with ambitions to promote social inclusion and develop social capital' (2010: 124). This redefinition of the coach as 'an agent of the welfare state' is important for the case study presented below on Magee's experiences of engaging with socially excluded homeless individuals.

A key reference point for the present chapter is the inclusive coaching models developed in relation to sport and physical activity for people with disabilities (see also Chapter 8). Inclusion Spectrum is one such model that was developed in the late 1990s in the UK and initially aimed at teachers and support staff members working in mainstream schools to improve the social inclusion of young people with special educational needs in physical education (Black 2011). Stevenson (2009) also provides understanding of the application of the Inclusion Spectrum based on experiences in delivering sport and game activities to children with disabilities in secondary schools in the UK. Importantly, in drawing on this experience Black (2011: 203) notes how flexibility is key to successful inclusive coaching practice:

> ... tasks are set and adapted, and support is provided to reflect the needs of the learner. The key factor is the flexibility of these systems ... the systems empower coaches, allowing them to change their approach or modify their delivery to provide optimum opportunities for the athletes.

The importance of a flexible approach is further highlighted in Chapter 8, where we illustrate how disability inclusion can be achieved in practice in community sport settings. For coaches working toward inclusive practice, Black (2011: 210) argues that fundamentally 'the solutions lie with the enquiring mind and adaptable imagination of the coach'. This should be borne in mind in terms of the case study that follows.

The social inclusion agenda and the community coach: a case study of the Homeless World Cup

The football program that preceded the 2003 Homeless World Cup (HWC) was initiated by the street paper *The Big Issue* with assistance from three social workers from local social services. These social workers not only recruited participants by embedding the program within their rehabilitation support program, but also attended the program to offer professional care and assistance should it be required. The program design was two-hour weekly sessions over ten weeks, with three purposes in mind. First, it aimed to use football activity to improve the physical and mental health of the participants (akin to the mental health case study discussed in Chapter 5). Second, it sought to add some structure to the lives of the homeless individuals by encouraging regular attendance. Third, the program endeavoured to provide enough participants to enter a team to attend the 2003 HWC to be held in Graz, Austria not long after the program ended. Funding issues proved difficult, however, and attendance at the HWC was only confirmed in the week leading up to the tournament, at which point a squad of six players, a coach and three social workers agreed to attend.

The coach and participants

I (Magee) agreed to be volunteer coach on the program following an approach from *The Big Issue*. As a UEFA A Licence coach with considerable experience delivering football sessions and coaching a variety of teams, the opportunity to work on the program appealed to me. Permission was granted from the social workers to simultaneously conduct research during the program and at the ensuing HWC. A logbook of observations about all attendees and activities was collated during the program, and in-depth interviews were held with the six participants who went to the HWC. On occasion certain information or instances were removed and have never been part of any published research emerging from this databank, including here.

Participant attendance throughout the program was fluid as numbers ebbed and flowed each week from six and 12 participants, with some participants more regular attendees than others. In the end, the six most regular attendees were selected in the squad to attend the HWC. All participants were males aged between 16 and 29 years, lived in either hostels or social services accommodation, were unemployed and at various stages had spent time living rough on the streets. They shared common themes such as a lack of family support, impermanent accommodation and spiralling mental and physical health problems. Personal situations included depression, anxiety, mood swings, anger control and schizophrenia, sometimes in combination. Some participants were on prescribed medication and members of the same rehabilitation program, while all had alcohol issues and were heavy smokers, with the majority acknowledging a history of substance abuse.

Clearly all participants had varying issues to cope with on a daily basis and as a result experienced varying degrees of social exclusion. Homelessness represents a continuum, one that views a homeless person as holding a multitude of often shifting positions from completely roofless and living on the streets, to living in shelters and support accommodation or temporarily accommodated by family and friends (Magee and Jeanes 2013). All individuals involved in this football program remained on the homelessness continuum, with the personal and situational factors that paved each individual's route into homelessness typically reflecting the archetypal homeless individual covered in mainstream literature (Yeich 1994; Ravenhill 2008). This football program, then, was designed to assist these individuals' return to mainstream society. Detailed participant experiences of the program and the HWC can be found in Magee (2011) and Magee and Jeanes (2013).

Coaching as relationship-building: expectations and realities

Relationship-building is key to the coaching process (Lyle 2002; Jones *et al.* 2004). While the sports coaching literature provides strong support for the importance of relationship-building, this is almost exclusively focused on coach–athlete relations within the performance coaching setting (e.g. Jones *et al.* 2004; Jowett 2007). So far, little has been written about coach–participant relationships and relationship-building within the community coaching context where the coach is delivering to individuals who are, for example, homeless, mentally ill or criminal offenders. However, some important insights can be gleaned from Crabbe's (2009) work with socially excluded individuals as part of the Positive Futures program that we also briefly discuss in Chapter 8. The first objective for program staff members, then, is to establish social relationships with participants. Crabbe (2009) further emphasizes that program staff members need to appreciate the dynamic nature of the engagement process and recognize individual circumstances. These are important issues for the community coach and have key relevance to the case study of a football program and its focus on the engagement process and the development of social relationships between Magee as a sports coach and homeless individuals as socially excluded participants.

Working in the coach–athlete context and establishing the coach–athlete relationship were basic aspects of my varied previous coaching roles and experiences prior to the homeless program, but ultimately this caused a significant and immediate problem. Prior to the first session on the program, I compiled a week-by-week coaching program and at the first session turned up early to set up. In other words, I prepared as I typically did and expected nothing to be different. This was my first challenge, as a problem materialized in terms of how my expectations had not prepared me for the reality of this experience, as the logbook explains:

> I waited nervously for the players. I always get nervous before meeting a new group and taking a session for the first time. The minibus turned up and parked. The back doors opened and out climbed a group of bedraggled blokes, most wearing jeans and shoes and they all lit up a cigarette. They were unkempt, a bit scruffy, scrawny and I kept waiting, looking at them and ashamedly thought that if I saw them smoking at a street corner I would cross the road fearing for my safety. They finished and made their way slowly to the pitch and edged their way toward me, keeping a bit of a distance, eyeing me up and looking at the cones I had set out. [Social worker] came up and said they were ready to go. I asked if they were getting changed and he said they were. No one was kitted out for football. [Social worker] turned round and said, 'Lads this is Jon, your coach I was telling you about. He is going to take you for football. Over to you, Jon.' [Social worker] walked off, the group looked at me. I looked at them. 'What the f***?' was all I could think.

At this point, and for the first time in a long and varied coaching career, I felt out of my depth and desperately isolated as I had totally misunderstood the setting in which this coaching would take place and the type of participants involved. Not only that, I felt fear: fear based on how my various accredited awards, wide range of football knowledge and various coaching experiences rendered me incapable and clueless here. This sense of inadequacy was fuelled in part by the relaxed attitude of the social workers. At the program sessions and training sessions at the HWC, the social workers were present at the edge of the pitch, usually sitting down watching the session from a distance, often as far away as 50 or 60 metres. However, during the 12-day visit to the HWC, I was often left with participants without social workers present – in the dormitory room we shared, in the canteen, on trams, in cafes and bars, watching other matches – and thus was 'in charge of them'. The social workers considered the good relationship I had with the group to be enough for me to be placed 'in charge' of the participants (either individually or in small groups). It was at these moments that I, who was not a trained health professional, felt most exposed and isolated.

In hindsight, I understand that the exposure resulted in moving me away from my coaching comfort zone and I was unprepared for this, especially as in previous coaching situations I had worked with appropriately kitted out participants. In this program I knew the participants would be homeless individuals but I still expected them to turn up appropriately dressed as a sign of an interest in football and thus be part way on the road to being a football player. My predetermined view was, 'if they are not football players then why are they on a football program?' Clearly I was wrong. The logbook continues:

> I was left standing there, racking my brains. My first thought was about how I could get out of this and how I should only have committed to one session to see how it went. I could then have bailed out. As I was thinking of this, they [participants] were looking me up and down, looking at my training kit, looking over at the cones I laid out. I felt they were almost laughing that I thought I would get them to play football. No one was dressed for it and we all knew that. I was wondering if they were thinking of stealing the kit on me, as it would not have surprised me as they looked a shifty bunch.

Evident here is a blatant and shameful act of how I 'judged a book by its cover' based purely on personal appearance. I had had no prior dealings with homeless individuals beyond purchasing *The Big Issue*, yet still expected football players of some sort to attend even if they were homeless. The logbook excerpts relay how wrong this position was for an experienced coach. The actual situation was different from my expectations, and I experienced 'reality shock' (Cassidy *et al.* 2009: 10) for almost the first time in my coaching career.

This account is an honest and shameful reflection; however, it is also a critical lesson for the community coach to learn: that is, they need to prepare for the encounter according to the type of participant that will attend. Although I had never met homeless individuals before (other than vendors of *The Big Issue*), I still felt capable of delivering a football program to them because I was confident (or arrogant?) enough to believe that my football knowledge and experience would see me right with the participants as they had never failed before. Further, as a football coach I expected that it would be football players who would attend – low level skilled ones arguably but players nonetheless, with previous experience of competitive football. In reality, while some participants had played football recreationally on the street or in the school playground, only one participant had played competitive football, and that was for a school team years previously. Hence, the community coach needs to appreciate this aspect of such programs: do not expect experienced athletes to attend. To learn from this, and in hindsight, I should have staved off the reality shock by spending time with homeless individuals prior to the first session, which would have better prepared me for what to expect. I would recommend that any community coach should seek this familiarization experience.

Given that I was thrown by my expectations of the individuals who would attend the program, I later probed each participant on the reasons they were there. It materialized that attendance was voluntary for all and even though social workers were embedding the program within a wider rehabilitation program, participants could choose not to attend at any time. Reasons for attending are summarized by the following comments from two participants:

I was told to come along to the program by my social worker as part of trying to cut down on my drinking. You know, get fit and all that. I was not interested in football as if I was, I would have joined a team but he [social worker] told me to come along. Instead of having a meeting to chat about things we went along to your program. To be honest, it beat sitting in a room with the social worker talking about my drinking.

I had played football at school and heard about the program in the hostel from a mate so I thought why not come along as he seemed to enjoy it and said it was fun. I mentioned it to [social worker] and she ran it by [another social worker] who you were involved with and I came with my mate. It was on a day I had nothing else to do so gave me something to do.

The lure of possible attendance at the 2003 HWC was also a reason to attend the program. One participant commented that:

I was in the same hostel as [player] and he said he was going to a football thing his social worker had asked him to join and there was a free holiday at the end of it. Abroad as well and I had never been on a plane before!

These varied comments of reasons for attending again reinforced my misunderstanding of the program and my expectations regarding it. Only one participant, quoted above, identified the football aspect as a reason for attendance. The community coach thus needs to appreciate that, as in this case, the football dimension of the program is often low down on the list of reasons to attend, if even a reason at all, and that most likely attendance will be influenced by a social worker, or be a peer-driven rather than a self-driven desire to take part. This is critical to relationship-building as part of the over-all engagement process, and is a further factor in understanding that the community coach may be taken out of their comfort zone in terms of expectations when delivering to socially excluded individuals.

The crucial first impression

The previous section relays my (shameful) feelings at the very start of the program and how the outward appearance of the participants created a reality shock. Crucially, though, I realized at that juncture that these feelings, as off-putting as they were, nonetheless were inward rather than outward feelings. Yes, I felt graphically exposed for the first time in my coaching career but no, I do not think the participants could detect that. Within relationship-building, and not just in the sporting context, attention needs to be paid to making a positive first impression, something a tutor on communication skills had driven home on a coaching course I had attended: that is, 'You only get one chance to make a first impression so make it count.'

During the introduction to the group I contemplated how to get out of the program, but dropped such thoughts and returned to the task at hand:

> I tore up my session plan in my head, pretending I had not written it and that it was not in my pocket. The warm-up I had planned where I would find out the names of the participants was irrelevant now. What now? They were looking at me, waiting on me to say something. So I thought, get over yourself and get on with it. You signed up for this. You knew they were homeless. Who knows how many people have turned their backs on them, not given them a chance. Don't be another one. This is your chance to make a good first impression and your only chance.

The situation I was in and my route out of it are succinctly portrayed by Cassidy *et al.* (2009: 11), who argue that 'coaches should treat each situation, inclusive of its many variables, on its merits, assess it, carefully weigh the options and choose the most appropriate course of action'. On various teaching and sports coaching courses I had been schooled in the benefits of using icebreakers as a way of engaging positively with a new group and its importance in establishing positive relationships. Even though the setting was different from my other coaching experiences, I calculated that a icebreaker was appropriate even though I had not planned one, so in effect I took what I felt was the appropriate action and became adaptable (Black 2011).

I decided to use an icebreaker activity loosely called 'speed dating' whereby the coach goes around the group, makes an introduction to each individual, offers up a piece of football information about themselves and asks for one back from the participant. So far my early observations had scoped a group not dressed for football and I believed that football talk would be unlikely to 'break the ice'. I also observed that most of the group appeared shy, were not engaging with others, and avoided eye contact while shifting from foot to foot or looking down at the ground. I thought that a friendly, engaging manner was required to seek to relax the participants in a way that reduced our collective nervousness. I decided to be adaptable, and, rather than impart football-related information as an initial engagement task, sought to offer and ask personal information.

Subsequently, I introduced myself to the group as a whole then went around each individual, shook them by the hand, told them something personal about myself – basic information like first primary school, name of my brother, favourite food – and asked them to tell me something about themselves. Additionally, I got the participants to introduce themselves to each other. I was not sure if they already knew each other, but it was too easy to assume they did because they were all homeless and had travelled to the venue on the same minibus.

As well as paying close attention to the type of information I imparted in this dialogue – personal things without giving too much away – I was careful to seek to create a personal vibe that would not only connect with the participants by taking an interest in their life (Jones *et al.* 2004; Jowett 2007) but also relax them – and myself – at the same time. Thus, I paid close attention to the tone and volume of my voice and the language I used while listening intently to each response, greeting it with a smile on my face and treating it with great importance. This was not necessarily my usual style and not something I had given that much attention to in other coaching settings; however, I felt that it was appropriate with this group and more suited to breaking the ice than football-related discussions. The following participant comment reflects upon the icebreaker and the approach I took to it:

> You remember at the first session, when we stood there and [social worker] introduced you and we stood around, looking at you, you remember what you did? You walked round and shook our hands. I didn't know you but that said to me, you respected me and I was made up with that. I just thought you would tell us about football, give us orders but you made me feel like a person. We [homeless individuals] don't get that too often. When I was selling the [*Big Issue*] paper on the street, I would get strangers come up and spit at me; that is what I thought strangers were like. You were different and I liked that. We all liked it and liked you. You treated us like people.

As well as relaxing the individuals (and myself), the icebreaker not only created an initial bond on which a relationship could develop between me and individual participants, it also created bonds among participants, as the following comment confirms:

> I had known [participant] as he had been in a hostel I had been in for a while and we had not got on really, sort of kept to ourselves, so I was

not that keen when he came to the first session. You got us to talk to each other though and I found out he was okay. We were partners for a game you did with us and he was alright to be with and we got on a lot better.

Each time a new participant joined the group over the ensuing weeks we performed the icebreaker exercise and they received the same instant welcome from myself and from the group that we initiated at the very first meeting.

The icebreaker in itself may not be that remarkable, but it had a significant impact on the participants and was critical in establishing a positive first impression that permitted a bond to quickly establish that could be built on as part of the wider engagement process. It is evidence of how the community coach needs to be aware of the importance of the first meeting, the role the icebreaker plays, and how it is delivered. A favourable impression through an icebreaker that is engineered around the person and delivered in an amenable, welcoming and friendly manner puts the coach in a better position to bond with the group and develop relationships than an unfavourable one. This was especially important in a program such as this as participants were able to remove themselves at any time. Hence it was critical to get off to a good start – something I managed to do despite my inner feelings of exposure and desperation.

Developing coach–participant relationships

With regard to establishing personal relationships, the sports coaching literature emphasizes the importance of getting to know athletes and 'what makes them tick' (Jones *et al.* 2004: 18) by treating them as 'unique and individual beings' (Cassidy *et al.* 2009: 93) and not as a homogeneous group (Jones 2000; Jowett 2007). The approach I took to developing relationships with each participant was deliberately personal and as each week progressed I got to know more and more about them. As noted above, one participant commented how my approach, manner and demeanour made him 'feel like a person'. However, with that came personal life histories and in-depth information that I found difficult to cope with, especially some of the more harrowing material. This experience suggests that those who advocate the get-to-know-them approach need to err on the side of caution regarding the community coach.

What community coaches will duly find out about their participants when they treat them as 'unique and individual beings' was a difficult part of the engagement process to manage, as I became familiar with deeply personal information about substance abuse and alcohol dependency, living on the streets, complex family situations, intricate personal and social relationship difficulties and various mental health problems. I was pleased that relationships developed over the weeks and that the participants trusted me enough to allow me 'inside' their group and lives. However, when there I found it difficult to manage the details about the type of lives they had led, the various problems they faced and the demons they fought on a daily basis. On occasion

I was able to seek advice from the appropriate social worker on how to deal with the information and how to react to it within the coaching session.

An incident that illustrates this point occurred during a session when a player was disruptive within a fun game. He became sufficiently argumentative with me and some of his peers and threatened physical harm on one before storming off the pitch, swearing loudly. The social worker went after him and we carried on. Soon after he returned to the group, asked me to stop the session, and apologized to the group, saying he was 'out of order but had been off alcohol for a week and it was really getting to him'. After the session he further apologized to me and asked for a private conversation in which he detailed his drinking problems and how it had caused significant problems in personal relationships with females. I then asked the social worker to join us, and we had a lengthy discussion that resulted in the participant and the social worker agreeing to pay greater attention to alcohol-related issues and anger management in the rehabilitation program.

There were other incidents within the coaching setting that I could draw upon to indicate how developing meaningful and trusting relationships through the engagement process exposes the community coach to the inner workings of individuals with fragile states of mind. This is particularly the case with individuals who have the more serious issues, such as recovering schizophrenics who are susceptible to episodes that can occur almost without warning and without any visible signs for the coach to pre-empt. As noted earlier, I was placed in situations where I was in isolation with some of the more fragile individuals; in hindsight I should not have placed myself – or been placed – in sole care of any participants regardless of how deeply personal our relationship had become. My experience of working on this program and attending the HWC leads me to conclude that any future coaches working with socially excluded homeless individuals should receive professional training regarding how to deal with fragile individuals who are either still experiencing or recovering from mental illness or alcohol and substance abuse. Advocating the need for sports coaches to get to know who they are delivering to needs to be treated with caution when applied to community coaches dealing with socially excluded individuals, as there are wider implications at play for the coach in developing meaningful personal relationships with such individuals than the literature currently acknowledges.

Seeking the middle ground between antagonism and reverence

A final issue to address regarding the engagement process and relationship-building concerns 'hostile' participants and 'worshipper' participants and how the coach deals with these polar extremes. The hostile participant displays an outward dislike of the coach and is reluctant to engage with the coach, their peers and the activity. Simple requests are met with a mix of aggression, incredulity, disdain and, at times, foul language, which causes problems in the delivery of the session, its ambience, flow and peer group relations. The self-reported reason for this is that the hostile participant has been instructed to attend the program, views it as an extension of the 'state', and is therefore reluctant to accept or respect it. The hostile participants I dealt with in this setting were disengaged from their rehabilitation program and regarded me as another state figure bestowed upon them to fix their problems.

Hostile participants frequently tested my coaching ability and the associated disciplinary boundaries, seeking a negative reaction from me whenever they could. Tempted as I was to order one participant to leave a session – I would have done this is in another setting – I considered this to be the wrong thing to do as I was not certain of its ramifications not only on this participant but also on his peers. I thus sought to work with the participant, and as difficult as that was I placated their hostility and sought to operate as normally as I could. No hostile participant attended more than one session, however, and feeling a sense of failure about this I discussed it with one of the social workers who commented that 'at times you just have to accept some people are just a lost cause no matter how much you try to help them so you learn not to take it personally and help those who want to help themselves'.

Opposite to the hostile participant is the 'worshipper' participant who causes issues of a different nature by idolizing the coach; this is something I also found difficult to deal with. On one occasion I was told by a participant that a peer in the group had been describing me as his best mate to his hostel colleagues, while on another occasion a participant said to me: 'I was telling my mates about you and how great you are. You have a house, a job, a car. You did well at school and uni[versity]. You have all the things I don't have. I think you are the best.' Another participant said in an interview: 'I have none of the things you have. I wish I could be like you but I won't as I have failed at everything I have done so I look up to you for that and would do anything for you.' Comments like these were uncomfortable to deal with and left me with guilt pangs about my life circumstances and sympathy for the very different lives of the participants. Simply by coming from outside of the daily spheres in which each participant lived, I was elevated by some to a status that was unwelcome and in my view undeserved in the circumstances.

The community coach therefore needs as best as possible to find a middle position where they neither provoke hostility nor encourage worship status. However, in practice such a position is difficult to negotiate as establishing relationships with socially excluded individuals is a complex, dynamic and fluid as well as a situational process. The individuality of life circumstances cannot be underestimated in terms of how socially excluded participants view and subsequently treat the community coach, but what is sure is that personal fragility and a sense of failure will be dominant among the group.

Critical reflections

The data and discussion presented in this chapter are only starting points in a wider research agenda dedicated to investigating community coaching and its place in sports programs aimed at engaging socially excluded individuals. The chapter has paid key attention to the engagement process and the importance of relationship-building. We have highlighted how the sports coaching literature is almost exclusively skewed towards the performance coach, and this is problematic because existing coaching models have different applications and implications for practice and delivery in a community coaching setting. While the case study offers some initial insight into the latter, further research is required into the relationships among community coaches, the programs they deliver, and the challenges they face when seeking to engage with socially excluded individuals. It is important to note for future research that the case study only covered one socially excluded group. Thus, the experiences of coaches engaging with other socially excluded groups need further investigation. In doing so, greater veracity, capacity and tenacity will be given to the research portfolio regarding coaches who deliver in the community setting and how they engage with socially excluded individuals across the spectrum of social exclusion.

A central conclusion to draw from the case study is how Magee felt qualified, experienced and prepared enough to embark on the program, yet when there actually found himself to be unprepared, exposed and out of his depth for the first time in a long and varied coaching career. A key admission here is how the UEFA Coach Accreditation Schemes largely unprepared Magee for the complexities of his role as a community coach. Clearly what he had learnt on various accredited courses had reduced relevance and importance when applied to the community coaching setting. Moreover, varied experiences within the performance setting counted for little when it came to working on a sports program for homeless individuals. Recently, criticisms of coach education accreditation schemes have emerged within sports coaching literature that question the education and preparation processes of the coach for the coaching workplace (Culver and Trudel 2006; Piggott 2012; Nelson *et al.* 2013). Although these criticisms are solely focused on those seeking to work in the performance environment, they are equally appropriate to the community coaching setting.

It is our contention that to better equip sports coaches in the community setting to work on programs for socially excluded individuals, respective national governing bodies need to create a separate accreditation scheme dedicated solely to preparing a coach for the community setting. Such a scheme should expose the prospective community coach to a variety of settings in which to learn (Cushion 2006) in ways that allow the individual to gain hands-on practical knowledge and experience (Cassidy *et al.* 2004) rather than, as Magee did, suffer from a reality shock when they actually start working. Thus, experience on coach education courses with groups such as people with disabilities, homeless people with mental illness and offenders, to name a few, is necessary to steel the community coach for the realities of what lies ahead.

Given the growth of community coaching and associated employment opportunities, especially in the UK, national governing bodies subsequently need to overhaul their coach accreditation schemes and introduce courses specifically tailored to the demands and requirements faced by the community coach (Jeanes 2010). This will be the first step to better prepare coaches to deliver, for example, sports programs for homeless individuals and prevent as much as possible a repeat of Magee's situation. Much of the sports coaching literature indicates the complexities that surround the role of the coach, yet the case study illustrates that those complexity levels go far and beyond those that have been considered up to now within sports coaching. These core issues regarding the engagement process within community coaching are worthy of future research.

In this chapter we have referred to a number of existing approaches to engaging socially excluded young people in and through sport. The relationship-building approach that has been most comprehensively formulated by Crabbe and his colleagues (Crabbe *et al.* 2006; Crabbe 2008, 2009) is of particular significance in this regard. As noted, central to this approach is the need to develop meaningful and mutually respectful relationships between program staff members and socially excluded young people, as well as to facilitate access to opportunities that are not currently available to them so that they are placed 'in a stronger position to make positive life choices from a wider range of options' (Crabbe *et al.* 2006: 15). This approach can inform sport-focused social inclusion programs such as those discussed in this chapter and in Chapters 5 and 6. It arguably has the potential to be mobilized as a force for progressive social inclusion in and through sport. The imperative here is to identify theoretical orientations that advocate the role of sport in wider community development strategies (Crabbe 2008). The potential synergies between relationship-building strategies and wider community development approaches, as reflected in this chapter's focus on the community coaching setting, will be explored in depth in Chapter 8. As will be seen in that chapter, it is this type of synergy that has the potential to engender significant culture change within sporting environments to facilitate greater social inclusion.

With regard to the engagement process detailed in this chapter, sports coaching in its broadest sense could consider learning from other fields and disciplines. Critical pedagogy is a key domain to draw from, again with clear connections to wider critical community development (Macdonald 2002; Spaaij and Jeanes 2013), as it stresses the need to give voice and devolve power to participants. This approach is particularly significant for the contemporary policy context in which the community sports coach has come to be defined as an agent of the welfare state (Taylor and Garratt 2010). The Homeless World Cup case study illustrates this point well. The hostility and disaffection that some participants displayed towards the program were based on their perception of the program as an extension of the 'state', and this further reinforced their sense of a loss of agency and autonomy associated with the imposition of top-down policies and programs. A key challenge here is to create and implement programs that participants respect and find rewarding. From a critical pedagogical perspective, educators or facilitators – in this case the community coach – ought to play a key role in this process by developing and nurturing bonds of sincerity and authenticity that in turn build partici-pants' respect, trust and mutual caring (Freire 2005).

However, critical pedagogy takes this approach a step further. One concern that emerges from the above discussion of the relationship-building approach is that while it encourages the active engagement of socially excluded youth, it does not tackle the deeper causes of social exclusion at any (localized) structural or community level. Not only does it tend to favour engagement at the individual level over more collective forms of learning and acting, it also operates on a very pragmatic basis in its attempt to allow young people to actively participate in wider social, economic and political spheres, rather than to durably transform these spheres (Spaaij and Jeanes 2013). As noted in Chapters 5 and 6, this is limiting because, as they are presently structured, these spheres tend to create, condone or exacerbate social exclusion for certain individuals and groups. Sport is no exception to this, as is demonstrated throughout this book. From a critical pedagogical viewpoint, sports programs and the coaches working on them should move beyond the goal of merely (re-)engaging participants, and instead strive to create social change by developing critical and reflective capacities in partic-ipants. The questioning and reflective frame of mind that critical pedagogy generates urges us to ask uncomfortable questions regarding barriers to participation and exclusionary discourses, and these do need to be addressed if more just and inclusive sporting practices are to be created (Macdonald 2002). In the next chapter, we unpack these ideas to consider how more inclusive sports communities can be developed and sustained.

8 Building inclusive sports communities

Introduction

In Chapter 7 we considered how coaches are able to engage and build relationships with socially excluded young people within a community sport setting. In the present chapter, we consider the sporting landscape more broadly by examining how inclusive sports communities can be developed and sustained. Inclusive coaches who are capable of working in a critical way with socially excluded persons are a key aspect of such sports communities. However, we also consider the broader processes that are required to engender significant culture change within sport environments to facilitate greater social inclusion. In this chapter, we review broader policy and practice that are aimed at facilitating inclusive sports communities, and discuss some of the limitations of current approaches. Concepts from community development are then presented as a potential alternative to traditional approaches to sport development. The chapter also explores how community development principles can be operationalized in practice, and the value of doing so, via two case studies. One case study explores the engagement of young people with disabilities in sport while the other examines the integration of people with culturally and linguistically diverse (CALD) backgrounds in sports contexts.

The central argument developed in this chapter is that creating inclusive sports communities essentially requires a shift in how sport, and particularly organized competitive sport, is understood and valued within society. Azzopardi (2012: 48) suggests that fostering social inclusion within society is 'inherently problematic because it challenges the very way in which society is structured and organised'. Indeed, as we argued in Chapter 2, it is precisely 'normal' society which creates or maintains social exclusion; thus any attempt to tackle social exclusion requires a much more fundamental approach than merely enhancing people's ability to participate in prescribed institutions of society. Similar conclusions could be drawn regarding sports contexts. Chapter 4 outlined the many ways in which current sports communities are often elitist, exclusionary and unwelcoming to particular groups and individuals who do not reflect the dominant white, male, high socio-economic status, high ability hegemonic discourses that continue to be pervasive within sport.

The Janus-faced character of sport in relation to its possibilities to both reproduce and combat exclusionary attitudes, behaviours and cultural values is well established in recent research (Corboz 2012). There is an inherent tension between the perception of sport as a competitive activity that thrives on winners and losers, and the idea of an inclusive community whereby everyone is respected, equal and has the same opportunities to take part (Long *et al.* 2005; Spaaij *et al.* in press). The concepts of sport (as it is commonly understood) and social inclusion are therefore somewhat incongruous (Burnett 2009). As such, we ought to critically address how the structure and culture of sport often give rise to or condone social exclusion, and how they may be transformed to become more inclusive. For Long *et al.* (2005: 55), this process necessarily involves sports organizations 'surrendering control over the myths associated with their sport and allowing counter-hegemonic movements and resistance to arise'.

Before moving forward, it is helpful to define what we understand as inclusive sports communities. As with definitions of social exclusion, there is no singular definition of an 'inclusive community', with both 'inclusive' and 'community' being contested terms (Azzopardi 2012). In this chapter we draw on a definition provided by the Canadian Centre for Disability Studies (CCDS) as we consider it to be directly relevant to sports contexts. According to CCDS (2013), within inclusive communities all people regardless of any observable or unobservable difference: (1) have access to quality community necessities and amenities; (2) have the same opportunities to take part in all aspects of community life; and (3) have a sense of belonging and respect in the community. Within a sports context we would understand these criteria as:

- All people having access to the same sports opportunities, facilities and resources, for example, women not having to play on a substandard pitch because the male team takes priority (Caudwell 1999).
- All people having the opportunity not only to play sport but also to participate in administration and organization, irrespective of who they are. Hallinan and Judd's (2009a) work provides a useful example of how Indigenous Australians have been welcomed as players within the Australian Football League (AFL) but not necessarily within powerful administrative and coaching positions.
- All people feeling part of the sports community they participate in and experiencing a sense of belonging within it. Krane and Romont (1997), for instance, highlight how gay athletes who have not publicly announced their sexuality participate regularly in mainstream sport but do not feel as though they belong within that sports community.

These criteria emphasize the point made in Chapter 2 that participation alone does not equate to social inclusion. In relation to sport, while the involvement of marginalized groups in playing sport is an important first step, genuinely inclusive communities require the involvement of traditionally excluded participants at all levels of provision. However, recent research indicates that this criterion if often not met. Similar to Hallinan and Judd's (2009a) finding that the number of Indigenous Australians in managerial and coaching positions within the AFL remains low, Cashmore and Cleland (2011) stress the under-representation of black managers and coaches within professional football in the UK. In the same vein, Black (2011) highlights the almost complete absence of coaches and administrators with disabilities within sport unless such individuals are specifically connected to disability provision. In Chapter 4 we further showed that while participation of women and girls continues to increase across a range of traditionally masculine sports (e.g. football, rugby and cricket), women remain under-represented in managerial and senior administrative positions within sport (see also Knoppers and Anthonissen 2008).

Our understanding of these criteria is further informed by the idea that we developed in Chapter 2 that it is not non-participation itself that constitutes social exclusion, but rather the lack of the *opportunity* to participate in sports activities that one has reason to value. Our reference to 'all people' thus includes not only those who would like to participate in sports communities, but those who are denied the opportunities to participate in an equitable and meaningful way.

The role of policy and practice in facilitating inclusive sports communities

Chapter 3 provided an overview of the key policies that intertwine sport and social inclusion at a national level across three countries. The purpose of this section is to discuss research examining various policies and practices that seek to support the development of inclusive sports communities. This section is not intended to be exhaustive; rather, it is illustrative of the types of policies that have been created by the governing bodies of sport. It examines their application and, in particular, provides a critique of their impact. We do this by reviewing the critiques of other scholars as well as using our own primary data.

Recent international research raises concerns about the capacity of top-down policy to facilitate the significant cultural shifts within sport deemed necessary to foster more inclusive environments. May *et al.* (2012) examine the impact of policies on community sports clubs in England, and suggest that volunteers are mostly unaware of current sport policy objectives, both those highlighted in national policy documents and those specified within a governing body. Long *et al.* (2005) and Corboz (2012) contend that while policy is potentially an important catalyst to encourage sports administrators, volunteers and participants to consider issues of social exclusion and inclusion, it cannot on its own facilitate the shift in exclusionary values and beliefs imbued within sport. Long *et al.* (2005) analyse the impact of the *Racial Equality Charter for Sport* and the subsequent *Achieving Racial Equality: A Standard for Sport* on the practices of sports organizations in the UK. The Charter was published by Sporting Equals in March 2000 and signified a public commitment by sports leaders to tackle racial discrimination. Launched in December 2000, the Standard provides a framework of good racial equality good practices for governing bodies and key sports organizations. However, although the Standard has led to greater recognition of the importance of racial equality policies in sport, they were still not a high priority for sports organizations. This led the authors to question the capacity of inclusion policies to be more than a 'paper trail', suggesting that 'it is possible for procedures to be superficially accommodated without there being any necessary organic change' (Long *et al.* 2005: 54). In Australia, Corboz's (2012: 3) exploration of the AFL's Respect and Responsibility policy, instigated in 2004 to encourage the development of 'safe and inclusive environments for women at all levels of the game', suggests that policy does not necessarily lead to any significant cultural change, despite prompting scrutiny of particular issues.

In our own research among community sports clubs in Australia (Spaaij *et al.* in press), we find that although many clubs, under guidance of their State Sports Associations, have developed policies that state a clear commitment to equality and inclusive principles, many do not know how to enact these in practice. Hanlon and Coleman (2006) similarly outline that while managers within sports organizations may understand the needs of people from diverse backgrounds, they are not clear how this knowledge can be used to effectively recruit and retain diverse groups into their club. Our interviews with clubs' committee members and coaches also suggest that clubs struggle to engage effectively with excluded communities and are unsure how to integrate them fully within the club environment. There are several examples where individuals within clubs worked hard to establish opportunities for young people with disabilities and successfully created teams; however, these often sat outside what was described as the 'main focus' of the club, which was usually to field able-bodied junior teams in local leagues and tournaments. As one volunteer coach (male, 60s) explains, the club committee allowed the establishment of a team for people with disabilities so long as 'it didn't interfere with anything else' within the club environment. In this particular club, people with disabilities are accommodated more as an add-on rather than integrated within club life.

A broader issue affecting sports clubs' commitment to equality and inclusive principles is that, as most club committee members and coaches suggest during the interviews, team and club success (i.e. winning games, leagues, tournaments) is their priority. As one coach (male, 40s) points out, 'we're a competitive soccer club. We need to be in the best league we can be.' Thus, club administrators and coaches may consider that developing an inclusive sports context compromises this competitive, success-driven focus. That said, where it is felt that being inclusive may assist in the achievement of success by recruiting talented players from a previously untapped pool, sports may become more open to the inclusion of previously socially excluded groups (Spaaij *et al.* in press).

Existing studies would therefore point to the frailties of policy that impede the significant cultural change necessary for the development of inclusive sports communities. We now develop this issue further by considering some of the issues of current sport development practice, and outlining how a community development orientation may be more suitable for encouraging the more radical change required for inclusivity.

Social inclusion and sport development practice

Traditionally, the translation of policies aimed at addressing social exclusion in sport has resulted in top-driven practice whereby initiatives and projects are imposed on particular groups. These are often focused on increasing the participation opportunities for minority groups with limited consideration of the structural and cultural constraints that prevent regular engagement in existing sports environments (Long 2002). The Active Sports program in the UK, for example, aims to improve the range and quality of sport opportunities available for young people, particularly those from disadvantaged backgrounds, and tends to organize 12-week blocks of activity in target areas with limited consultation with the population the activity is intended to reach. Similarly, projects developed to use sport to alleviate broader social exclusion are rarely constructed with the target group. For example, the mental health and worklessness programs discussed in Chapter 5 were largely devised by health professionals and local government officials, respectively, with limited guidance or support from those they were intended to benefit.

As Chapter 5 demonstrated, while providing valuable individual benefits and potentially contributing to an enhanced quality of life for some individuals, sport-based social inclusion programs may not necessarily produce the social transformation intended. Indeed, Frisby *et al.* (2007) argue that programs aimed at addressing the social exclusion of particular groups within sport and recreation are generally ineffective because they are largely designed by bureaucrats with little or no input from those encountering structural barriers to participation. In a similar vein, Vail (2007) suggests that sports development professionals have long relied on traditional sport development strategies of launching top-down national programs to increase sport participation delivered in a uniform manner across the country for a fixed period of time. In Chapter 3 we provided clear examples of this from sport development policy and practice in the UK, China and Zambia. As Frisby *et al.* (2007) and Vail (2007) conclude, these strategies have been largely ineffective in terms of increasing the presence of marginalized groups within sport and, in particular, sustaining their participation. A key reason for this is that, as indicated, they fail to address the broader structural inequalities and hegemonies that currently restrict the access of certain groups to mainstream sports communities.

Integrating community development principles into sport development work offers an alternative to ineffective top-down policy and practice that fail to take into account the complexity of social exclusion (Vail 2007; Jeanes and Magee 2012). While there is no scope within this chapter to provide a full discussion of community development, we do acknowledge that the meaning of community development is contested (Ledwith 2005). However, the following section outlines some of the key principles of community development before using case studies to illustrate how these have been integrated within a sports context.

Community development: an alternative sport development praxis?

Community development is founded on the principles of local empowerment, participation, change from below and enhanced local capacity (Kenny 1999), with its ultimate objective being positive social transformation (Ledwith 2005). Utilizing a community development approach provides the target community with the opportunity to express their views on what activities they would like to participate in and the constraints to participation they face. Adopting this approach also provides the opportunity for the target community to develop personal and collective capacity among the group through partnerships with service providers to begin to organize and manage opportunities that meet their needs (Henderson and Salmon 2001). There is a key emphasis in community development on encouraging community decision-making, the development of goals that suit the community rather than external agencies, and the development of strategies that the community feels will help them to overcome the challenges they face (Phillips and Pittman 2009).

Community development, however, should be not be interpreted either as the community being left to solve its own problems, or as an offloading of responsibility by service providers onto that community. Rather, the purpose of community development is to connect communities with local service providers in a way that ensures the networks that develop suit the community's needs and not those of the service providers (Phillips and Pittman 2009). As Frisby and Millar (2002: 210) suggest, such an approach

> ... challenges taken-for-granted power relations reflected in traditional organisational structures of sport and recreation by advocating new roles for managers as facilitators and enablers, who work in partnership 'with' individuals and groups instead of making decisions 'for' them.

Critical community development is focused on supporting individuals and communities to understand their current situation, recognize the current causes of exclusion and marginalization, and equip them with skills to address these issues. The process of community development therefore reflects the principles of critical pedagogy that we discussed in Chapter 7. One major aspect of community development that strongly resonates with critical pedagogy is the centrality of participation and democratization. In both critical community development and critical pedagogy, participation involves the active engagement of people who are intended to benefit from services and actions in the making of relevant decisions. Participation does not serve simply to improve the operation of projects; rather, it can empower people and act as a catalyst for democratic decision-making and governance. This occurs when the community or user group sets up a process to control its own development (Nelson and Wright 1995). This approach to community development involves the transfer of power from power holders to project recipients, a loss of central control and the proliferation of local diversity (Chambers 1995).

Community development has been used in other areas, particularly health and international aid, as a process to tackle social exclusion (Schuftan 1996). In Chapter 6, we reflected on how it may be used in sport for development programs in the Global South by critiquing the control and decision-making powers that are often afforded to external agents in such programs. The existing literature offers further examples of how more inclusive sports communities have been established in various contexts.

Maxwell and Taylor (2010) demonstrate how an Australian community sport organization used a community development approach to engage Muslim women in both participation and administrative roles. They outline the process by which the club moved from having no Muslim female participants to engaging young Muslim women regularly and involving them in the managerial aspects of the club. As the aforementioned critiques of policy and practice suggest is necessary, this process began with a commitment from existing club and committee members to engender change and also consultation with the target population, initially via another community organization (the local Muslim Women Association), acting as go-between for the club and target community. The club initially sought to work with Muslim families who already had male children participating to find out what they could do to encourage more female participation. Crucially, many club members recognized that changing the club's culture was vital if they were to engage more participants and survive as a club. Accordingly, the club provided female-only practices led by a female coach, negotiated with the local football association to allow females to play in hijabs, and also ensured that culturally appropriate food was available in the canteen. As Maxwell and Taylor (2010) observe, these practical adaptations indicate that cultural difference had become recognized and accepted by the community sport organization, and that club practices had been modified accordingly. The experience of this community sport organization resonates with our own research on local sport provision for young people with disabilities and for people with culturally and linguistically diverse (CALD) backgrounds, as discussed in the case studies below.

Other studies further demonstrate the critical importance of partnerships with community groups to create inclusive communities, as well as the value of sports providers seeking advice from service providers who work regularly with different groups (Lawson 2005; Olliff 2008). The UK initiative Positive Futures referred to in Chapter 7 is a noteworthy example. The project builds on a broader community development approach to promote the social inclusion of disadvantaged young people. Activities organized through Positive Futures are characterized by their flexibility and informality (Skinner *et al.* 2008). Leaders encourage young people to share their views on what type of sports activities they would like to engage with, and these tend to (initially at least) take place away from traditional sports environments. Rather, leaders use spaces that young people feel comfortable within, for instance community halls, parks and youth clubs, in an attempt to move away from traditional sports environments that disadvantaged young people feel alienated from (Crabbe *et al.* 2006).

Programs such as Positive Futures, however, also suggest that the notion of an inclusive sports community is inherently challenging, and the question remains as to whether some groups and individuals remain excluded. For example, Kelly's (2011) analysis of Positive Futures discusses how the specific case study projects she examined were unable to effectively engage girls and young women. To appeal to disadvantaged young men, masculine discourses tended to dominate, and this consequently made the initiative unappealing to females.

At a more competitive level, the Gay Games provides a valuable example of how a major sporting event can potentially be reshaped and reimagined around inclusive principles (Symons 2010). In Chapter 7 we questioned the connection between inclusive principles and competitive tournaments using the Homeless World Cup as a case study; however, the tensions between inclusion and competition appear to be less within the Gay Games, which seek to offer a mega event participation experience for all. The Gay Games were founded on a commitment to create inclusivity; hence, they are open to participants of any skill level, age, ethnicity, nationality and sexual orientation (Krane and Romont 1997). The principles on which the Gay Games were established – focused on 'unifying people in their ability to participate in a festival of sports' (Waitt 2003: 168) – certainly provide a contrast to the discourses established and perpetuated at more traditional global sporting events. Waitt (2003: 168) suggests that the Games have become a site where marginalized groups 'attempt to challenge cultural norms that are oppressive and constrain the bodily performances of those who identify as gay, lesbian, bisexual, transgender and intersex'.

The transformative potential of sporting events such as the Gay Games is not lost on critics of the exclusivist tendencies of competitive sport. Indicative of this are the calls for alternative competitions such as the Gay Games to continue to challenge the hegemony of competitive sport mega events, especially with regard to how 'sport for all' is to be imagined, and what a more progressive role for sport in fostering social inclusion might look like (Kidd 2005; Spaaij and Burleson 2012). Still, some scholars question how inclusive the Gay Games actually are. Waitt (2003), for example, argues that despite social inclusion being the foundation concept of the event, in reality the Games reinforce traditional tenets of sporting exclusion:

> Despite the stress upon sports across the limits, participants have been predominantly North American males, from white, middle-class backgrounds. Important constraints over participation are leisure time and disposable incomes for sports, registration fees and travel costs. Equally, the sports disciplines represented are exclusionary, almost solely of European and North American origin. Tensions are created because orthodox understandings of competitive sports persist ... values of faster, higher, stronger and winning are still prized.
>
> (Waitt 2003: 172)

In sum, recent studies that have explored inclusive sports communities illustrate the importance of developing a culture of inclusivity and participation from the outset. Working with excluded groups and establishing what they need and then responding to this is absolutely critical to foster genuinely inclusive sports communities. In the following sections, we examine these principles in action via case studies of sport participation among young people with disabilities and people with CALD backgrounds, respectively.

Creating inclusive sports communities for young people with disabilities

The club involved in this first case study is a football club located in a medium-sized town in the north of England. In 2009, the club ran six junior boys' teams and three junior girls' teams with approximately 110 junior members in total, as well as three senior men's sides and one women's team. Both male and female senior teams competed in local leagues and achieved some success with both the first-team men and the women's team winning their respective leagues once in the last five years. As demonstrated by the presence of female teams, the club was already showing some commitment to inclusive practice. There was a female representative on the club committee and the club had supported the development of two female coaches, one of whom now managed the women's senior team while the other ran one of the male junior teams.

A range of factors led to the club seeking to develop opportunities for young people with disabilities. One committee member had first-hand experience of disability as the father of a son with cerebral palsy and moderate intellectual disabilities. The committee member's son had recently expressed an interest in playing sport outside of school. The committee member was in contact with other parents of children with various physical and intellectual disabilities, and these parents similarly recognized that there was a lack of inclusive sport and leisure activities available for their children.

There was also something of a policy catalyst as the club had just moved training venues to a new purpose-built facility with an all-weather pitch and changing facilities. This was funded externally by a charitable group. To secure funding for the projects, local authorities, schools and community partners had to demonstrate how they would use the new facilities to promote social inclusion via sport in the local area. One of the conditions of access was a demonstrated commitment to providing or developing inclusive opportunities. As the club president explains, the existing girls' section could have been enough for the club to 'tick this particular box'. However, the committee member mentioned above provided the impetus, and when it became apparent that other parents were encountering similar difficulties in accessing inclusive sports opportunities for their children, the club was encouraged to explore in greater detail how they might provide for these young people at the club. Use of the new facility meant that the club did not face the common barrier of inaccessible changing rooms/pavilion, with both the all-weather pitch and the pavilion providing full access for individuals with physical and sensory disabilities.

As discussed in Chapter 4, while barriers relating to access do need to be overcome, doing so does not ameliorate the attitudinal exclusion that prevents many people with disabilities from participating in sport (Jeanes and Magee 2012). Prompted by the key committee member, one of the most important actions the club committee undertook was to organize an open meeting with parents to discuss what provisions at the club might look like and what might be most appropriate for them and their children. On the committee member's advice, the meeting was scheduled at a time when parents could bring their children, considering that finding childcare for children with disabilities at the time needed could be challenging. Twelve families attended the initial meeting, all with at least one child aged 7–14 years. The club president, committee members and junior team coordinator also attended the meeting.

The composition of young people at the meeting reflected the realities that voluntary clubs face when seeking to work with young people with disabilities. Some of the young people were wheelchair users, several had moderate to severe intellectual disabilities, one was visually impaired and two had high-functioning autism. In our recent research with Australian junior sports clubs (Spaaij *et al.* in press), we find that many club personnel are daunted by the range of disabilities they may be required to work with. Indeed, in the case study at hand, the club president admits to feeling overwhelmed during the first meeting. He points out that he initially asked parents to outline what their experiences had been in attempting to access sport opportunities for their children, and what they felt were the most common barriers. He explains:

> This was a real eye opener, you can imagine it was difficult but some of the stories of the way they'd been treated at different places, had other

kids laugh at them. Even parents getting funny with them because their kid looks different or is shouting a lot ... They didn't talk about it in a 'you should feel sorry for me' way either, it was very practical; these are the problems, this is what we want doing about it.

(Male, 30s)

As well as providing committee members with a first-hand description of challenges faced, parents also discuss how this initial meeting encouraged them to believe that the club was genuine and serious about issues of social inclusion. Reflecting the principles promoted within community development, they discuss how they felt that they were engaged from the outset in shaping provision rather than having to continually participate in activities that were not suitable for them or their children. As one mother (30s) puts it:

I can't think of any time before that someone has actually asked us about the barriers we face and how they can do things better. I was a bit sceptical before the meeting that it might be just a token thing but the committee members genuinely wanted to hear about our experiences and see how they could make things better.

At this meeting, it was decided that the club would look at developing a mixed-ability team that was open for all young people regardless of their abilities. One of the key issues highlighted by parents was that young people had different expectations for their participation; some just wanted to play football and had no desire or interest to play competitively, while others wanted to 'play properly' and have access to training and competitive games. With agreement from the parents, the club decided to initially run a generic mixed-ability team that would have sessions twice a week; from this, if there was sufficient interest the club would develop a competitive team to participate in a local mixed-ability league. The committee also felt that it was important to offer the opportunity for young people with disabilities to integrate into existing junior teams if they wished. Again there were diverging views from parents depending on their child's disability. For example, one parent whose son was autistic discussed how she felt he would like to be within a mainstream team but would need additional support from the coaches to process information and cope with team dynamics. Another whose daughter was a wheelchair user with moderate intellectual disabilities felt that a mainstream setting would be too structured.

The meeting also identified two key issues. First, from the club perspective there was a concern about the practicalities of coaching and working with young people with disabilities. Second, parents were concerned about exposing their children to yet another setting where they would be on the receiving end of negative attitudes and ridicule. After discussing possible strategies to overcome these problems, it was decided that the club would run a Football Association disability coaching course for all coaches, wherein parents would run sessions to discuss the practical realities of working with young people with disabilities. It was also agreed that the club would hold a disability awareness evening to be led by parents of children with disabilities and open to all parents and players within the club. Many parents were initially concerned about their capability to provide such education but, again reflecting community development principles, ultimately found it an empowering experience. One father (40s) expresses this as follows:

> I was a bit like at first, what do I know? Obviously I've got [disabled son] but training others about disability? I was a bit concerned but I worked with four other parents and we planned it all out. We just focused on what life is like, just explaining how much other people's attitudes can limit what we can do and what we need from them to help us get involved … On the actual evening it was an amazing feeling; they were asking so many questions and I just felt like I was helping to change the club for the better.

As this comment indicates, both the disability awareness and coach education were successful not only in improving understanding within the club of disability issues, but also in demonstrating to the club's membership and volunteers that the club was serious about engaging people with disabilities and doing so in a way that fully included them. Where parents agreed, disabled young people were involved in the sessions, sharing their experiences and outlining how to work with them most effectively. As one coach (male, 40s) comments:

> I was a bit worried about how I mix kids with visual impairments with those kids that can see but [visually impaired young person] just said that all he'd need is for me to be really specific with my instructions and he can work out the rest. It gave me a lot of confidence.

After the education sessions, the club began to run a mixed-ability session twice a week. These were held on the same night as several of the junior boys' teams to ensure integration with the club and allow young people with disabilities the opportunity to mix with able-bodied youth and vice versa. The club president explains how the coaches of the three teams would seek to plan aspects of the session, such as warm-ups or various drills that they could all do together, and how this 'makes the kids work together, and particularly for the able-bodied ones, they stop thinking of disability as something weird; it just becomes normal'. The president further outlines how he utilized the initial training sessions to insist on particular values being upheld within the club. There were a number of seemingly minor changes that he instigated that assisted with creating a feeling of inclusivity. The mixed-ability team was provided with the same uniform as the other junior teams, they were included within all club socials, and just generally viewed as part of the club. Moreover, the club instigated a zero-tolerance policy towards any type of prejudice, towards disability or otherwise, that was communicated in the club. The club committee and coaches were tasked with implementing this policy. Several coaches discuss how initially they had to talk to young people who were making fun of the players with disabilities. Coaches outline how they took young people aside and explained why their attitudes were problematic and needed to change if they wished to continue being involved in the club. Again, they felt that having the opportunity to work alongside young people with disabilities within the club helped with this process because, as one coach (female, 20s) puts it, 'they get to see that they are not so different than them and start to lose some of the fear they have towards them being different'.

The financial costs of participating in sport are often prohibitive for families with children with disabilities. To address this barrier to participation, the club not only agreed to offer reduced membership fees based on what parents outlined they could afford, but also discussed how it would like to be more proactive in terms of generating external funding to support the development of disability participation. Two parents and two committee members volunteered to explore possible funding opportunities; subsequently, via working with the local council, they secured grants to procure specialist equipment, including lightweight wheelchairs, to support the growth of disability participation. For one mother (40s) this was again an empowering process. As she explains:

> Finance is always a big thing but here we were actually working to get our own money. I'm a stay-at-home mum and you sort of forget you have any skills. Working with [council employee] I realized I was quite good at putting together the grant applications and it's a skill now I've got. I've started doing all the grant work for the club now, not just for the disability group.

A key aspect of community development is equipping excluded groups with the skills and expertise to begin to change their situation. As the mother above comments, rather than feeling she has to accept that her son cannot do activities because of the expense, she has been able to develop skills to overcome this particular barrier and in doing so help to support other families and the club more broadly.

When the research on which this case study is based was completed in 2011, the club had 34 members with disabilities. Approximately ten of these were playing within mainstream teams and the remainder were part of three mixed-ability teams, one of which played in a competitive league. Several parents had joined the club committee, and two had subsequently gained coaching qualifications to be able to lead the mixed-ability sessions. When speaking to parents, they discussed how much they valued the club and the environment that had been fostered via the work of the club president and committee. In these terms, the mother (30s) of a child with a disability observes that:

> It has become a really central part of our lives, all the kids are playing here and it is so good not having to worry about [child] not being able

to take part. We come down for the social evenings and everyone is welcoming. It's been so good to know we can just do normal things as a family ... the club has been really excellent in how they've gone about ensuring we are included. We just feel part of the club, not this 'special group' any more.

Parents with non-disabled children also reflect positively on the development of disability provision. One father (40s) says: 'It's been so good for my son to mix regularly with kids with disabilities. He's realizing they are just as capable as he is and he's learnt to not see them as any different to himself.'

The value of an inclusive sports community for both the previously excluded group and for participants more broadly emerges in this case study. The club provides an example of how social inclusion in sport may begin to challenge wider attitudes and beliefs promoting social exclusion within wider society. An example of this is parents discussing how, via contact in sport, their children's attitudes are beginning to change towards young people with disabilities. The club committee and the president are also positive about their experiences. The president discusses how from a business perspective social inclusion has been beneficial; it has led to additional grants, increases in membership and social members at the club, as well as a larger pool of adults from whom to recruit volunteers. However, the president is keen to stress that the benefits to the club have moved beyond a business model, and suggests that the club had been enriched socially by the increased involvement of young people with disabilities:

It's just given everyone a different experience; I've learnt so much about disabled people through working with parents and the kids. They've made me a better coach and a much more thoughtful person generally. And I hope we've given something back in terms of having that opportunity to be part of a team and a club that maybe wasn't there before.

The case study provides a useful example of a community development approach in action. The importance of working with excluded groups from the outset and avoiding being tokenistic in this consultation is highlighted. The experiences of the club illustrate the necessity of 'whole of club change' if sports communities are to shift from exclusionary to welcoming environments for minority groups. The leadership demonstrated by the president and the early involvement of the club committee with families were essential for communicating to those in the club that change was occurring, and that they wanted club members to be a part of this. Education was another key aspect of fostering a change in culture and values. The involvement of young people with disabilities and their families in this change process not only provided an empowering experience for them, it also made the issue of social inclusion and its importance 'real' to parents and coaches. Involvement of families was critical to ensuring that provision was developed that reflected need and was not imposed on young people with disabilities. Key to this process was the 'community champion' (Vail 2007) and 'group insider' – in this case the committee member with a disabled son – who was able to provide that connection between families and what the sports club was seeking to achieve. Another critical aspect of ensuring the ongoing sustainability of provision was supporting parents to gain skills to begin to secure further funding. This increased feelings of empowerment among families; that they did not need to rely on 'handouts' and were more in control of provision also had knock-on benefits for the club more generally.

The case study highlights that if inclusive provision is established that meets the needs of excluded groups, word-of-mouth advertising is particularly effective at encouraging others to attend. The important aspect of the process is working to create cultural change, so that as soon as excluded groups are involved in the community they feel welcome and supported. This theme is explored further in the second case study, which examines how people from CALD backgrounds have been effectively engaged in community sport.

Engaging people from CALD backgrounds in organized sport

Organized sport, and particularly club-based sport, is firmly embedded in government policy as a strategy for promoting the settlement and wellbeing of newly arrived migrants (Walseth and Fasting 2004; Doherty and Taylor 2007; Spaaij 2013c). From a policy perspective, sport offers new arrivals the opportunity to learn about and connect with a new culture. To facilitate this acculturation process, policy-makers in several Global North countries seek to promote sustainable opportunities for people from CALD backgrounds to participate in sport within local communities. In Australia, this objective is shared and supported by a range of community-based organizations, including Sports Without Borders, the Refugee Council of Australia (2010), the Settlement Council of Australia (2012) and the Centre for Multicultural Youth (2007).

However, as noted earlier, we know that the policy objective of social inclusion is often not translated into practice, with some groups and individuals remaining marginalized or subordinated in sports communities. Our own research in Australia shows that people with CALD backgrounds may face multiple barriers to sport participation, especially when 'participation' is considered holistically in line with the three criteria for inclusive sports communities outlined at the start of this chapter. As shown in Chapter 4, key barriers to participation can be found at the structural and interpersonal levels. These include a lack of time, financial cost, transport, language difficulties, a lack of or inappropriate information provision, as well as socio-cultural constraints such as stigmatization and a lack of social support (Centre for Multicultural Youth 2005; Spaaij 2013a). Women with CALD backgrounds often face heightened barriers that can reduce their desire to participate or change the kinds of sports activities they would choose. These include a lack of culturally appropriate facilities, high costs, family responsibilities or a lack of transport (e.g. Sawrikar and Muir 2010). They are also less likely than their male counterparts to feel that they have the freedom and opportunity to participate in organized sport (Cortis 2009).

Even when these barriers to participation are overcome, participation in sport can itself be an alienating experience, especially when it involves a misalignment or conflict of values and expectations. Hence, as we also noted in the mental health case study in Chapter 5, the internal structure and logic of sporting competition can highlight and even exacerbate differences rather than overcome them (Hutchins 2007), and in so doing can reinforce interpersonal or inter-group boundaries and tensions instead of bridging them. Experiencing discrimination, aggression and violence on the playing field can even lead to the reinforcement in individuals of group boundaries outside of sport, with negative implications for community engagement and settlement (Spaaij 2012b).

The needs and interests of people with CALD backgrounds are highly diverse. Given this, a key challenge for sport organizations is to understand and cater for these diverse needs (Hanlon and Coleman 2006; Tirone *et al.* 2010). As the previous case study demonstrates, a critical community development approach can be particularly instructive to develop an understanding of what inclusive provision entails on the ground. In our research we identify a few cases where a community development approach has been employed to engage people with CALD backgrounds in mainstream sports communities. Below we discuss one such case: a cricket club located in Melbourne.

The cricket club under study has a strong tradition of the involvement of people with CALD backgrounds, both as players and in administration and coaching roles. Providing low-threshold and inclusive participation opportunities has been a club objective from its foundation in the mid-1950s. Over time the local area experienced a major influx of immigrants from Southern and Eastern Europe. Some migrant youth who were introduced to cricket and other sports in school developed a strong interest in the game, not only to have fun and socialize with their peers, but also as a way to settle in their new country. The club's vice-president (50s) is one of these individuals and expresses this sentiment in a personal interview with the authors:

> It became a game that, for us, was a way to make us equal with the other kids, and it was a way we could be on an equal footing, and also help us liaise, because if we showed sporting prowess suddenly you were accepted.

He goes on to outline how the club made him and his peers feel welcome and accepted: 'They really welcomed us into the club; they nurtured our involvement ... Basically everything that we needed to take to this sport of cricket was provided.'

This sense of belonging and inclusion is shared by other committee members who also joined the club as recently arrived migrant youth. As one committee member (male, 40s) explains:

> I know what it's like to be at a club and not have my parents there, not have support from an adult, and you know to speak another language and all that ... Now, we're fortunate at the [club], there's probably 20 or 30 people like that, maybe even more, that have that same sort of philosophy, the same journey.

Hence, their experiences strongly inform the philosophy of the present club leadership. It is something that is considered critical to the club's attitude towards people with CALD backgrounds, as the following comment by the vice-president indicates:

> I know for me personally, and for a lot of other people at the club, that lesson remained with us. It was a strong lesson, even though we probably didn't realize it at the time, but on reflection they did us a huge service, because they helped us integrate into the local community, they helped us learn a sport that was a huge iconic sport in Australia, and that empowered us. That was a lesson that remained with us, and with the current committee I know that's something that we often talk about, how it's our duty now to embrace new migrants, and embrace anybody that wants to come into the club and play, that we will try and minimize all the barriers so they can successfully participate in cricket, and not only to become good cricketers and to strengthen our cricket, but to become good community members.

The club's approach to minimizing the barriers to participation for people with CALD backgrounds is multi-pronged and can be understood as both needs-based and assets-focused. Recognizing that financial cost is a often a potent barrier, the club actively applies for grants, seeks sponsorship and raises money from within the club to be able to offer reduced membership fees to make access to the game as easy as possible. More broadly, the club leadership seeks to challenge the deficit discourse that is often associated with CALD communities. The vice-president describes this challenge as follows:

> We don't say, 'Oh, they're just unreliable,' or some generalization, and then we move on. What we've said is ... what are the issues there? And we actually delve into it and try and work out how our club can include them ... And then what we try and do is also have an outlook where we ... what can we learn from people; what can we learn from each other? ... So what we actually do there is, what we're saying is, we're celebrating that culture, and we're elevating it to a level, and it sends out an important message to our young people, and to our adults, and to

some of our members that don't get it as well ... It's about, you know, hopefully the leadership at the club is exposing to people, and getting rid of myths and fears by creating a platform where people can have those conversations.

Many people with CALD backgrounds who have joined the club in recent years consider this approach critical in encouraging inclusive sports communities. For example, a Sudanese Australian man (30s) recalled his previous experiences at other sports clubs that lacked such an approach by criticizing their 'rigid way of thinking' and for being 'stuck in their way'. He comments: 'They do not want to engage in a dialogue, to learn from others. They don't want to adapt. So if you want to play you have to accept how things are done; you have to take it the way it is.' In contrast, he praises the cricket club's willingness to engage in a dialogue and to learn from, and with, people like him.

The club's ongoing efforts to engage Indian and Pakistani immigrants living in the local area illustrate how a flexible, needs-based approach can help foster a more inclusive sports environment. A group of Indian and Pakistani students had been regularly using the cricket nets, which are open and accessible to anyone. Observing the students' passion for cricket, club members engaged them in a dialogue and invited them to come along to the club to play or just to train. The club recognized that the students were financially constrained and also had limited time available to play cricket. Some of the students had previously approached another cricket club to see if they could join it; however, they found the club's attitude to be unwelcoming in that it was based on a deficit model of having to chase the students for money and of their not being available regularly. The approach of the cricket club under study, however, was radically different. Rather than requiring the students to play every week and commit to a full season, in consultation with the students the club established a one-day team that allowed the students to play irregularly and only pay for the games in which they played (e.g. four or five games per season). The club also offered the students a flexible membership based on their needs (i.e. actual games played), rather than having to pay a full annual membership fee to join the club. A male club committee member (40s) explains this approach as follows:

> You're suiting the needs. You've got to see what the needs are of people, because cricket's changing, people's time constraints are changing, and that way you're still keeping ... your membership is growing, and you're tailoring it to the needs of different people who've got different sort of requirements.

In addition to being needs-based, the club's engagement with the students is also assets-driven in the sense that the club leadership believes that the students' involvement in the club enriches the culture and structure of the club as a whole. As the vice-president argues:

> We actually take the time to talk to people and learn about their culture, you know, and see how they can contribute. You know, we know that people with Indian heritage love their cricket … we don't have to sell the game to them. But we can learn a lot about Indian culture, and we've had nights at our club where they actually presented on where they're from, what are some of the customs.

Another male committee member (40s) adds:

> When we find people who may be, you know, from a different background or whatever, we want to nurture that, we see the passion that they have for the sport, and we sort of tie into that and try and get them involved, and learn about them at our club … And then it just helps to integrate all of us, because we're all there just enjoying each other's company, and enjoying cricket, of course. And that you get these bonds, and I think it just makes us so much healthier as a club.

Another strategy that the cricket club has initiated to improve its engagement with people from CALD backgrounds is the use of cultural aids. The role of the 'cultural aid' is broadly comparable to that of the 'cultural intermediary' that we discussed in Chapter 5. Within the context of the cricket club's objective to provide an inclusive environment for people with CALD backgrounds, the cultural aid is a person who reflects the target group (i.e. having the same CALD background and sharing their first language) in order to support and build trust with CALD communities and to enhance the club's awareness of the needs and expectations of these communities. The role of the cultural aid in building a relationship of trust with parents is considered of vital import. Again, this belief is based on club members' own experiences as migrant youth growing up in Australia. As the vice-president puts it:

> Our parents obviously didn't understand the sport, but they wanted to know that we were safe wherever we were going. [My coach] actually came and saw my dad, and he took the time to come and see him. My dad appreciated that. So that was a real … that was a powerful act, to come, knock on the door, speak to him and say, 'Look, [your son], I'm his coach, this is what I look like, this is what we stand for,' and my dad appreciated that gesture … some sort of trust was established. And then we were OK, when we went to cricket they knew we were safe, and we were doing something that was popular in Australia.

Cultural aids at the club take on a similar role as the coach described above by the vice-president. Moreover, the cultural aids serve as 'a knowledge bank of that community', a 'great first point of call' for the club to learn about the community. The club has been successful in obtaining financial support from the State Sports Association and raising money itself, and this has enabled the club to employ multiple cultural aids at the club at training and on game days. Further, the cultural aids have built trust with and buy-in from the parents. For families facing transport difficulties, the cultural aids gather the children and bring them to training or the matches, and afterwards take them home.

The abovementioned strategies are all part of the cricket club's community development approach to building an inclusive sports environment for people with CALD backgrounds. A powerful illustration of this approach is the club's partnership with a group of Sudanese Australian footballers. This particular group of footballers, numbering 10 to 30 men at any time, commenced as an informal social club that played football at a local park. A few years later, they approached the local government to see if they could register as a formal sports club and participate in a local football league. Their requests were knocked back due to a lack of space and venues for clubs already having been taken. In 2010, however, their luck changed when a local government official put them in contact with the cricket club under study, who were immediately welcoming and willing to discuss the options. From the cricket club's perspective, it was believed that the team would fit in well because the club already had some Sudanese Australian members as well as a number of football teams.

From the outset, both parties agreed that the collaboration should be a partnership between equals. In line with the critical community development approach discussed earlier in this chapter, the cricket club invited the team to develop a proposal and committed to accommodating the approach that would work best for the team. The football team was allowed to keep its own name and to keep playing together; over time some players also moved on to other teams within the club. The team members are consulted and involved in all decision-making at the club, an approach that is valued greatly by the Sudanese Australian players. One player (30s) expresses this as follows:

> We are all involved in the decision-making so we don't feel like being outsiders or just a participant. We are part of it; we are not participants. We are part of the club and feel valued and we also feel obliged to play a role because we're not just there as participants.

The football team's involvement in decision-making processes within the club is formalized through its representation on the club committee. Three out of ten committee members are drawn from this team, which affords them both an opportunity to voice their needs or concerns and to make relevant decisions in partnership with other club leaders. The sense of equality and inclusion that this sharing of decision-making powers evokes in the

Sudanese Australian players is not to be underestimated, as the following comment by one of the players (30s) indicates:

> We're equal and that's how I accept it to be involved in the project because my approach, or my view, is always I don't deal with people who see me as a victim or someone to be helped. I want to work with someone who will treat me as equal and deal with issues on an equal level rather than just saying, 'You guys, we understand what you have gone through, well, we'll do our best to help you.' Well, we don't really need help, all we need is just mentoring and guidance to be able to work together.

Again, the importance of an assets-based as opposed to a deficit approach is emphasized here. The cultural appropriateness of such an approach is further highlighted by another player (20s), who points out:

> [The cricket club] took us in as partners, rather than, you know, some others ... rather than a team or individual that have issues to deal with, and we appreciate that ... 'cause some clubs here all interpret the newly arrived and especially the African as having common issues, would be unable to fit in or it's going to take them ... they have to do extra initiative to accommodate them. So I think it did make a big difference because the people that we're dealing with have an insight, or I guess are aware of what was going on and not too, I guess ... they don't see us in a different context.

Although this comment indicates that the cricket club's attempts to foster an inclusive environment for people with CALD backgrounds are considered highly successful by those involved, it also suggests that this type of practice may well be the exception rather than the rule. The players' narratives of their experiences at some other sports clubs are decidedly less positive and frequently refer to being 'an outsider' and not feeling fully accepted. Negative experiences at mainstream sports clubs can lead prospective participants to give up sport altogether, or to look for alternative forms of sport participation (Spaaij 2012b, 2013a). One alternative is the relatively informal programs run by community-based organizations such as migrant resource centres. These programs often offer low-cost or free recreational sports activities including basketball, indoor football and swimming, which are delivered in culturally sensitive ways by multicultural development workers (e.g. Centre for Multicultural Youth 2005, 2007).

For people with CALD backgrounds who prefer to engage in organized competitive sport, mono-ethnic sports clubs that are organized and dominated by members of a particular minority ethnic group can serve an important social function as a way to connect with people with similar experiences and values and to deal with some of the stresses of everyday life. They are places where minority ethnic groups can find acceptance and familiarity among individuals with whom they share a culture and language (Tirone *et al.* 2010; Spaaij 2012b). Yet, there is a long-standing perception that multicultural sports clubs that comprise different ethnic groups or identities stimulate the social inclusion of CALD groups in ways that mono-ethnic sports organizations do not, with the practices of mono-ethnic sports clubs typically inhibiting the connection of their members to the wider society (Pooley 1976). Hence, this can result in further segregation, the erosion of community cohesion and self-exclusion.

These concerns relate to broader questions regarding the inclusivity of sports environments that contain large proportions of an excluded group – not just in relation to CALD groups but also, for example, gay and lesbian athletes (e.g. Caudwell 2007; Symons *et al.* 2010; Drury 2011), or to people with learning disabilities (Southby 2011). For example, Long (2002) highlights how dominant groups frequently hold a perception that minority groups would rather have separatist provision and 'stick together', a perception that devalues the segregated safe spaces that marginalized individuals have created for themselves where they can develop their own sense of community and be treated with dignity and respect. From a social exclusion perspective, however, this perception is seriously flawed, as it ignores the fact that mono-ethnic clubs are often relatively well suited to facilitate social networks within migrant communities on which new arrivals rely for practical and emotional support (Spaaij 2011, 2012b). It also undervalues the desire among some people with a CALD background to spend their leisure time with those for whom social interaction is uncomplicated, symmetrical and meaningful. Indeed, close relationships with members of one's ethnic group and a common language can be important for a sense of belonging and trust, for social learning and for accessing support (Spaaij 2011).

Research further shows that this ostensible self-exclusion is, in reality, often a consequence of experienced exclusion and prejudice in other sports communities and in other societal domains. Bradbury's (2011) analysis of black and minority ethnic (BME) communities within English football stresses the complexity of understanding social inclusion. He discusses how many BME communities, as a result of the continuing exclusion they experienced within traditional footballing contexts, created their own sports environments that they 'owned' and in which they felt included. Such spaces do not necessarily represent 'cultural separatism' or 'voluntary self-segregation'; rather, they provide 'valuable participation opportunities in organized football for a range of marginalized communities for whom access to local competitive football infrastructures has been historically limited' (Bradbury 2011: 40). In doing so, such clubs redefine social exclusion. Inclusion is essentially available to any community that has historically not been able to engage in established sports communities, but it is not necessarily available for those who have traditionally been the perpetuators of exclusion. Maynard's (2011) account of Indigenous sportsmen and sportswomen in Australia who found acceptance and a haven from prejudice within the post-World War Two football organizations established by European migrant communities provides further evidence of this. It also reiterates the importance of promoting inclusive sports communities in which all people can experience a sense of belonging, acceptance and equity.

Conclusion

The case studies presented in this chapter illustrate how it is possible to alter the sports context to foster more inclusive experiences for persons with diverse backgrounds and needs. The examples demonstrate, however, that this is not an easy process and essentially depends on redistributing power and redefining dominant discourses within sports spaces (Lawson 2005). A willingness to relinquish power by those in authority and critique hegemonic practices is essential in moving beyond tokenistic attempts to engage socially excluded groups (Ledwith 2005). As the case studies suggest, when sport is inclusive it can facilitate broader perceptions of social inclusion, and enable individuals and groups that feel on the fringes of society within their everyday lives to feel connected to a social group and able to participate in the broadest sense. It can also begin to reshape dominant values held about particular groups that contribute to their marginalization and exclusion. In the first case study, both the football club president and parents discuss how regular contact with young people with disabilities altered their understanding of people with disabilities as incompetent and less capable. In the second case study, the innovative ways in which the cricket club sought to engage people with CALD backgrounds enhanced club members' understanding of CALD communities' needs as well as the skills and talents they possess, and how these could enrich the quality of experience in sports communities.

The process, however, is challenging. Within community development literature more broadly there are critiques of the capacity of a bottom-up approach to facilitate the wider structural change essential to creating genuinely inclusive settings. For example, Ledwith (2005) argues that even when adopting a bottom-up approach that encourages participation and seeks to empower a disempowered group, the results can remain localized. This critique echoes our conclusions in Chapters 5 and 6, which indicate that individuals involved in a sports program may see some changes in their situation for a short period of time, but ultimately they are unable to significantly change the wider socio-political factors that contribute to their social exclusion. Similarly, a small number of clubs or projects that do seek to provide inclusive sports communities will not necessarily shake the foundations of sporting hegemony sufficiently to engender wider change. Additionally, while marginalized groups may have the opportunity to experience inclusion within a sports community, their experiences of exclusion elsewhere remain the same. They are essentially 'included within an excluded community' (Jeanes and Magee 2011b), with everyday life remaining restrictive and challenging.

Engaging socially excluded individuals or groups in a bottom-up approach can also be difficult. As Skinner *et al.* (2008) point out, for under-resourced sports clubs serviced largely by volunteers, the work entailed in supporting the development of an inclusive sports environment is often a bridge too far. Although we argue that it should be an embedded part of everyday practice, even those volunteers who would like to work towards more inclusive environments often see it as too much effort. Such sentiments are continually expressed in our own research with Australian sports club representatives, who frequently refer to social inclusion as important but 'too much to take on' (Spaaij *et al.* in press). Another issue is that even where proactive social inclusion efforts are exerted, different axes or forms of inclusion are typically treated in isolation from one another. For example, while the sports clubs in the case studies seek to extend themselves by engaging people with disabilities and CALD groups, respectively, they are not equally committed to, at least thus far, providing a safe and inclusive environment for other groups that remain marginalized or subordinated in organized competitive sport, such as gay and lesbian athletes. This highlights the still narrow confines within which broader social inclusion practice is addressed in sport. It also reveals some of the practical complexities of the type of needs-based approach discussed in the case studies. In the final chapter, we reflect on the implications of these findings for the relationship between sport and social exclusion.

9 Looking back, looking forward

Reflections on sport and social exclusion in global society

Introduction

The preceding chapters illuminate the multifaceted processes through which individuals and groups experience and negotiate social exclusion in the realm of sport. Our discussion has focused specifically on the factors, mechanisms and contexts that affect people's ability to participate in sport and the lived experiences of social inclusion/exclusion of those who play sport, as well as the wider social outcomes that sports policies and programs aim to achieve. In this book, we have situated these themes within a theoretical understanding of social exclusion as a (set of) process(es) that negatively affects the rights, recognition and/or resources of targets of social exclusion and/or their opportunity to participate in key activities in different societal domains. This chapter draws together our main arguments and findings, proposes avenues for future research, and considers how sport might be organized and provided in a way that, to quote Sonia Sotomayor (2013: 163), promotes 'a sense of belonging among those who formerly would have been considered and felt themselves outsiders'. We do so by returning to the initial three questions raised in Chapter 1, and consider these questions in relation to our theoretical underpinning and the various empirical studies presented.

How does social exclusion affect participation and non-participation in sport?

Despite an increasing number of policies and regulations that address social exclusion in sport, in most countries there remain considerable discrepancies in sport participation rates among diverse population groups. As Chapter 4 shows, organized competitive sport is exclusionary across multiple axes of diversity and this can lead to large numbers of non-participants. Gender, class, ethnicity, disability and other axes of diversity continue to mediate participation, with the highest rates of sport participation noted in able-bodied, majority ethnic, middle-class males. Where disparities in participation rates signal an enforced lack of access to sport, this is problematic because 'without access, any discussion of social inclusion is moot' (Bailey 2008: 91).

However, social exclusion from sport need not be involuntary. We know that sport does not appeal to everyone to the same extent and in the same way. Many people simply have no interest in playing, spectating, working or volunteering in sport, or afford it a low priority relative to their other pursuits. Given this, non-participation in sport arising from personal choice cannot be considered problematic, or arguably only when it has significant negative externalities for the long-term wellbeing of the individual(s) involved or for society more broadly. Yet, it is often precisely the latter idea that drives the 'will for inclusion' (Macdonald *et al.* 2012: 9): that is, the enduring belief that non-participants should become participants so that they are 'included'. As such, even those individuals who might be excluded from the practices of sport are never fully excluded from the pervasive *discourses* of sport (Macdonald *et al.* 2012).

Our understanding of social exclusion as a dynamic, relational process is valuable when considering self-exclusion from sport as it highlights the complex interplay between choosing exclusion and being excluded. Chapters 4 and 8 illustrate how some marginalized groups choose to exclude themselves from traditional mainstream sport settings; instead, they choose to participate in alternative sport settings where they can claim a sense of belonging that they feel is not available to them in mainstream settings. This suggests that the distinction between self-exclusion and involuntary social exclusion in sport is less clear-cut than is often assumed. What may appear as self-exclusion is, more often than not, shaped by an *enforced* lack of participation emanating from exclusionary processes that are beyond an individual's control.

A relational approach to social exclusion directs attention towards the nuanced ways in which mechanisms of social exclusion can affect participation experiences. In this book, we have illustrated that participation is not necessarily a signifier of social inclusion. Individuals and groups can feel excluded within sports spaces despite the fact that they are present within them and may seem included to the outsider. As Chapter 2 shows, conceptualizing social exclusion as a fluid continuum is valuable for understanding the subjective experiences of those who seek full and equitable inclusion in sport. For example, while the young Zambian women we discuss in Chapter 4 regularly participate in a sport (i.e. football) that is traditionally dominated by males, their participation is heavily regulated and restricted. Various structural, socio-normative and organizational mechanisms still shape how often they are able to play, the resources available to them, and whether their participation is tolerated or valued within their local communities. Hence, although these women do have opportunities to participate in sport, their participation tends to be characterized by an enforced lack of rights, recognition and resources which are constitutive elements of the definition of social exclusion proposed in this book. We conclude, therefore, that while absolute and complete social exclusion from sport is rare at this point in the twenty-first century, particular mechanisms of social exclusion continue to shape (non-)involvement at all levels of sports competition.

In Chapter 2 we also highlight the value of understanding social exclusion as a process driven by unequal power relations. As Chapter 4 demonstrates, inequalities within the governance of sport, and consequently how sport is structured, play a key role in shaping experiences of social exclusion for some participants. Within the governance of sport there is clear evidence of the marginalization of certain individuals and groups. Hence, the unwillingness of those who govern sport to embrace diversity and social inclusion maintains the unequal power relations that perpetuate exclusion within everyday sports spaces. We will reflect on the implications of this further on in the chapter.

How is social exclusion produced, experienced, resisted and managed in sport?

Our second question has allowed for a much more detailed exploration of how social exclusion that exists within sport manifests in practice. This exploration shows that while poverty and material deprivation are important aspects of social exclusion, they are not the only mechanisms via which it occurs. This understanding of social exclusion challenges the view that poverty is *the* core of exclusion, a view that is held by leading scholars in this field of research (Collins with Kay 2003; Collins 2012). Understanding social exclusion as multidimensional allows us to examine how structural, socio-cultural, institutional and interpersonal mechanisms interlink to affect individual experiences. It also urges us to focus on those doing the excluding rather than on just the excluded: that is, on social exclusion as a process rather than a state or situation. From this perspective, cultural stigmatization, civil rights violations, institutional discrimination and other social processes all play their part in producing the enforced lack of participation that is experienced by many individuals and groups across the world, notwithstanding that the exact combination of mechanisms that shape this experience is specific to particular contexts at particular points in time.

In Chapter 2 we emphasize the importance of recognizing and responding to Global South perspectives on social exclusion. These perspectives are instructive, for example, for deconstructing Global North assumptions that social exclusion is something that affects only a small minority of people in a society and can be comprehensively understood within exclusively national terms of reference, rather than within the broader context of global power relations that can graft themselves on to discourses and practices of inclusion/exclusion operating at the local level. A Global South understanding also places greater emphasis, *inter alia*, on human dignity, cultural recognition and personal security in the conceptualization of social exclusion. The experiences of the Zambian young women in Chapter 4 illustrate the importance of recognizing the nuances between Global North and Global South experiences of social exclusion. While the women identify mechanisms of social exclusion that are similar to those discussed by Global North scholars, the consequences of challenging these mechanisms usually negatively affect their human dignity and personal safety in ways that will not necessarily impact women in the Global North.

This case study and the broader issues that we discuss in Chapter 4 further illustrate that while individuals and groups may experience profound social exclusion, they also tend to develop strategies to cope with, resist and contest their exclusion. Indeed, targets of social exclusion are not passive victims of existing power relations. Socially excluded individuals and groups do exert agency, albeit in constrained ways, to be able to participate in sport in a meaningful way. The construction of alternative sports spaces by marginalized groups that resist the social exclusion they experience within pre-existing mainstream sports provision is a clear example of this (see Chapter 7).

In answering the second question, we examined policy as a possible strategy to manage or transform social exclusion in sport. Chapter 3 demonstrates that in both the Global North and the Global South, in rhetoric at least, there is a governmental commitment to addressing social exclusion in sport and broadening sport participation. Chapter 8 explores this further, specifically in relation to policies developed by sports organizations and governing bodies. We illustrate that while such policies are an important aspect of awareness raising and action towards social exclusion in sport, they have actually done very little in terms of prompting significant shifts in the structure and culture of (organized competitive) sport. Theoretically, we need to realize that the policy objective of social inclusion tends to relate only to involvement in predefined mainstream social spaces; this therefore conceals the complex social relations that drive social exclusion and the strategies that socially excluded individuals or groups develop to create alternative forms of inclusion. The implied assumption in much of the policy thinking around social inclusion is that society is itself fundamentally sound and inclusive, whereas, in reality, it is precisely 'normal' society that creates and condones the types of social exclusion that are being addressed (Byrne 2005; Gough *et al.* 2006). Thus, social inclusion policies and programs that merely seek to adapt socially excluded people to the needs of prescribed mainstream institutions of society are fatally flawed; instead, their aim should be to regulate or change these institutions to the needs of those experiencing social exclusion. From this critical perspective, genuine social inclusion can be achieved only when society changes.

For sports organizations, this means that they ought to critically reflect on and be willing to change their own structures, values and practices to meet community needs, based on critical awareness of the fact that the way sport is organized or delivered can create institutional barriers to inclusive participation. Chapter 8 shows that a willingness by those in authority to relinquish power and critique and alter hegemonic practices is essential to move beyond tokenistic attempts to engage socially excluded groups in sport. Where this is done successfully, sport can facilitate broader perceptions of social inclusion and enable subordinated or marginalized individuals and groups to feel connected to a sports community and able to participate in it in a way that is both meaningful and equitable. This can also begin to reshape dominant perceptions and prejudices towards particular groups that contribute to their social exclusion. Put differently, it can contribute to the process of challenging and transforming the pejorative judgements that dominant social groups often bring to bear on those who are 'different' from themselves or deviate from the social norm, which play a key role in separating (symbolically, but often also literally) these groups, both within and outside of sport.

How is sport used to combat social exclusion in other life domains?

Chapters 5 and 6 outline the diverse ways in which sport is used to address the social exclusion experienced by individuals and groups within broader societal domains. Sport can offer an alternative platform to engage with those experiencing social exclusion in ways that can be appealing and motivating for some individuals. The case studies that we outline in Chapters 5 and 6 illustrate that, at an individual level, some of those who participate in sports programs can experience considerable benefits that potentially contribute to their feeling less socially excluded within mainstream society. In both the Global North and the Global South some participants consider that involvement in sports programs has provided them with various outcomes ranging from improved social connectedness, employment skills, better mental health, improved knowledge and increased resilience. Returning to the concept of social exclusion as a continuum, we argue that while engagement in the programs discussed in Chapters 5 and 6 did not address social exclusion in absolute terms, the benefits gained did assist some participants to move away from more acute forms of social exclusion within their everyday lives. The programs also provided a space within which participants felt included, valued and welcomed, often in contrast to their experiences in other aspects of their daily lives. That such safe spaces are valued is particularly evident in the responses of Global South participants.

There are further differences in how sport is used to tackle wider social exclusion in the Global North and South. Within our Global North case studies, sport is generally used to work with excluded groups alongside services that have a specific remit to work with disadvantaged groups. Within the Global South such services rarely exist; rather, NGOs run the sports programs as holistic support services for disadvantaged young people in their own right. As we discuss in the next section, this potentially reduces the capacity to bring about broader structural change as NGOs operate within such localized contexts.

At the same time, however, the research presented in this book shows that the evangelical rhetoric (Coalter 2013) that often surrounds sport policy is deeply problematic. Although the case studies confirm that sport, especially when delivered within a broader personal and social development model, can alleviate experienced social exclusion for some people in some circumstances, the broader constraints and limitations of programs using sport to address social exclusion cannot be ignored. One particular aspect that is pertinent to both the Global North and the Global South is that the 'power of sport' to transform people's lives is often directed at individual, interpersonal and, at best, inter-group levels of social exclusion, while the broader social contexts, including exclusionary processes operating in the global political economy, are left unaltered. This is problematic because, as noted in Chapter 6, extra-local drivers of social exclusion tend to act as a structuring context or pretext for local experiences, with significant implications for program impacts and outcomes.

Policy interventions typically focus on 'fixing' or engaging socially excluded individuals to enhance their economic or social participation through developing their knowledge, skills and attributes. As we discuss in Chapter 6, this focus corresponds to a weak conception of social exclusion that explains social exclusion as an outcome of the individual's handicapping characteristics. In contrast, the relational approach to social exclusion that we propose in this book directs attention to the question of who or what is doing the excluding, and thereby encourages a more realistic appraisal of the role that sport, and sports organizations, play or can play in tackling social exclusion. This approach recognizes that rather than simply seeking to enhance individuals' agency, sports policies and programs designed to address social exclusion are also a form of social control and regulation (Spaaij 2009a; Coakley 2011). Moreover, as noted, sports organizations and sport-related policies can, albeit often unwittingly or unknowingly, foster institutional barriers that impede access to or the attractiveness of existing sports provisions to diverse population groups (Allison and Hibbler 2004). In the case of SFD initiatives in the Global South, a related concern is that programs are often dominated by external actors and consequently fail to afford adequate voice, recognition and decision-making power to local recipients and their communities. In so doing, they may actually contribute to experienced social exclusion rather than alleviate it.

The above highlights the still narrow confines within which social exclusion is addressed in sport. Not only do we need to unpack and critically examine the concept and hidden assumptions of 'social inclusion', we also need to creatively rethink how social exclusion in sport may be addressed more effectively and how sport can be used in a meaningful way to encourage social and cultural change, as well as the inherent limitations thereof. The latter is a complex challenge that essentially necessitates the redistribution of power and the deconstruction of dominant discourses within sports spaces. In Chapters 7 and 8, we explore different ways in which this complex challenge may be confronted and, through case study analyses, offer specific approaches and strategies that we consider appropriate for the task. Both chapters stress the significance of a bottom-up approach to engagement, relationship-building and inclusivity, drawing upon insights from community development, critical pedagogy and sports coaching. The case studies that we present in Chapters 5–8 demonstrate the merits of this approach. Indeed, they show that local practices are by no means powerless in the face of global practices of social exclusion; rather, they can actually construct, mediate or reform such global practices (Palmer 2013).

However, the opposite is also true. Our theoretical understanding of social exclusion highlights the limitations that a bottom-up approach is likely to have, particularly in terms of its capacity to facilitate the deep, long-term structural change that is required to create genuinely inclusive sports communities. The adoption of a community development approach focused on transforming power relations that are at the heart of social exclusion as it unfolds on the ground often means that its results remain localized. Any such approach therefore needs to be considered in relation to extra-local mechanisms that co-shape objective and subjective experiences of inclusion/exclusion. As we theorize in Chapter 2, this relationship between local and extra-local drivers of social exclusion is particularly relevant in terms of the discrepancy that may exist between the opportunities for full and equitable participation that marginalized individuals and groups can experience within an inclusive sports community and their everyday experiences of social exclusion in other societal domains, such as unemployment and a lack of access to public goods. Clearly, social exclusion is a multidimensional and multi-scalar phenomenon and, as such, the way in which sport is implicated in both of these characteristics needs to be critically considered.

Implications for policy and practice

The above discussion of the three questions that have guided this book highlights a number of issues pertinent for policy and practice aimed at promoting inclusive sports environments for people of all backgrounds and abilities, an objective that should be central to sports policy and practice. First, our findings call for a more critical understanding of the role that sport may play in tackling social exclusion. Rather than focusing attention on the use of sport as a potential vehicle for social inclusion in other societal domains, policy-makers and practitioners first need to recognize that sport, as a powerful social and cultural institution, is itself a site of multiple and diverse exclusionary processes. Existing sports policies have often done little to turn social inclusion rhetoric into reality, and to do so will require greater consideration by policy-makers and planners as to how they can more effectively engender cultural change in sport via such policies. In particular, this requires addressing inequity within the governance of sport as a key starting point for creating the cultural change necessary for inclusive sports communities to flourish. As noted, it further requires that sports organizations should reflect critically on and be willing to change their own structures, values and practices in order to reduce organizational barriers to inclusive participation. Chapter 8 illustrates a number of ways in which this might be done.

In this book we have considered how, at a local level, exclusionary spaces within sport can become more inclusive. Ideas from critical pedagogy and community development provide important insights into how one could work more effectively with socially excluded groups and individuals within the realm of sport. Our case studies in the Global South suggest that community development approaches are more typical within sport and social exclusion work in the Global South than they are in the Global North. There is therefore an opportunity for practitioners in the Global North to learn from their Global South counterparts how to develop and implement a bottom-up approach to tackling social exclusion.

Our research further highlights the importance of sport coaches/leaders in both creating inclusive sports environments and delivering sport in a way that can begin to challenge aspects of wider social exclusion. Critical pedagogy not only provides a valuable framework for understanding how to work inclusively, it also encourages excluded groups to develop critical awareness of and challenge the social exclusion they face. However, the development and application of such critical educational strategies is still in its infancy in sport (Macdonald 2002; Spaaij and Jeanes 2013). Given this, we suggest that formal coach education provision needs to move beyond a focus on preparing coaches for the performance setting to recognizing that some coaches may opt for coaching in alternative settings. The case study in Chapter 7 is one such setting and by no means unique. We therefore contend that formal coach education needs to better support and equip coaches to work in settings where they are expected to deliver on the ambitious policy objective of social inclusion.

Directions for future research

The book highlights a number of avenues for future research. In Chapter 1, we argue that social exclusion can occur or be challenged at any level of sports competition, from the foundation/participation levels through to the performance/excellence levels. While our own research has primarily focused on experiences and mechanisms of social exclusion at the foundation/participation levels, we recognize that there is a gap in knowledge about the causes and effects of social exclusion in professional sport. The limited existing research on social exclusion in professional sport examines, for instance, how socio-economic disadvantage affects young people's opportunities to become elite athletes (Collins and Buller 2003) and how black athletes fare in professional sport (McGuire *et al.* 2001; Burdsey 2005). However, detailed analysis of social exclusion in professional sport as a multidimensional, relational process is lacking.

A life-course approach holds particular promise for the study of social exclusion in professional sport, and is consistent with our theoretical understanding of social exclusion as a fluid continuum that is subject to changes over time. Almost all professional athletes have worked their way up the professional sport ladder to the riches on offer. However, their career is necessarily short-term, performance-driven and reliant on form and injury, with the prospect of it ending never far away. And when it does, most return to mainstream society unable to afford the lifestyle to which they have become accustomed once the earnings cease. At that stage, former professional sports stars are just as susceptible to degrees of social exclusion as the next person. This has been well documented in the post-career struggles of former professional athletes (Barker-Ruchti *et al.* 2011), for example, in Paul Gascoigne's battle against depression and alcoholism (Gascoigne 2005). Thus, research into experiences of social exclusion among (former) professional athletes would broaden our perspective on the relationship between sport and social exclusion, and potentially highlight the considerable inequity that exists in elite sport.

A second direction that future research should take is 'studying up' on social exclusion in sport: that is, to scrutinize the processes whereby power and responsibility are exercised. Studying up traces and deconstructs the processes that produce 'the normal' in sport, hence making power and privilege visible. Our analysis in this book provides a starting point for this type of research by theorizing social exclusion as a relational process that directs attention to the ways in which boundaries separating the included from the excluded arise from the interactions and interdependencies between social actors with unequal power. However, given that our aim has been to explore diverse population groups' subjective experiences of social exclusion and give recognition and voice to individuals and communities that are frequently ignored within research in this field, the bulk of the empirical analysis presented in this book has been concerned with 'studying down': that is, with the lived experiences of those who face social exclusion. Studying up as well as down can facilitate superior theory development by leading us to ask many questions in reverse (Nader 1972). If we were to principally study those who govern the global sports industrial complex (Maguire 2005), our view of, for example, Zambian women's football, the Homeless World Cup, SFD programs, and community development initiatives in sport might be largely in terms of power relationships larger than the micro-level experiences highlighted in the case studies. As Chapter 6 shows, our understanding of those relationships can be further informed by Global South perspectives that highlight how socially excluded people are incorporated within broader formations of power in ways that marginalize them and undermine their ability to control and impact upon the systems into which they are locked (e.g. Du Toit 2004).

The development and application of Global South perspectives on sport and social exclusion also constitute a promising area for future research in its own right. This book has sought to engage with and synthesize ideas and experiences from both the Global North and the Global South, and builds on broader attempts in the social sciences to take social theory and research from the world periphery seriously (e.g. Connell 2007). Such global dialogue, we argue, requires more than merely bridging different geopolitical areas through the incorporation of research data from multiple and diverse parts of the world. Rather, it invites us to engage more fully with alternative ideas and perspectives that may challenge or complement dominantly Eurocentric approaches to social exclusion. In this book, we have sought to demonstrate the importance that Global South perspectives have for understanding and explaining social exclusion and its relations to sport. While Global North theories of social exclusion do have relevance for understanding sport and social exclusion in the Global South, they do not necessarily capture the complexity, nature or causes of social exclusion in Global South settings.

This book provides a useful starting point for further global analysis of sport and social exclusion. However, in terms of empirically grounded analysis we have only been partially successful in this effort because the majority of our work has been undertaken in Global North contexts. Further research is necessary to move beyond a narrow focus on the SFD agenda and how sport may 'solve' particular social problems to consider how social exclusion in sport may be more adequately conceptualized, understood and responded to by drawing on knowledge and approaches from the Global South (e.g. Mwaanga and Mwansa 2013). We acknowledge our own positions here as Global North researchers and recognize the importance of academics from the Global South leading and contributing to an improved understanding of sport and social exclusion within Global South contexts.

The case studies that we present in the book tackle the relationship between sport and social exclusion in a diverse and rigorous way that extends and deepens contemporary research debates and agendas. We acknowledge, however, that some aspects of our research may be considered as 'snapshot'. The research discussed in this book ranges from long-term ethnographic studies to short-term research and evaluation projects (see Chapter 1). As we did not spend an extended period of time in all research settings, we are not in a position to provide longitudinal data regarding the experience and mechanisms of social exclusion in such short-term research and evaluation projects. Future research would benefit from researchers spending extended periods within research settings to gather longitudinal data that would enhance the intellectual and policy understanding of how objective and subjective experiences of social exclusion change over time, as well as answer the perennial calls of Coalter (2007, 2013) for more robust evidence on the capacity of sport to create long-term social change. We hope that this book will add impetus to the research agenda on sport and social exclusion and encourage other scholars not only to contribute, but also to do so with the longer game in mind.

References

Abramovay, M., Castro, M.G., Pinheiro, L., Lima, F.S. and Martinelli, C.C. (2002) *Juventude, violência e vulnerabilidade social na América Latina: Desafios para políticas públicas*. Brasília: UNESCO.

Abrams, D., Hogg, M.A. and Marques, J.M. (2005) 'A social psychological framework for understanding social inclusion and exclusion', in D. Abrams, M.A. Hogg, J.M. Marques (eds) *The Social Psychology of Inclusion and Exclusion*. New York: Psychology Press, 1–23.

Adair, D. and Stronach, M. (2011) 'Natural-born athletes? Australian Aboriginal people and the double-edged lure of professional sport', in J. Long and K. Spracklen (eds) *Sport and Challenges to Racism*. London: Palgrave Macmillan, 117–34.

Aitchison, C. (2005) 'Feminist and gender research in sport and leisure management: Understanding the social-cultural nexus of gender-power relations', *Journal of Sport Management*, 19(4): 422–41.

Alcock, C., Payne, S. and Sullivan, M. (2004) *Introducing Social Policy*. Harlow: Pearson.

Alcock, P. (1997) *Understanding Poverty*. Basingstoke: Macmillan.

Allison, M. and Hibbler, D. (2004) 'Organizational barriers to inclusion: Perspectives from the recreation professional', *Leisure Sciences*, 26: 261–80.

Anderson, E. (2005) 'Orthodox and inclusive masculinity: Competing masculinities among heterosexual men in a feminized terrain', *Sociological Perspectives*, 48(3): 337–55.

Anderson, E. (2008) '"I used to think women were weak": Orthodox masculinity, gender segregation, and sport', *Sociological Forum*, 23(2): 257–80.

Anderson, E. (2009a) 'The maintenance of masculinity among the stakeholders of sport', *Sport Management Review*, 12(1): 3–14.

Anderson, E. (2009b) *Inclusive Masculinity: The Changing Nature of Masculinities*. New York: Routledge.

Anderson, E. (2010) *Sport, Theory and Social Problems*. London: Routledge.

Andreasen, N., Carpenter, W.T., Kane, J., Lasser, R., Marder, S. and Weinberger, D.A. (2005) 'Remission in schizophrenia: Proposed criteria and rationale for consensus', *American Journal of Psychiatry*, 162: 441–9.

Ansell, N. (2005) *Children, Youth and Development*. London: Routledge.

Apffel-Marglin, F. and Marglin, S. (eds) (1996) *Decolonizing Knowledge: From Development to Dialogue*. Oxford: Clarendon Press.

Arias, E.D. (2006) *Drugs and Democracy in Rio de Janeiro: Trafficking, Social Networks, and Public Security*. Chapel Hill, NC: University of North Carolina Press.

Aristotle (1908) *Nicomachean Ethics*, trans. W.D. Ross. Oxford: Clarendon Press.

Arthurson, K. and Jacobs, K. (2004) 'A critique of the concept of social exclusion and its utility for Australian social housing policy', *Australian Journal of Social Issues*, 39(1): 25–40.

Askonas, P. and Stewart, A. (eds) (2000) *Social Inclusion: Possibilities and Tensions*. Basingstoke: Palgrave Macmillan.

Atkinson, A.B. (1998) 'Social exclusion, poverty and unemployment', in A.B. Atkinson and J. Hills (eds) *Exclusion, Employment and Opportunity*. London: Centre for Analysis of Social Exclusion, London School of Economics, 9–24.

Atkinson, R. and Flint, J. (2004) 'Fortress UK? Gated communities, the spatial revolt of the elites and time–space trajectories of segregation', *Housing Studies*, 19(6): 875–92.

Australian Government (2009) *A Stronger, Fairer Australia*. Canberra: Commonwealth of Australia.

Australian Sports Commission (2012) *Women on Boards Report*. Available at: www. ausport.gov.au/participating/women/get_involved/leadership_register/women_ on_boards2 (accessed 9 October 2013).

Azzarito, L. (2009) 'The panopticon of physical education: Pretty, active and ideally white', *Physical Education and Sport Pedagogy*, 14(1): 19–39.

Azzopardi, A. (2012) 'Spaces for inclusive communities', in A. Azzopardi and S. Grech (eds) *Inclusive Communities: A Critical Reader*. Rotterdam: Sense, 41–54.

Bailey, P. (1978) *Leisure and Class in Victorian England*. London: Routledge & Kegan Paul.

Bailey, R. (2005) 'Evaluating the relationship between physical education, sport and social inclusion', *Educational Review*, 57(1): 71–90.

Bailey, R. (2008) 'Youth sport and social inclusion', in N. Holt (ed.) *Positive Youth Development through Sport*. London: Routledge, 85–96.

Bairner, A. and Shirlow, P. (2003) 'When leisure turns to fear: Fear, mobility, and ethno-sectarianism in Belfast', *Leisure Studies*, 22: 203–21.

Bakilana, A. and de Waal, A. (2002) 'Child survival and development in Africa in the 21st century', in A. de Waal and N. Argenti (eds) *Young Africa: Realising the Rights of Children and Youth*. Trenton, NJ: Africa World Press, 29–54.

Banda, D. (2010) 'Zambia: Government's role in colonial and modern times', *International Journal of Sport Policy*, 2(2): 237–52.

Banda, D. (2011) 'International development through sport: Zambia', in B. Houlihan and M. Green (eds) *International Handbook for Sport Development*. London: Routledge, 323–36.

Barker, G.T. (2005) *Dying to be Men: Youth, Masculinities and Social Exclusion*. New York: Routledge.

Barker-Ruchti, N., Barker, D., Lee, J. and Rynne, S. (2011) *Preparing Olympic Athletes for Lives Outside of Elite Sport: Towards Best Practice*. Lausanne: IOC.

Barry, B. (2002) 'Social exclusion, social isolation, and the distribution of income', in J. Hills, J. Le Grand and D. Piachaud (eds) *Understanding Social Exclusion*. Oxford: Oxford University Press, 13–29.

Bartlett, S. and Straume, S. (2008) *Sports-for-Development Monitoring and Evaluation Consultancy: Final Report*. Washington, DC: Inter-American Development Bank.

Bauman, Z. (2001) *The Individualized Society*. Cambridge: Polity.

Bauman, Z. (2004) *Wasted Lives*. Cambridge: Polity.

Baydar, M., Reid, J. and Webster-Stratto, C. (2003) 'The role of mental health factors and program engagement in the effectiveness of a preventive parenting program for head start mothers', *Child Development*, 74(5): 1433–53.

Beall, J. (2002) 'Globalization and social exclusion in cities: Framing the debate with lessons from Africa and Asia', *Environment and Urbanization*, 14(1): 41–51.

Becker, H.S. (1963) *Outsiders: Studies in Sociology of Deviance*. New York: Free Press.

Beebe, L., Tian, L., Morris, N., Goodwin, N., Allen, S. and Kuldau, J. (2005), 'Effects of exercise on mental and physical health parameters of persons with schizophrenia', *Issues in Mental Health Nursing*, 26: 661–76.

Béland, D. (2007) 'The social exclusion discourse: ideas and policy change', *Policy & Politics*, 35(1): 123–39.

Berkman, H. (2007) *Social Exclusion and Violence in Latin America and the Caribbean*. New York: Inter-American Development Bank.

Bernstein, A. (2002) 'Is it time for a victory lap? Changes in the media coverage of women in sport', *International Review for the Sociology of Sport*, 37(3/4): 415–28.

Beutler, I. (2008) 'Sport serving development and peace: Achieving the goals of the United Nations through sport', *Sport in Society* 11(4): 359–69.

Bhalla, A. and Lapeyre, F. (1997) 'Social exclusion: Towards an analytical and operational framework', Development and Change, 28: 413–33.

Bhalla, A. and Lapeyre, F. (2004) *Poverty and Exclusion in a Global World*, 2nd edn. Basingstoke: Palgrave Macmillan.

Black, K. (2011) 'Coaching disabled children in sport', in I. Stafford (ed.) *Coaching Children in Sport*. London: Routledge, 215–26.

Blackshaw, T. and Long, J. (2005) 'What's the big idea? A critical exploration of the concept of social capital and its incorporation into leisure policy discourse', *Leisure Studies*, 24: 239–258.

Blakely, E.J. and Snyder, M.G. (1997) 'Divided we fall: Gated and walled communities in the United States', in N. Ellin (ed.) *Architecture of Fear*. New York: Princeton Architectural Press, 85–100.

Blakemore, K. and Griggs, E. (2007) *Social Policy: An Introduction*. Berkshire: Open University Press.

Bloyce, D. and Smith, A. (2010) *Sport Policy and Development: An Introduction*. London: Routledge.

Bourdieu, P. (1978) 'Sport and social class', *Social Science Information*, 17(6): 819–40.

Bourdieu, P. (1998) *Contre-feux: propos pour servir à la résistance contre l'invasion néo-libérale*. Paris: Raisons d'Agir.

Bourdieu, P. (2000) *Pascalian Meditations*. Stanford, CA: Stanford University Press.

Bowring, F. (2000) 'Social exclusion: Limitations of the debate', *Critical Social Policy*, 20(3): 307–30.

Bradbury, S. (2011) 'From racial exclusions to new inclusions: Black and minority ethnic participation in football clubs in the East Midlands of England', *International Review for the Sociology of Sport*, 46(1): 23–44.

Breman, J. (2004) 'Social exclusion in the context of globalization', Working Paper No. 18. Geneva: World Commission on the Social Dimension of Globalization, International Labour Office.

Burchardt, T., Le Grand, J. and Piachaud, D. (1999) 'Social exclusion in Britain 1991–1995', *Social Policy and Administration*, 33(3): 227–44.

Burchardt, T., Le Grand, J. and Piachaud, D. (2002) 'Degrees of exclusion: Developing a dynamic, multi-dimensional measure', in J. Hills, J. Le Grand and D. Piachaud (eds) *Understanding Social Exclusion*. Oxford: Oxford University Press, 30–43.

Burdsey, D. (2005) 'Social identity', in D. Levinson and K. Christensen (eds) *Berkshire Encyclopaedia of World Sport* (4 vols). Berkshire: Berkshire Publishing Group.

Burdsey, D. (2011a) 'They think it's all over … it isn't yet! The persistence of structural racism and racialised exclusion in twenty-first century football', in D. Burdsey (ed.) *Race, Ethnicity and Football: Persisting Debates and Emergent Issues.* London: Routledge, 1–18.

Burdsey, D. (2011b) 'That joke isn't funny anymore: Racial microaggressions, color-blind ideology and the mitigation of racism in English men's first-class cricket', *Sociology of Sport Journal,* 28(3): 261–83.

Burnett, C. (2009) 'Engaging sport-for-development for social impact in the South African context', *Sport in Society,* 12(9): 1184–97.

Burnett, C. (2010) 'Sport-for-development approaches in the South African context: A case study analysis', *South African Journal for Research in Sport, Physical Education and Recreation,* 32(1): 29–42.

Byrne, D. (2005) *Social Exclusion,* 2nd edn. Maidenhead: Open University Press.

Campbell, C. (2004) 'Creating environments that support peer education: Experiences from HIV/AIDS-prevention in South Africa', *Health Education,* 104(4): 197–200.

Campbell, C. and MacPhail, C. (2002) 'Peer education, gender and the development of critical consciousness: Participatory HIV prevention by South African youth', *Social Science and Medicine,* 55(2): 331–45.

Carless, D. (2007) 'Phases in physical activity initiation and maintenance among men with serious mental illness', *International Journal of Mental Health Promotion,* 9(2): 17–27.

Carless, D. and Douglas, K. (2008) 'Narrative, identity and mental health: How men with serious mental illness re-story their lives through sport and exercise', *Psychology of Sport and Exercise,* 9(5): 576–94.

Carless, D. and Sparkes, A. (2008) 'The physical activity experiences of men with serious mental illness: Three short stories', *Psychology of Sport and Exercise,* 9(2): 191–210.

Caritas Aotearoa New Zealand (2011) *On a Level Playing Field: Fair Play and the Common Good.* Wellington: Caritas Aotearoa New Zealand.

Carrington, B. (1986) 'Social mobility, ethnicity and sport', *British Journal of Sociology of Education,* 7(1): 3–18.

Carrington, B. (2010) *Race, Sport and Politics: The Sporting Black Diaspora.* London: Sage.

Cashmore, E. and Cleland, J. (2011) 'Why aren't there more black football managers?', *Ethnic and Racial Studies,* 34(9): 1594–607.

Cashmore, E. and Cleland, J. (2012) 'Fans, homophobia and masculinities in association football: Evidence of a more inclusive environment', *British Journal of Sociology,* 63(2): 370–87.

Cassidy, T., Jones, R. and Potrac, P. (2004) *Understanding Sports Coaching: The Social, Cultural and Pedagogical Foundations of Coaching Practice.* London: Routledge.

Cassidy, T., Jones, R. and Potrac, P. (2009) *Understanding Sports Coaching: The Social, Cultural and Pedagogical Foundations of Coaching Practice,* 2nd edn. London: Routledge.

Castro, M.G. and Abramovay, M. (2002) 'Jovens em situação de pobreza, vulnerabilidades sociais e violências', *Cadernos de Pesquisa,* 116: 143–76.

Caudwell, J. (1999) 'Women's football in the United Kingdom: Theorizing gender and unpacking the butch lesbian image', *Journal of Sport and Social Issues,* 23(4): 390–402.

Caudwell, J. (2007) 'Hackney women's football club: Lesbian United?', in J. Magee, J. Caudwell, K. Liston and S. Scraton (eds) *Women, Football and Europe: Histories, Equity and Experiences.* Aachen: Meyer & Meyer, 64–84.

Caudwell, J. (2011) '"Does your boyfriend know you're here?" The spatiality of homophobia in men's football culture in the UK', *Leisure Studies,* 30(2): 123–38.

Central Council for Physical Recreation (CCPR) (1960) *Sport and the Community*. London: CCPR.

Centre for Multicultural Youth (2005) *Report into Good Practice Sports Inclusion Models for Young People from Culturally and Linguistically Diverse Communities*. Melbourne: CMY.

Centre for Multicultural Youth (2007) *Playing for the Future: The Role of Sport and Recreation in Supporting Refugee Young People to 'Settle Well' in Australia*. Melbourne: CMY.

Chambers, R. (1995) 'Paradigm shifts and the practice of participatory research and development', in N. Nelson and S. Wright (eds) *Power and Participatory Development: Theory and Practice*. London: Intermediate Technology Publications, 30–42.

Chan, A. (2001) *China's Workers under Assault: The Exploitation of Labour in a Globalising Economy*. Armonk, NY: M.E. Sharpe.

Chan, C.K., Ngok, K.L and Phillips, D. (2008) *Social Policy in China: Development and Well-being*. Bristol: Policy Press.

Chan, K.W., Liu, T. and Yang, Y. (1999) 'Hukou and non-Hukou migrations in China: Comparisons and contrasts', *International Journal of Population Geography*, 5: 425–8.

China Disabled Persons' Federation (CDPF) (2012) *Sports*. Available at: www.cdpf.org.cn/english/sports/content/2012-11/02/content_84857.htm (accessed 23 April 2013).

Clark, S. and Paechter, C. (2007) 'Why can't girls play football?' Gender dynamics and the playground', *Sport, Education and Society*, 12(3): 261–76.

Claringbould, I. and Knoppers, A. (2008) 'Doing and undoing gender in sport governance', *Sex Roles*, 58: 81–92.

Coakley, J. (2011) 'Youth sports: What counts as "positive development"?', *Journal of Sport and Social Issues*, 35: 306–24.

Coalter, F. (2000) 'Public and commercial leisure provision: Active citizens and passive consumers?' *Leisure Studies*, 19(3): 163–81.

Coalter, F. (2007) *A Wider Social Role for Sport: Who's Keeping the Score?* London: Routledge.

Coalter, F. (2013) *Sport for Development: What Game are we Playing?* London: Routledge.

Cockburn, C. and Clarke, G. (2002) '"Everybody's looking at you!" Girls negotiating the "femininity deficit" they incur in physical education', *Women's Studies International Forum*, 25(6): 651–65.

Coghlan, J. (1990) *Sport and British Politics since 1960*. London: Falmer Press.

Collard, D. and Hoekman, R. (2013) *Sportdeelname in Nederland: 2006–2012*. Utrecht: WJH Mulier Institute.

Colley, H. (2003) 'Engagement mentoring for socially excluded youth: Problematising an "holistic" approach to creating employability through the transformation of habitus', *British Journal of Guidance and Counselling*, 31(1): 77–100.

Colley, H., Boetzelen, P., Hoskins, B. and Parveva, T. (eds) (2007) *Social Inclusion for Young People: Breaking Down the Barriers*. Strasbourg: Council of Europe Press.

Collins, M. (2007) 'Sport, physical activity and social exclusion', *Journal of Sports Science*, 22(8): 727–40.

Collins, M. (2008) 'Social exclusion from sport and leisure', in B. Houlihan (ed.) *Sport and Society*, 2nd edn. London: Routledge, 77–105.

Collins, M. (2010) 'From "sport for good" to "sport for sport's sake" – not a good move for sports development', *International Journal of Sport Policy and Politics*, 2(3): 367–9.

Collins, M. (2012) 'Understanding social exclusion and sport for children', in S. Dagkas and K. Armour (eds) *Inclusion and Exclusion Through Youth Sport*. London: Routledge, 24–39.

Collins, M. and Buller, J. (2003) 'Social exclusion from high-performance sport: Are all talented young sports people being given an equal opportunity of reaching the Olympic podium?', *Journal of Sport and Social Issues*, 27(4): 420–42.

Collins, M. with Kay, T. (2003) *Sport and Social Exclusion*. London: Routledge.

Collins, S. (2011) 'Finland', in M. Nicholson, R. Hoye and B. Houlihan (eds) *Participation in Sport: International Policy Perspectives*. London: Routledge, 109–25.

Connell, R. (1995) *Masculinities*. Berkeley, CA: University of California Press.

Connell, R. (2007) *Southern Theory: The Global Dynamics of Knowledge in Social Science*. Sydney: Allen & Unwin.

Corboz, J. (2012) 'Commercial sport and culture change: lessons from respect and responsibility – A primary prevention of violence against women policy implemented in the Australian Football League'. Available at: www.inter-disciplinary.net/probing-the-boundaries/wp-content/uploads/2012/10/corbozsportpaper.pdf (accessed 12 March 2013).

Correa-Velez, I., Spaaij, R. and Upham, S. (2013) '"We are not here to claim better services than any other": Social exclusion among men from refugee backgrounds in urban and regional Australia', *Journal of Refugee Studies*, 26(2): 163–87.

Corrigan, P. (2004) 'How stigma interferes with mental health care', *American Psychologist*, 59(7): 614–25.

Cortis, N. (2009) 'Social inclusion and sport: Culturally diverse women's perspectives', *Australian Journal of Social Issues*, 44(1): 91–106.

Costa Ribeiro, C.A. (2003) *Estrutura de classe e mobilidade social no Brasil*. São Paulo: EDUSC-ANPOCS.

Costanzi, R.N. (2009) *Trabalho decente e juventude no Brasil*. Brasília: OIT.

Crabbe, T. (2008) 'Avoiding the numbers game: Social theory, policy and sport's role in the art of relationship building', in M. Nicholson and R. Hoye (eds) *Sport and Social Capital*. Oxford: Elsevier Butterworth-Heinemann, 21–37.

Crabbe, T. (2009) 'Getting to know you: Using sport to engage and build relationships with socially marginalised young people', in R. Levermore and A. Beacom (eds) *Sport and International Development*. Basingstoke: Palgrave Macmillan, 176–97.

Crabbe, T., Bailey, G., Blackshaw, T., Brown, A., Choak, C., Gidley, B., Mellor, G., O'Connor, K., Slater, I. and Woodhouse, D. (2006) *Knowing the Score: Positive Futures Case Study Research. Final Report*. London: Home Office.

Crawford, A. (2013) 'Adam Goodes "gutted" by racist slur but wants fan educated'. Available at: www.abc.net.au/news/2013-05-25/goodes-gutted-but-places-no-blame/4712772 (accessed 17 September 2013).

Crisp, R., Batty, E., Cole, I. and Robinson, D. (2009) *Work and Worklessness in Deprived Neighbourhoods*. York: Joseph Rowntree Foundation.

Culver, D. and Trudel, P. (2006) 'Cultivating coaches' community of practice: Developing the potential for learning through interactions', in R. Jones (ed.) *The Sports Coach as Educator: Re-conceptualising Sports Coaching*. London: Routledge, 97–112.

Cushion, C. (2006) 'Mentoring: Harnessing the power of experience', in R. Jones (ed.) *The Sports Coach as Educator: Re-conceptualising Sports Coaching*. London: Routledge, 128–44.

Dagkas, S. and Armour, K. (eds) (2012) *Inclusion and Exclusion Through Youth Sport*. London: Routledge.

Dagnino, E. (2005) '"We all have rights, but …": Contesting concepts of citizenship in Brazil', in N. Kabeer (ed.) *Inclusive Citizenship: Meanings and Expressions*. London: Zed Books, 149–63.

Daimon, A. (2010) 'The most beautiful game or the most gender violent sport? Exploring the interface between soccer, gender and violence in Zimbabwe', in J. Shehu (ed.) *Gender, Sport and Development in Africa: Cross-cultural Perspectives on Patterns of Representations and Marginalization.* Dakar: CODESRIA, 1–12.

Darnell, S. (2007) 'Playing with race: Right to Play and the production of whiteness in "development through sport"', *Sport in Society*, 10(4): 560–80.

Darnell, S. (2010) 'Power, politics and "Sport for Development and Peace": Investigating the utility of sport for international development', *Sociology of Sport Journal*, 27(1): 54–75.

Darnell, S. (2012) *Sport for Development and Peace: A Critical Sociology.* London: Bloomsbury Academic.

Darnell, S. and Hayhurst, L. (2012) 'Hegemony, postcolonialism and sport-for-development: A response to Lindsey and Grattan', *International Journal of Sport Policy and Politics*, 4(1): 111–24.

Dashper, K. and Fletcher, T. (2013) 'Introduction: Diversity, equity and inclusion in sport and leisure', *Sport in Society*, 16(10): 1227–32. Published online first, 15 August 2013: DOI:10.1080/17430437.2013.821259.

Davidson, L. and Roe, D. (2007) 'Recovery from versus recovery in serious mental illness: One strategy for lessening confusion plaguing recovery', *Journal of Mental Health*, 16(4): 459–70.

De Haan, A. (1998) '"Social exclusion": An alternative concept for the study of deprivation?', *IDS Bulletin*, 29(1): 10–19.

De Haan, A. and Maxwell, S. (1998) 'Poverty and social exclusion in North and South', *IDS Bulletin*, 29(1): 1–9.

De Haan, J. (2010) 'Transities in de levensloop als context voor sport', in A. Tiessen-Raaphorst, D. Verbeek, J. de Haan and K. Breedveld (eds) *Sport: een leven lang. Rapportage Sport 2010.* The Hague/'s-Hertogenbosch: Social and Cultural Planning Office/WJH Mulier Institute, 28–44.

Department for Culture, Media and Sport (DMCS) (1999) *Arts and Sports: A Report to the Social Exclusion Unit.* London: DCMS.

Department for Culture, Media and Sport (DCMS) (2000) *Creating Opportunities.* London: DCMS.

Department for Culture, Media and Sport (DCMS) (2008) *Playing to Win: A New Era for Sport.* London: DCMS.

Department for Culture, Media and Sport (DCMS) and Strategy Unit (2002) *Game Plan: A Strategy for Delivering Government's Sport and Physical Activity Objectives.* London: DCMS/Strategy Unit.

Department of Health (DH) and Department of Children, Schools and Families (DCSF) (2008) *Healthy Health? Choosing Activity: A Consultation on How to Increase Physical Activity.* London: Department of Health.

DePauw, K. (2009) 'Disability sport: A historical context', in H. Fitzgerald (ed.) *Disability and Youth Sport.* London: Routledge, 11–23.

DePauw, K. and Gavron, S. (2005) *Disability Sport.* Champaign, IL: Human Kinetics.

Devine, M. and Parr, M. (2008) '"Come on in, but not too far": Social capital in an inclusive leisure setting', *Leisure Sciences*, 30(5): 391–408.

Doherty, A. and Taylor, T. (2007) 'Sport and physical recreation in the settlement of immigrant youth'. *Leisure/Loisir*, 31(1): 27–55.

Doidge, M (2013) '"If you jump up and down, Balotelli dies": Racism and player abuse in Italian football', *International Review for the Sociology of Sport.* Published online first, 27 March 2013: DOI:10.1177/1012690213480354.

Donnelly, P. and Coakley, J. (2002) *The Role of Recreation in Promoting Social Inclusion.* Toronto: Laidlaw Foundation.

Dorsey, J. (2013) 'Saudi Arabia mulls granting women access to stadia'. Available at: http://mideastsoccer.blogspot.com.au/search/label/Women (accessed 8 September 2013).

Drury, S. (2011) '"It seems really inclusive in some ways, but … inclusive just for people who identify as lesbian": Discourses of gender and sexuality in a lesbian-identified football club', *Soccer and Society*, 12(3): 421–42.

Du Toit, A. (2004) '"Social exclusion" discourse and chronic poverty: A South African case study', *Development and Change*, 35(5): 987–1010.

Durkheim, E. (1895) *The Rules of Sociological Method.* New York: Free Press.

Eaton, G. (2011) 'Cameron searches for the "root cause" of the riots', *New Statesman*, 10 August.

Eitzen, D.S. (2006) *Fair and Foul: Beyond the Myths and Paradoxes of Sport*, 3rd edn. Lanham, MD: Rowman and Littlefield.

Eitzen, D.S. (ed.) (2011) *Sport in Contemporary Society*, 9th edn. Oxford: Oxford University Press.

Elling, A. (2002) *"Ze zijn er [niet] voor gebouwd": In- en uitsluiting in de sport naar sekse en etniciteit.* Nieuwegein: Arko Sports Media.

Elling, A. (2007) *Het voordeel van thuis spelen: Sociale betekenissen en in- en uitsluitings-mechanismen in sportloopbanen.* Nieuwegein: Arko Sports Media.

Elling, A. and Claringbould, I. (2005) 'Mechanisms of inclusion and exclusion in the Dutch sports landscape: Who can and wants to belong?', *Sociology of Sport Journal*, 22: 498–515.

Elling, A. and Knoppers, A. (2005) 'Sport, gender and ethnicity: Practices of symbolic inclusion/exclusion', *Journal of Youth and Adolescence*, 34(3): 257–68.

Elling, A, De Knop, P. and Knoppers, A. (2003) 'Gay/lesbian sport clubs and events: Places of homo-social bonding and cultural resistance?', *International Review for the Sociology of Sport*, 38(4): 441–56.

English, L.M. (2005) 'Third-space practitioners: Women educating for justice in the Global South', *Adult Education Quarterly*, 55(2): 85–100.

Enoch, N. (2010) 'Towards a contemporary national structure for youth sport in England', in M. Collins (ed.) *Examining Sports Development.* London: Routledge, 45–71.

ERASS (2010) *Participation in Exercise, Recreation and Sport Report.* Canberra: Australian Sports Commission.

Estivill, J. (2003) *Concepts and Strategies for Combating Social Exclusion: An Overview.* Geneva: ILO.

Esu-Williams, E., Schenk, K., Geibel, S., Motsepe, J., Zulu, A., Bweupe, P. and Weiss, E. (2006) '"We are no longer called club members but caregivers": Involving youth in HIV and AIDS caregiving in rural Zambia', *AIDS Care: Psychological and Socio-Medical Aspects of AIDS/ HIV*, 18(8): 888–94.

European Commission (2007) *White Paper on Sport.* Brussels: European Commission.

European Commission (2010) *Youth on the Move.* Brussels: European Commission.

European Commission (2012) *Europe 2020 Targets: Poverty and Social Exclusion Active Inclusion Strategies.* Available at: http://ec.europa.eu/europe2020/pdf/themes/25_poverty_and_social_inclusion.pdf (accessed 25 April 2013).

European Foundation for the Improvement of Living and Working Conditions (1995) *Public Welfare Services and Social Exclusion: The Development of Consumer Oriented Initiatives in the European Union.* Dublin: The Foundation.

Eurostat (2013) *Unemployment Statistics*. Available at: http://epp.eurostat.ec.europa.eu/statistics_explained/index.php/Unemployment_statistics (accessed 20 July 2013).

Evans, J. and Penney, D. (2008) 'Levels on the playing field: The social construction of physical "ability" in the physical education curriculum', *Physical Education and Sport Pedagogy*, 13(1): 31–47.

Fan, H. and Lu, Z. (2011) 'China', in M. Nicholson, R. Hoye and B. Houlihan (eds) *Participation in Sport: International Policy Perspectives*. London: Routledge, 160–82.

Fan, H. and Lu, Z. (2012) 'Representing the New China and the Sovietisation of Chinese sport (1949–1962)', *International Journal of the History of Sport*, 29(1): 21–9.

Faulkner, G. and Sparkes, A. (1999) 'Exercise as therapy for schizophrenia: An ethnographic study', *Journal of Sport & Exercise Psychology*, 21(1): 52–69.

Fitzgerald, H. (2005) 'Still feeling like a spare piece of luggage? Embodied experiences of (dis)ability in physical education and school sport', *Physical Education and Sport Pedagogy*, 10(1): 41–59.

Fletcher, T. and Spracklen, K. (2013) 'Cricket, drinking and exclusion of British Pakistani Muslims?', *Ethnic and Racial Studies*. Published online first, April 2013: DOI:10.1080/01419870.2013.790983.

Fogarty, M. and Happell, B. (2005) 'Exploring the benefits of an exercise program for people with schizophrenia: A qualitative study', *Issues in Mental Health Nursing*, 26: 341–51.

Football Task Force (1999) *Investing in the Community*. London: Football Task Force.

Fraser, N. (1997) *Justice Interruptus: Critical Reflections on the 'Post-Socialist' Condition*. London: Routledge.

Freire, P. (2005) *Teachers as Cultural Workers: Letters to Those Who Dare Teach*, expanded edn, trans. D. Macedo, D. Koike and A. Oliveira. Boulder, CO: Westview Press.

Frisby, W. and Millar, S. (2002) 'The actualities of doing community development to promote the inclusion of low-income populations in local sport and recreation', *European Sport Management Quarterly*, 3: 209–33.

Frisby, W., Reid, C. and Ponic, P. (2007) 'Levelling the playing field: Promoting the health of poor women through a community development approach to recreation', in K. Young and P. White (eds) *Sport and Gender in Canada*. Don Mills, ON: Oxford University Press, 121–36.

Fu, Z. and Dong, X. (2008) 'Problems of sports poverty' (体育贫困问题初探), *Sports Culture Guide*, 3: 73–4.

Gacitúa Marió, E. and Woolcock, M. (eds) (2008) *Social Exclusion and Mobility in Brazil*. Washington, DC: World Bank.

Galabuzi, G.-E. (2004) 'Social exclusion', in D. Raphael (ed.) *Social Determinants of Health: Canadian Perspectives*. Toronto: Canadian Scholars' Press, 235–51.

Galabuzi, G.-E. (2006) *Canada's Economic Apartheid: The Social Exclusion of Racialized Groups in the New Century*. Toronto: Canadian Scholars' Press.

Gallie, D. and Paugam, S. (eds) (2000) *Welfare Regimes and the Experience of Unemployment in Europe*. Oxford: Oxford University Press.

Gascoigne, P. (2005) *Gazza: My Story*. London: Headline.

Gasparini, W. and Vieille-Marchiset, G. (2008) *Le sport dans les quartiers*. Paris: Presses Universitaires de France.

General Administration of Sport (2011) *Outlines of the Olympic Strategy, 2011–2020* (2011–2020 年奥运争光计划纲要). Beijing: General Administration of Sport.

General Administration of Sport, National Development and Reform Commission, and Ministry of Finance (2007) *Policies on the Promotion of Sports among People in*

Rural Areas ("十一五"农民体育健身工程建设规划). Beijing: General Administration of Sport.

Giddens, A. (1998) *The Third Way: The Renewal of Social Democracy*. Cambridge: Polity.

Giulianotti, R. (2011) 'Sport, peacemaking and conflict resolution: A contextual analysis and modelling of the sport, development and peace sector', *Ethnic and Racial Studies*, 34(2): 207–28.

Glyptis, S. (1989) *Leisure and Unemployment*. Milton Keynes: Open University Press.

Goffman, E. (1963) *Stigma*. Englewood Cliffs, NJ: Prentice Hall.

Goodin, R.E. (1996) 'Inclusion and exclusion', *Archives of European Sociology*, 2: 343–71.

Gordon, D., Adelman, L., Ashworth, K., Bradshaw, J., Levitas, R., Middleton, S., Pantazis, C., Patsios, D., Payne, S., Townsend, P. and Williams, J. (2000) *Poverty and Social Exclusion in Britain*. York: Joseph Rowntree Foundation.

Gore, C. and Figueiredo, J.B. (eds) (1997) *Social Exclusion and Anti-Poverty Policy: A Debate*. Geneva: International Institute for Labour Studies.

Gough, J., Eisenschitz, A. and McCulloch, A. (2006) *Spaces of Social Exclusion*. London: Routledge.

Gough, K. (2008) '"Moving around": The social and spatial mobility of youth in Lusaka', *Geografiska: Series B, Human Geography*, 90(3): 243–55.

Gray, J. (2000) 'Inclusion: A radical critique', in P. Askonas and A. Stewart (eds) *Social Inclusion: Possibilities and Tensions*. Basingstoke: Palgrave Macmillan, 19–36.

Green, B. (2008) 'Sport as an agent for social and personal change', in V. Girginov (ed.) *Management of Sports Development*. Oxford: Butterworth-Heinemann, 130–45.

Green, M. (2004) 'Power, policy, and political priorities: Elite sport development in Canada and the United Kingdom', *Sociology of Sport Journal*, 21(4): 376–96.

Greendorfer, S. (1993) 'Gender role stereotypes and early childhood socialisation', *Psychology of Women Quarterly*, 18: 85–104.

Guest, A. (2009) 'The diffusion of development-through-sport: Analysing the history and practice of the Olympic Movement's grassroots outreach to Africa', *Sport in Society*, 12(10): 1336–52.

Guillén, M.F. (2001) 'Is globalization civilizing, destructive or feeble? A critique of five key debates in the social science literature', *Annual Review of Sociology*, 27: 235–60.

Hallinan, C. and Judd, B. (2009a) 'Change in the assumptions about Indigenous Australian footballers', *International Journal of the History of Sport*, 26(16): 2358–76.

Hallinan, C. and Judd, B. (2009b) 'Race relations, indigenous Australia and the social impact of professional Australian football', *Sport in Society*, 12(9):1220–36.

Hallman, K. (2005) 'Gendered socioeconomic conditions and HIV risk behaviours among young people in South Africa', *African Journal of AIDS Research*, 4(1): 37–50.

Hanlon, C. and. Coleman, D. (2006) 'Recruitment and retention of culturally diverse people by sport and active recreation clubs', *Managing Leisure*, 11(1): 77–95.

Hansen, K. (1997) *Keeping House in Lusaka*. New York: Columbia University Press.

Hansen, K. (2005) 'Getting stuck in the compound: Some odds against social adulthood in Lusaka, Zambia', *Africa Today*, 51(4): 2–16.

Hao, X. (2010) 'The evolution of the sports policy for disabled people in China' (中国大陆残疾人体育政策研究之变迁:从权利保障到权利救济), *Chinese Journal of Special Education*, 9: 38–42.

Hargreaves, J. (1994) *Sporting Females: Critical Issues in the History and Sociology of Women's Sports*. London: Routledge.

Hartmann, D. (2001) 'Notes on midnight basketball and the cultural politics of recreation, race and at-risk urban youth', *Journal of Sport and Social Issues*, 25: 339–71.

Hasenbalg, C. and Silva N.V. (eds) (2003) *Origens e destinos: Desigualdades sociais ao longo da vida.* Rio de Janeiro: Topbooks.

Hashem, M. (1995) 'Patterns and processes of social exclusion in the Republic of Yemen', in G. Rodgers, C. Gore and J. Figueiredo (eds) *Social Exclusion: Rhetoric, Reality, Responses.* Geneva: International Institute for Labour Studies, 175–84.

Hayes, A., Gray, M. and Edwards, B. (2008) 'Social inclusion: Origins, concepts and key themes', paper prepared by the Australian Institute of Family Studies for the Social Inclusion Unit, Department of the Prime Minister and Cabinet. Canberra: Commonwealth of Australia.

Haywood, L., Kew, F., Bramham, P., Spink, J., Capenerhurst, J. and Henry, I. (1990) *Understanding Leisure.* Cheltenham: Stanley Thomas.

Henderson, P. and Salmon, H. (2001) *Social Exclusion and Community Development.* London: Community Development Foundation.

Herd, R. (2010) 'A pause in the growth of inequality in China?', OECD Economics Department Working Paper No. 748. Paris: OECD.

Hickey, C. (2008) 'Physical education, sport and hyper-masculinity in schools', *Sport Education and Society,* 13(2): 147–61.

Hickey, S. and Du Toit, A. (2007) 'Adverse incorporation, social exclusion and chronic poverty', CPRC Working Paper 81. Manchester: Chronic Poverty Research Centre.

Hill, M. (2003) *Understanding Social Policy.* Oxford: Blackwell.

Hills, J., Le Grand, J. and Piachaud, D. (eds) (2002) *Understanding Social Exclusion.* Oxford: Oxford University Press.

Hills, L. (2006) 'Playing the field(s): An exploration of change, conformity and conflict in girls' understandings of gendered physicality in physical education', *Gender and Education,* 18(5): 539–56.

Hoeber, L. (2007) 'Exploring the gaps between meaning and practice of gender equity in a sport organisation', *Gender, Work and Organisation,* 14(3): 260–80.

Holt, R. (1989) *Sport and the British: A Modern History.* Oxford: Oxford University Press.

Houlihan, B. (2011) 'England', in M. Nicholson, R. Hoye and B. Houlihan (eds) *Participation in Sport: International Policy Perspectives.* London: Routledge: 10–24.

Houlihan, B. and White, A. (2002) *The Politics of Sports Development: Development of Sport or Development through Sport?* Oxford: Butterworth-Heinemann.

Howe, D. (2003) 'Kicking stereotypes into touch: An ethnographic account of women's rugby', in A. Bolin and J. Granskog (eds) *Athletic Intruders: Ethnographic Research on Women, Culture and Exercise.* Albany, NJ: State University of New York Press, 227–46.

Hunter, B. (2008) 'Indigenous social exclusion: Insights and challenges for the concept of social inclusion', presented at the Social Inclusion Down Under Symposium, 26 June. Melbourne: Brotherhood of St Laurence.

Hutchins, B. (2007) 'The problem of sport and social cohesion', in J. Jupp and J. Nieuwenhuysen (eds) *Social Cohesion in Australia.* Melbourne: Cambridge University Press, 170–81.

Hylton, K. (2010) 'How a turn to critical race theory can contribute to our understanding of "race", racism and anti-racism in sport', *International Review for the Sociology of Sport,* 45(3): 335–54.

Hylton, K. and Totten, M. (2013) 'Developing "sport for all"', in K. Hylton (ed.) *Sport Development: Policy, Process and Practice,* 3rd edn. London: Routledge, 37–77.

Information Office of the State Council (2011a) *New Progress in Development-oriented Poverty Reduction Program for Rural China.* Beijing: State Council.

Information Office of the State Council (2011b) *Assessment Report on the National Human Rights Action Plan of China (2009–2010)*. Beijing: State Council.

Jahoda, M., Lazarsfeld, P.F. and Zeisel, H. (1971) *Marienthal: The Sociography of an Unemployed Community*. Chicago, IL: Aldine.

Jeanes, R. (2010) 'The role of leadership in sports programmes aimed at addressing social exclusion', presented at the Leisure Studies Association Annual Conference, July, Leeds, UK.

Jeanes, R. (2011a) 'Family leisure experiences in families with children with disabilities', in R. Jeanes and J. Magee (eds) *Children, Youth and Leisure*. Brighton: Leisure Studies Association, 123–42.

Jeanes, R. (2011b) '"I like high heels and make up but I'm still into football": Negotiating gender and football, the experiences of pre-adolescent girls', *Soccer and Society*, 12(3): 401–19.

Jeanes, R. (2013) 'Educating through sport? Examining HIV/AIDS education and sport-for-development through the perspectives of Zambian young people', *Sport, Education and Society*, 18(3): 388–406.

Jeanes, R. and Geddes, N. (2010) *Evaluation of the Street Chance Initiative*. Loughborough: Institute of Youth Sport, Loughborough University.

Jeanes, R. and Kay, T. (2007) 'Can football be a female game? An examination of girls perceptions of football and gender identity', in J. Magee, J. Caudwell, K. Liston and S. Scraton (eds) *Women and Football in Europe: Histories, Equity and Experience*. Oxford: Meyer & Meyer, 105–31.

Jeanes, R. and Magee, J. (eds) (2011a) *Children, Youth and Leisure*. Brighton: Leisure Studies Association.

Jeanes, R. and Magee, J. (2011b) 'Social exclusion and access to leisure in Northern Ireland communities: Examining the experiences of parents with disabled children', *Loisir et Société/Society and Leisure*, 33(2): 221–50.

Jeanes, R. and Magee, J. (2012) 'Can we play on the swings and roundabouts? Creating inclusive play spaces for disabled young people and their families', *Leisure Studies*, 31(2): 193–210.

Jeanes, R. and Nevill, M. (2010) *Evaluation of the New Opportunities in Sport Initiative, Northern Ireland Final Report*. Loughborough: Institute of Youth Sport, Loughborough University.

Jeanes, R., Magee, J., Kay, T. and Banda, D. (2013) 'Sport for development in Zambia: The new or not so new colonisation?', in C. Hallinan and B. Judd (eds) *Native Games, Indigenous Peoples and Sport in the Post-Colonial World*. Bingley: Emerald, 127–46.

Jeanes, R., Musson, H. and Kay, T. (2009) *Chance to Shine Evaluation, Year 2 Report*. Loughborough: Institute of Youth Sport, Loughborough University.

Jeanes, R., Magee, J., Spaaij, R., Farquharson, K., Lusher, D. and Gorman, S. (2012) 'Junior sports clubs and disabled young people', paper presented at the ANZALS Equity and Diversity Symposium, November, University of Technology, Sydney, Australia.

Jones, R. (2000) 'Toward a sociology of coaching', in R. Jones and K. Armour (eds) *The Sociology of Sport: Theory and Practice*. London: Addision Wesley Longman, 33–43.

Jones, R. (2009) 'Coaching as caring (the smiling gallery): Accessing hidden knowledge', *Physical Education and Sport Pedagogy*, 14(4): 377–90.

Jones, R., Armour, K. and Potrac, P. (2004) *Sports Coaching Cultures: From Practice to Theory*. London: Routledge.

Jordan, B. (1996) *A Theory of Poverty and Social Exclusion*. Cambridge: Polity.

Jowett, S. (2007) 'Interdependence analysis and the 3 + 1 C's in the coach-athlete relationship', in D. Jowett and D. Lavallee (eds) *Social Psychology in Sport*. Champaign, IL: Human Kinetics: 15–28.

Kabeer, N. (2000) 'Social exclusion, poverty and discrimination: Towards an analytical framework', *IDS Bulletin*, 31(4): 83–97.

Kalunde, W. (1997) 'HIV/AIDS and sexual behaviour amongst youth in Zambia: Health', *Transition Review*, Supplement 3 to volume 7: 91–5.

Kaufman, C. and Stavrou, S. (2004) '"Bus fare please": The economics of sex and gifts among young people in urban South Africa', *Culture, Health and Sexuality: An International Journal for Research Intervention and Care*, 6(5): 377–91.

Kay, T. (2000) 'Sporting excellence: A family affair?', *European Physical Education Review*, 6(2): 151–69.

Kay, T. (2006) 'Daughters of Islam: Family influences on Muslim young women's participation in sport', *International Review for the Sociology of Sport*, 41(3): 357–73.

Kay, T. (2009) 'Developing through sport: Evidencing sport impacts on young people', *Sport in Society*, 12(9): 1177–91.

Kay, T. (2010) 'The reported benefits of sport: Local voices from Brazil', *Leisure Studies Association Newsletter*, 85: 34–40.

Kay, T. (2012a) 'Accounting for legacy? Monitoring and evaluation in sport in development relationships', *Sport in Society*, 15(6): 888–904.

Kay, T. (2012b) 'Sport and youth inclusion in the "Majority World"', in S. Dagkas and K. Armour (eds) *Inclusion and Exclusion through Youth Sport*. London: Routledge, 218–32.

Kay, T. and Jeanes, R. (2010) *International Inspiration Zambia Evaluation*. Loughborough: Institute of Youth Sport, Loughborough University.

Kay, T. and Jeanes, R. (2011) *Go Sisters Evaluation Year 2 Report*. London: Brunel University.

Kay, T. and Spaaij, R. (2012) 'The mediating effects of family on sport in international development contexts', *International Review for the Sociology of Sport*, 47(1): 77–94.

Kearns, K. (1997) 'Social democratic perspectives', in M. Lavalette and A. Pratt (eds) *Social Policy: A Conceptual and Theoretical Introduction*. London: Sage, 11–30.

Keech, M. (2003) 'England and Wales', in J. Riordan and A. Kruger (eds) *European Cultures in Sport: Examining the Nations and Regions*, Bristol: Intellect, 5–21.

Keim, M. (2003) *Nation Building at Play: Sport as a Tool for Social Integration in Post-Apartheid South Africa*. Oxford: Meyer & Meyer Sport.

Kell, P. (2000) *Good Sports: Australian Sport and the Myth of the Fair Go*. Sydney: Pluto Press.

Kelly, L. (2011) 'Social inclusion through sports-based interventions?', *Critical Social Policy*, 31(1): 126–50.

Kelly, M. and Gamble, C. (2005) 'Exploring the concept of recovery in schizophrenia', *Journal of Psychiatric & Mental Health Nursing*, 12: 245–51.

Kemp, P. (2005) 'Young people and unemployment', in M. Barry (ed.) *Youth Policy and Social Inclusion*. London: Routledge, 139–59.

Kenny, S. (1999) *Developing Communities for the Future: Community Development in Australia*. Melbourne: Thomas Nelson ITP Publishing.

Kerr, H., Ashton, H. and Carless, R. (1959) *The Challenge of Leisure*. London: Conservative Political Centre.

Kidd, B. (2005) '"Another world is possible": Recapturing alternative Olympic histories, imagining different games', in K. Young and K. Wamsley (eds) *Global Olympics*. Oxford: Elsevier, 143–58.

Kidd, B. (2008) 'A new social movement: Sport for development and peace', *Sport in Society*, 11(4): 370–80.

Kidd, B. (2011) 'Cautions, questions and opportunities in sport for development and peace', *Third World Quarterly*, 32(3): 603–9.

Kim, H.S., Munson, M. and McKay, M. (2012) 'Engagement in mental health treatment among adolescents and young adults: A systematic review', *Child, Adolescent and Social Work Journal*, 29: 241–66.

Kingsbury, D. (2004) 'Community development', in D. Kingsbury, J. Remenyi, J. McKay and J. Hunt (eds) *Key Issues in Development*. Basingstoke: Palgrave Macmillan, 221–42.

Kirk, D. (2005) 'Physical education, youth sport and lifelong participation: The importance of early learning experiences', *European Physical Education Review*, 11(3): 239–55.

Knight, J. (2000) 'Trends in poverty, inequality and the achievement of international development targets in China', paper prepared for the DFID China Programme Retreat, 29 June.

Knoppers, A. and Anthonissen, A. (2008) 'Gendered managerial discourses in sport organizations: Multiplicity and complexity', *Sex Roles*, 58(1/2): 93–103.

Knoppers, A. and Elling, A. (2001) 'Organising masculinities and feminities: The gendered sporting bodies', in J. Steenbergen, P. De Knop and A. Elling (eds) *Values and Norms in Sport*. Maidenhead: Meyer & Meyer, 171–92.

Krane, V. and Romont, L. (1997) 'Female athletes' motives and experiences during the Gay Games', *Journal of Gay, Lesbian and Bisexual Identity*, 2(2): 123–38.

Labonte, R. (2004) 'Social inclusion/exclusion: Dancing the dialectic', *Health Promotion International*, 19(1): 115–21.

Labour Party (1959) *Living for Leisure*. London: Labour Party Publications.

Lafferty, Y. and McKay, J. (2004) 'Suffragettes in satin shorts: Gender and competitive boxing', *Qualitative Sociology*, 27(3): 249–76.

Lake, R. (2013) '"They treat me like scum": Social exclusion and established-outsider relations in a British tennis club', *International Review for the Sociology of Sport*, 48(1): 112–28.

LaVoi, N. and Dutove, J. (2012) 'Barriers and supports for female coaches: An ecological model', *Sports Coaching Review*, 1(1): 17–37.

Lawson, H. (2005) 'Empowering people, facilitating community development, and contributing to sustainable development: The social work of sport, exercise, and physical education programs', *Sport, Education and Society*, 10(1): 135–60.

Le Clair, J. (2011) 'Global organisational change in sport and the shifting meaning of disability', *Sport in Society*, 14(9): 1072–93.

Le Grand, J. (2003) 'Individual choice and social exclusion', CASE Paper 75. London: Centre for Analysis of Social Exclusion, London School of Economics.

Ledwith, M. (2005) *Community Development: A Critical Approach*. Bristol: Policy Press.

Ledwith, M. (2011) *Community Development: A Critical Approach*, 2nd edn. Bristol: Policy Press.

Lemert, E.M. (1967) *Human Deviance, Social Problems and Social Control*. Englewood Cliffs, NJ: Prentice Hall.

Lenoir, R. (1974) *Les exclus: un Français sur dix*. Paris: Éditions du Seuil.

Levermore, R. (2008a) 'Sport: A new engine of development', *Progress in Development Studies*, 8(2): 183–90.

Levermore, R. (2008b) 'Sport in international development: Time to treat it seriously?', *Brown Journal of International Affairs*, 14(2): 55–66.

Levermore, A. and Beacom, A. (eds) (2009) *Sport and International Development.* Basingstoke: Palgrave Macmillan.

Levitas, R. (2005) *The Inclusive Society? Social Exclusion and New Labour,* 2nd edn. Basingstoke: Palgrave Macmillan.

Levitas, R., Pantazis, C., Fahmy, E., Gordon, D., Lloyd, E. and Patsios, D. (2007) *The Multi-Dimensional Analysis of Social Exclusion.* Bristol: University of Bristol.

Li, B. (2004) 'Urban social exclusion in transitional China', CASE Paper 82. London: Centre for Analysis of Social Exclusion, London School of Economics.

Li, B. (2005) 'Urban social change in transitional China: A perspective of social exclusion and vulnerability', *Journal of Contingencies and Crisis Management,* 13(2): 54–65.

Li, B. and Piachaud, D. (2004) 'Poverty and inequality and social policy in China', CASE Paper 87. London: Centre for Analysis of Social Exclusion, London School of Economics.

Liberman, R.P. and Kopelowicz, A. (2005) 'Recovery from schizophrenia: A criterion-based definition', in R.O. Ralph and P. Corrigan (eds) *Recovery in Mental Illness: Broadening our Understanding of Wellness.* Washington, DC: American Psychological Association, 101–29.

Light, R. and Wedgwood, N. (2012) 'Revisiting sport and the maintenance of masculine hegemony', *Asia-Pacific Journal of Health, Sport and Physical Education,* 3(3): 181–83.

Lindsey, I. and Banda, D. (2011) 'Sport and the fight against HIV/AIDS in Zambia: A "partnership" approach?', *International Review of the Sociology of Sport,* 46(1): 90–107.

Lindsey, I. and Gratton, A. (2012) 'An "international movement"? Decentring sport-for-development within Zambian communities', *International Journal of Sport Policy and Politics,* 4(1): 91–110.

Link, B. and Phelan, J. (2001) 'Conceptualizing stigma', *Annual Review of Sociology,* 27: 363–85.

Lister, R. (1998) 'From equality to social inclusion: New Labour and the welfare state', *Critical Social Policy,* 18: 215–25.

Liwena, R. (2006) *The Zambian Soccer Scene.* Lusaka: Liwena Publishing and Printing House.

Long, J. (2002) *Count Me In: The Dimensions of Social Inclusion through Culture and Sport.* London: DCMS.

Long, J. and Sanderson, I. (2001) 'The social benefits of sport: Where's the proof?', in C. Gratton and I. Henry (eds) *Sport in the City: The Role of Sport in Economic and Social Regeneration.* London: Routledge, 187–203.

Long, J. and Spracklen, K. (eds) (2010) *Sport and the Challenges to Racism.* Basingstoke: Palgrave Macmillan.

Long, J., Robinson, P. and Spracklen, K. (2005) 'Promoting racial equality in sports organisations', *Journal of Sport and Social Issues,* 29(1): 41–59.

Lu, W. and Henry, I. (2011) 'Historical review of sports policy in rural China (1949–2008)', *International Journal for the History of Sport,* 28(7): 1055–71.

Lu, Y. (2011) 'Chinese National Games for Disabled sparks hopes for London Paralympics', Xinhua News Agency, 20 October. Available at: http://news.xinhua-net.com/english2010/china/2011-10/20/c_131202017.htm (accessed 10 May 2013).

Lumby, C., Caple, H. and Greenwood, K. (2010) *Towards a Level Playing Field: Sport and Gender in Australian Media.* Canberra: Australian Sports Commission.

Luta Pela Paz (2012) *Manual de Metodologia do Programa.* Available at: www.lutapelapaz.net (accessed 12 October 2012).

Lyle, J. (2002) *Sports Coaching: A Framework for Coaches' Behaviour*. London: Routledge.

Macdonald, D. (2002) 'Critical pedagogy: What might it look like and why does it matter', in A. Laker (ed.) *Sociology of Sport and Physical Education: An Introductory Reader*. New York: Routledge Falmer, 167–89.

Macdonald, D., Pang, B., Knez, K., Nelson, A. and McCuaig, L. (2012) 'The will for inclusion: Bothering the inclusion/exclusion discourses of sport', in S. Dagkas and K. Armour (eds) *Inclusion and Exclusion Through Youth Sport*. London: Routledge, 9–23.

MacDonald, R. (2011) 'Youth transitions, unemployment and underemployment: Plus ça change, plus c'est la même chose?', *Journal of Sociology*, 47(4): 427–44.

Machado da Silva, L.A. (2006) 'Favela, crime violento e política no Rio de Janeiro', in F. Lopes de Carvalho (ed.) *Observatório da Cidadania n°10 – Arquitetura da exclusão*. Rio de Janeiro: IteM/Ibase, 76–81.

Madanipour, A. (1998) 'Social exclusion and space', in A. Madanipour, G. Cars and J. Allen (eds) *Social Exclusion in European Cities: Processes, Experiences and Responses*. London: Routledge, 75–94.

Magee, J. (2010) 'Developing people through sport: Personal and professional reflections on the Homeless World Cup', *Leisure Studies Association Newsletter*, 85: 50–5.

Magee, J. (2011) 'Disengagement, de-motivation, vulnerable groups and sporting inclusion: A case study of the Homeless World Cup', *Soccer and Society*, 12(2): 159–73.

Magee, J. and Jeanes, R. (2009) *Developing Women and Girls Football in Zambia: Challenges and Opportunities – A scoping report produced for the Football Association of Zambia*. Preston: University of Central Lancashire.

Magee, J. and Jeanes, R. (2010) *Stage 3 Evaluation of Community Projects*, Institute of Youth Sport and University of Central Lancashire Publication for the Football Foundation. Loughborough and Preston: Institute of Youth Sport and University of Central Lancashire.

Magee, J. and Jeanes, R. (2013) '"Football's coming home": A critical evaluation of the Homeless World Cup as an intervention to combat social exclusion', *International Review for the Sociology of Sport*, 48(1): 3–19.

Magnani, R., Mehryar Karim, A., Weiss, L., Bond, K., Lemba, M. and Morgan, G. (2002) 'Reproductive health risk and protective factors among youth in Lusaka, Zambia', *Journal of Adolescent Medicine*, 30: 76–86.

Maguire, J. (2005) *Power and Global Sport: Zones of Prestige, Emulation and Resistance*. London: Routledge.

Marjoribanks, T. and Farquharson, K. (2012) *Sport and Society in the Global Age*. Basingstoke: Palgrave Macmillan.

Markula, P. (2004) 'Tuning into one's self': Foucault's technologies of the self and mindful fitness', *Sociology of Sport Journal*, 21(3): 302–21.

Marsh, A. (2004) 'Housing and the social exclusion agenda in England', *Australian Journal of Social Issues*, 39(1): 7–23.

Mason, C. and Geddes, N. (2010) *Evaluation of the Prince's Trust Football-Linked Team and Get Started Programmes*. Loughborough: Institute of Youth Sport.

Massao, P. and Fasting, K. (2010) 'Race and racism: The experiences of black Norwegian athletes', *International Review for the Sociology of Sport*, 45(2): 147–62.

Mathieson, J., Popay, J., Enoch, E., Escorel, S., Hernandez, M., Johnston, H. and Rispel, L. (2008) *Social Exclusion: Meaning, Measurement and Experience and Links to Health Inequalities: A Review of Literature*. Geneva: WHO Social Exclusion Knowledge Network.

Maxwell, H. and Taylor, T. (2010) 'A culture of trust: Engaging Muslim women in community sport organisations', *European Sport Management Quarterly*, 10(4): 465–83.

May, T., Harris, S. and Collins, M. (2012) 'Implementing community sport policy: Understanding the variety of voluntary club types and their attitudes towards policy', *International Journal of Sport Policy and Politics*, 5(3): 397–419.

Maynard, J. (2011) *The Aboriginal Soccer Tribe: A History of Aboriginal Involvement with the World Game*. Broome: Magabala Books.

McGuire, B., Monks, K. and Halsall, R. (2001) 'Young Asian males: Social exclusion and social injustice in British professional football?', *Culture, Sport, Society*, 4(3): 65–80.

McIlwaine, C. and Moser, C.O.N. (2001) 'Violence and social capital in urban poor communities: Perspectives from Colombia and Guatemala', *Journal of International Development*, 13: 965–84.

Mean, L. and Kassing, J. (2008) '"I would just like to be known as an athlete": Managing hegemony, femininity, and heterosexuality in female sport', *Western Journal of Communication*, 72(2): 126–44.

Meekers, D. and Calves, A. (1997) '"Main" girlfriends, girlfriends, marriage, and money: The social context of HIV/AIDS risk behaviour in sub-Saharan Africa', *Health Transition Review*, 7 (supplement): 361–75.

Meier, M. and Saavedra, M. (2009) 'Esther Phiri and the Moutawakel effect in Zambia: An analysis of the use of female role models in sport-for-development', *Sport in Society*, 12(9): 1158–76.

Mennesson, C. (2009) 'Being a man in dance: Socialisation modes and gender identities', *Sport in Society*, 12(2): 174–95.

Merton, R.K. (1938) 'Social structure and anomie', *American Sociological Review*, 3: 672–82.

Messner, M.A. (2002) *Taking the Field: Women, Men, and Sports*. Minneapolis, MN: University of Minnesota Press.

Ministry of Social Affairs and Work [The Nertherlands] (2009) *Actieplan jeugdwerkloosheid*. The Hague: SZW.

Ministry of Sports [Brazil] (2010) *Brazil Insights Series: Sport*. Brasília: Ministry of Sports.

Ministry of Sports [Brazil] (2011) *Diretrises do Programa Segundo Tempo*. Brasília: Ministry of Sports.

Minujin, A. (1998) 'Vulnerabilidad y exclusión en América Latina', in E. Bustelo and A. Minujin (eds) *Todos entran: Propuesta para sociedades incluyentes*. Bogotá: UNICEF, 161–205.

Morgan, O. and Baker, A. (2006) 'Measuring deprivation in England and Wales using 2001 Carstairs scores', *Health Statistics Quarterly*, 31: 28–33.

Morgan, C., Burns, T., Fitzpatrick, R., Pinfold, V. and Priebe, P. (2007) 'Social exclusion and mental health: Conceptual and methodological review', *British Journal of Psychiatry*, 191: 477–83.

Mosley, P. and Dowler, E. (eds) (2003) *Poverty and Exclusion in North and South: Essays on Social Policy and Global Poverty Reduction*. London: Routledge.

Mother Jones (2012) 'Full transcript of the Mitt Romney secret video'. Available at: www.motherjones.com/politics/2012/09/full-transcript-mitt-romney-secret-video (accessed 19 September 2012).

Municipality of Rotterdam (2011) *'Ga gewoon door!' De Rotterdamse aanpak van de jeugdwerkloosheid 2011–2012*. Rotterdam: Municipality of Rotterdam.

Murray, C. (1982) 'The two wars against poverty', *The Public Interest*, 69 (Winter).

Murray, C. (1996) *Charles Murray and the Underclass: The Developing Debate*. London: IEA Health and Welfare Unit.

Mwaanga, O. and Mwansa, K. (2013) 'Indigenous discourses in sport for development and peace: A case study of the Ubuntu cultural philosophy in EduSport Foundation', in N. Schulenkorf and D. Adair (eds) *Global Sport-for-Development: Critical Perspectives.* Basingstoke: Palgrave Macmillan, 115–33.

Myrdal, G. (1944) *An American Dilemma: The Negro Problem and Modern Democracy.* New York: Harper & Row.

Nader, L. (1972) 'Up the anthropologist: Perspectives gained from studying up', in D. Hymes (ed.) *Reinventing Anthropology.* New York: Pantheon Books, 284–311.

Nelson, L., Cushion, C. and Potrac, P. (2013) 'Enhancing the provision of coach education: the recommendations of UK coaching practitioners', *Physical Education and Sport Pedagogy,* 18: 204–18.

Nelson, N. and Wright, S. (1995) 'Participation and power', in N. Nelson and S. Wright (eds) *Power and Participatory Development: Theory and Practice.* London: Intermediate Technology Publications, 1–18.

Nevile, A. (2007) 'Amartya K. Sen and social exclusion', *Development in Practice,* 17(2): 244–9.

Nfah Abbenyi, J (1997) *Gender in African Women's Writing: Identity, Sexuality, and Difference.* Bloomington, IN: Indiana University Press.

Noyoo, N. (2007) 'Corporate social responsibility and social policy in Zambia', paper presented at the Conference on Business, Social Policy and Corporate Political Influence in Developing Countries, November, Geneva, Switzerland.

Noyoo, N. (2008) *Social Policy and Human Development in Zambia.* Lusaka: UNZA Press.

NOWSPAR (2010) www.nowspar.org (accessed 15 December 2012).

Nshindano, C. and Maharaj, P. (2008) 'Reasons for multiple sexual partnerships: Perspectives of young people in Zambia', *African Journal of AIDS Research,* 7(1): 37–44.

Numerato, D. and Baglioni, S. (2011) 'The dark side of social capital: An ethnography of sport governance', *International Review of the Sociology of Sport,* 47(5): 594–611.

O'Brien, D., Wilkes, J., De Haan, A. and Maxwell, S. (1997) 'Poverty and social exclusion in North and South', IDS Working Paper 55. Brighton: Institute of Development Studies.

OECD (2012) *China in Focus: Lessons and Challenges.* Paris: OECD.

Ogbomo, O. (2005) 'Women, power and society in colonial Africa', *Lagos Historical Review,* 5: 49–74.

Olliff, L (2008) 'Playing for the future: The role of sport and recreation in supporting refugee young people to "settle well" in Australia', *Youth Studies Australia,* 27(1): 52–60.

Page, R. (2001) 'The exploration of social problems in the field of social policy', in M. May, R. Page and E. Brundson (eds) *Understanding Social Problems: Issues in Social Policy.* Oxford: Blackwell, 16–29.

Palmer, C. (2009) 'Soccer and the politics of identity for young Muslim refugee women in South Australia', *Soccer and Society,* 10(1): 27–38.

Palmer, C. (2011) 'Muslim women and sport', *Sport in Society,* 14(5): 726–8.

Palmer, C. (2013) *Global Sports Policy.* London: Sage.

Pantazis, C., Gordon, D. and Levitas, R. (eds) (2006) *Poverty and Social Exclusion in Britain: The Millennium Survey.* Bristol: Policy Press.

Parr, H., Philo, C. and Burns, N. (2004) 'Social geographies of rural mental health: Experiencing inclusions and exclusions', *Transactions of the Institute of British Geographers,* 29: 401–19.

Paugam, S. (1991) *La disqualification sociale.* Paris: Presses Universitaires de France.

Pease, B. (2009) 'The other side of social exclusion: Interrogating the role of the privileged in reproducing inequality', in A. Taket, B. Crisp, A. Nevill, G. Lamaro, M. Graham and S. Barter-Godfrey (eds) *Theorising Social Exclusion*. London: Routledge, 37–46.

Peck, J. and Theodore, N. (2000) '"Work first": Workfare and the regulation of contingent labour markets', *Cambridge Journal of Economics*, 24: 119–38.

Pelak, C. (2005) 'Negotiating gender/race/class constraints in the new South Africa: A case study of women's soccer', *International Review for the Sociology of Sport*, 40(1): 53–70.

Penedo, F. and Dahn, J. (2005) 'Exercise and well-being: A review of mental and physical health benefits associated with physical activity', *Current Opinion in Psychiatry*, 18(2): 189–93.

People's Republic of China (2008) *Law of the People's Republic of China on the Protection of Persons with Disabilities*. Beijing: People's Republic of China.

People's Republic of China (2012) 'Fifty-six ethnic groups'. Available at: http://english.gov.cn/2006-02/08/content_182626.htm (accessed 6 May 2013).

Percy-Smith, J. (2000) 'Introduction: The contours of social exclusion', in J. Percy-Smith (ed.) *Policy Responses to Social Exclusion*. Buckingham: Open University Press, 1–21.

Perlman, J. (2006) 'The metamorphosis of marginality: Four generations in the favelas of Rio de Janeiro', *The Annals of the American Academy of Political and Social Science*, 606: 154–77.

Perlman, J. (2010) *Favela: Four Decades of Living on the Edge in Rio de Janeiro*. Oxford: Oxford University Press.

Pfister, G. (2010) 'Women in sport: Gender relations and future perspective', *Sport in Society*, 13(2): 234–48.

Pfister, G., Lenneis, V. and Mintert, S. (2013) 'Female fans of men's football: A case study of Denmark', *Soccer and Society*. Published online first, 16 October 2013: DOI: 10.1080/14660970.2013.843923.

Phillips, R. and Pittman, R. (2009) 'A framework for community and economic development', in R. Phillips and R. Pittman (eds) *An Introduction to Community Development*. London: Routledge, 1–15.

Piggott, D. (2012) 'Coaches' experiences of formal coach education: A critical sociological investigation', *Sport, Education and Society*, 17(4): 535–44.

Pociello, C. (1995) *Les cultures sportives*. Paris: Presses Universitaires de France.

Polley, M. (1998) *Moving the Goalposts: A History of Sport and Society since 1945*. London: Routledge.

Pooley, J. (1976) 'Ethnic soccer clubs in Milwaukee: A study of assimilation', in M. Hart (ed.) *Sport in the Socio-Cultural Process*. Dubuque, IA: W.C. Brown, 475–92.

Popay, J., Escorel, S., Hernández, M., Johnston, J., Mathieson, J. and Rispel, L. (2008) *Understanding and Tackling Social Exclusion: Final Report to the WHO Commission on Social Determinants of Health from the Social Exclusion Knowledge Network*. Geneva: WHO Social Exclusion Knowledge Network.

Rao, Y., Zhang, Y. and Zu, H. (2007) 'Discussion on the characteristics of the National Minority Sports Policy in China' (论中国少数民族体育政策的特征与启), *Journal of China Sports Science*, 10: 56–60.

Ratna, A. (2011) '"Who wants to make aloo gobi when you can bend it like Beckham?" British Asian females and their racialised experiences of gender and identity in women's football', *Soccer and Society*, 12(3): 382–401.

Ravenhill, M. (2008) *The Culture of Homelessness*. Aldershot: Ashgate.

Ravenscroft, N. and Markwell, S. (2000) 'Ethnicity and the integration and exclusion of young people through urban park and recreation provision', *Managing Leisure*, 5(3): 135–50.

Refugee Council of Australia (2010) *A Bridge to a New Culture: Promoting the Participation of Refugees in Sporting Activities*. Sydney: RCOA.

Renold, E. (2002) 'Presumed innocence: (Hetero) sexual, heterosexist and homophobic harassment among primary school girls and boys', *Childhood*, 9(4): 415–34.

Repper, J. and Perkins, R. (2003) *Social Inclusion and Recovery: A Model for Mental Health Practice*. London: Baillière Tindall.

Republic of Zambia (2011) *Sixth National Development Plan 2011–2015: Sustained Economic Growth and Poverty Reduction*. Lusaka: Republic of Zambia Publications.

Resnick, S.G., Fontana, A., Lehman, A.F. and Rosenheck, R.A. (2005) 'An empirical conceptualization of the recovery orientation', *Schizophrenia Research*, 75, 119–28.

Rich, E. (2004) 'Exploring teachers' biographies and perceptions of girls' participation in physical education', *European Physical Education Review*, 10(2): 215–40.

Richardson, L. and Le Grand, J. (2002) 'Outsider and insider expertise: The response of residents of deprived neighbourhoods to an academic definition of social exclusion', *Social Policy and Administration*, 36(5): 496–515.

Rigg, J. (2007) *An Everyday Geography of the Global South*. London: Routledge.

Riots Communities and Victims Panel (2012) *5 Days in August: An Interim Report on the 2011 English Riots*. Available at: http://webarchive.nationalarchives.gov.uk/20121003195935/http://riotspanel.independent.gov.uk/wp-content/uploads/2012/04/Interim-report-5-Days-in-August.pdf (accessed 25 April 2013).

Roberts, G. and Wolfson, P. (2004) 'The rediscovery of recovery: Open to all', *Advances in Psychiatric Treatment*, 10: 37–49.

Roberts, K. (1983) *Youth and Leisure*. London: Allen and Unwin.

Roberts, K. (1992) 'Leisure responses to urban ills in Great Britain and Northern Ireland', in J. Sugden and C. Knox (eds) *Leisure in the 1990s: Rolling Back the Welfare State*. Eastbourne: Leisure Studies Association, 9–14.

Robertson, R. (1992) *Globalization*. London: Sage.

Rodgers, G. (1995) 'What is special about a "social exclusion" approach?', in G. Rodgers, C. Gore and J. Figueiredo (eds) *Social Exclusion: Rhetoric, Reality, Responses*. Geneva: International Institute for Labour Studies, 43–55.

Rookwood, J. and Palmer, C. (2011) 'Invasion games on war-torn nations: Can football help to build peace?', *Sport in Society*, 12: 184–200.

Room, G. (1999) 'Social exclusion, solidarity and the challenge of globalization', *International Journal of Social Welfare*, 8(3): 166–74.

Rowe, M. and Garland, J. (2012) 'Paying the price? Why football still has a problem', *Criminal Justice Matters*, 88(1): 30–1.

Russell, K. (2011) 'Compulsory heterosexuality and the construction of femininity and masculinity: Issues of performance versus presentation', in S. Georgakis and K. Russell (eds) *Youth Sport in Australia*. Sydney: Sydney University Press, 71–84.

Saavedra, M. (2009) 'Dilemmas and opportunities in gender and sport in development', in R. Levermore and A. Beacom (eds) *Sport and International Development*. Basingstoke: Palgrave Macmillan, 124–55.

Saith, R. (2007) 'Social exclusion: The concept and application to developing countries', in F. Stewart, R. Saith and B. Harriss-White (eds) *Defining Poverty in the Developing World*. Basingstoke: Palgrave Macmillan, 75–90.

Sandford, R., Armour, K. and Warmington, P. (2006) 'Re-engaging disaffected youth through physical activity programmes', *British Educational Research Journal*, 32: 251–71.

Sartorius, N. (2007) 'Mental health and stigma', *The Lancet*, 370(9590): 810–11.

Saunders, P. (2003) *Can Social Exclusion Provide a New Framework for Measuring Poverty?* Sydney: Social Policy Research Centre, University of New South Wales.

Saunders, P. (2008) 'Social exclusion: Challenges for research and implications for policy', *The Economic and Labour Relations Review*, 19(1): 73–92.

Sawrikar, P. and Muir, K. (2010) 'The myth of a "fair go": Barriers to sport and recreational participation among Indian and other ethnic minority women in Australia', *Sport Management Review*, 13(4): 355–67.

Schlyter, A. (1999) *Recycled Inequalities: Youth and Gender in George Compound, Zambia.* Motala: Nordiska Afrikainstitutet.

Schuftan, C. (1996) 'The community development dilemma: What is really empowering?', *Community Development Journal*, 31(3): 260–4.

Schulenkorf, N. (2010) 'The roles and responsibilities of a change agent in sport event development projects', *Sport Management Review*, 13(2): 118–28.

Schulenkorf, N. (2012) 'Sustainable community development through sport and events: A conceptual framework for sport-for-development projects', *Sport Management Review* 15(1): 1–12.

Schuyt, C.J.M. (2000) *Sociale uitsluiting.* Amsterdam: SWP.

Schuyt, C.J.M. (2006) *Steunberen van de samenleving: Sociologische essays.* Amsterdam: Amsterdam University Press.

Scottish Sports Council (1988) *Laying the Foundations: Report on School-Aged Sport in Scotland.* Edinburgh: Scottish Sports Council.

Scraton, S., Fasting, A., Pfister, G. and Bunuel A. (1999) 'It's still a man's game? The experience of top-level European women footballers', *International Review for the Sociology of Sport*, 34(2): 99–111.

Sen, A. (2000) *Social Exclusion: Concept, Application, and Scrutiny.* Manila: Asian Development Bank.

Settlement Council of Australia (2012) *Sport and Settlement.* SCOA Discussion Paper. Sydney: SCOA.

Shakib, S. (2003) 'Female basketball participation: Negotiating the conflation of peer status and gender status from childhood through to puberty', *American Behavioral Scientist*, 46(10): 1405–22.

Shan, J. (2011) 'Census: Population hits 1.37b', *China Daily*, 29 April.

Shaw, S. and Hoeber, L. (2003) '"A strong man is direct and a direct woman is a bitch": Gendered discourses and their influence on employment roles in sport organizations', *Journal of Sport Management*, 17(4): 347–75.

Shaw, S. and Slack, T. (2002) '"It's been like that for donkey's years": The construction of gender relations and the cultures of sports organisations', *Sport and Society*, 5(1): 86–106.

Shen, K., Zhou, X. and Tian, Y. (2009) 'Social exclusion and rural sports poverty', *Journal of Tianjin University of Sports*, 4: 282–92.

Shields, N., Synott, A. and Barr, M. (2012) 'Perceived barriers and facilitators to physical activity for children with a disability: A systematic review', *British Journal of Sports Medicine*, 46: 989–97.

Silver, H. (1994) 'Social exclusion and social solidarity: Three paradigms', *International Labour Review*, 133(5/6): 531–78.

Silver, H. (2007) 'Social exclusion', in G. Ritzer (ed.) *Blackwell Encyclopedia of Sociology.* Oxford: Blackwell Reference Online (accessed 27 January 2011).

Silver, H. (2010) 'Understanding social inclusion and its meaning for Australia', *Australian Journal of Social Issues,* 45(2): 183–211.

Silver, H. and Miller, S.M. (2003) 'Social exclusion: The European approach to social disadvantage', *Indicators,* 2(2): 5–21.

Simmel, G. (1955) *Conflict and the Web of Group Affiliations.* Glencoe, IL: Free Press.

Skinner, J., Zakus, D. and Cowell, J. (2008) 'Development through sport: Building social capital in disadvantaged communities', *Sport Management Review,* 11(3): 253–75.

Smyth, P. (2010) *In or Out? Building an Inclusive Nation.* Melbourne: Australian Collaboration.

Social Exclusion Unit (1998) *Bringing Britain Together.* London: Cabinet Office.

Social Exclusion Unit (2001) *Preventing Social Exclusion.* London: Cabinet Office.

Sotomayor, S. (2013) *Our Beloved World.* New York: Alfred A. Knopf.

Southby, K. (2011) 'Football fandom, social inclusion and learning disability: Opportunities and constraints', *World Leisure Journal,* 53(4): 322–31.

Souza, E.R. and Constantino, P. (2006) *Avaliação do Projeto Luta pela Paz – Maré – Rio de Janeiro.* Rio de Janeiro: Centro Latino Americano de Estudos de Violência e Saúde Jorge Careli.

Souza, M.L. (2008) *Fobópole: O medo generalizado e a militarização da questão urbana.* Rio de Janeiro: Bertrand Brasil.

Spaaij, R. (2009a) 'Sport as a vehicle for social mobility and regulation of disadvantaged urban youth', *International Review for the Sociology of Sport,* 44(2): 247–64.

Spaaij, R. (2009b) 'The social impact of sport: Diversities, complexities and contexts', *Sport in Society,* 12(9): 1101–9.

Spaaij, R. (2011) *Sport and Social Mobility: Crossing Boundaries.* London: Routledge.

Spaaij, R. (2012a) 'Building social and cultural capital among young people in disadvantaged communities: Lessons from a Brazilian sport-based intervention program', *Sport, Education and Society,* 17(1): 77–95.

Spaaij, R. (2012b) 'Beyond the playing field: Experiences of sport, social capital and integration among Somalis in Australia', *Ethnic and Racial Studies,* 35(9): 1519–38.

Spaaij, R. (2013a) 'Cultural diversity in community sport: An ethnographic inquiry of Somali Australians' experiences', *Sport Management Review,* 16(1): 29–40.

Spaaij, R. (2013b) 'Sport, social cohesion and community building: Managing the nexus', in P. Leisink, P. Boselie, M. van Bottenburg and D.M. Hosking (eds) *Managing Social Issues: A Public Values Perspective.* Brookfield and Cheltenham: Edward Elgar, 107–25.

Spaaij, R. (2013c) 'The ambiguities of sport and community engagement', *Ethos,* 21(2): 8–11.

Spaaij, R. (2013d) 'Changing people's lives for the better? Social mobility through sport-based intervention programmes: Opportunities and constraints', *European Journal for Sport and Society,* 10(1): 53–73.

Spaaij, R. (in press) 'Refugee youth, belonging and community sport,' *Leisure Studies.* Published online first, 5 March 2014: DOI:10.1080/02614367.2014.893006.

Spaaij, R. and Burleson, C. (2012) 'London 2012 and beyond: Reflections on peacemaking, sport and the Olympic movement', *Sport in Society,* 15(6): 905–13.

Spaaij, R. and Jeanes, R. (2013) 'Education for social change? A Freirean critique of sport for development and peace', *Physical Education and Sport Pedagogy,* 18(4): 442–57.

Spaaij, R., Farquharson, K., Magee, J., Jeanes, R., Lusher D. and Gorman S. (in press) '"A fair game for all?" How community sports clubs in Australia deal with diversity',

Journal of Sport and Social Issues. Published online first, 16 December 2013: DOI: 10.1177/0193723513515888.

Spaaij, R., Magee, J. and Jeanes, R. (2013) 'Urban youth, worklessness and sport: A comparison of sports-based employability programs in Rotterdam and Stoke-on-Trent', *Urban Studies,* 50(8): 1608–24.

Sport and Recreation South Africa (2005) *Participation Patterns in Sport and Recreation in South Africa.* Formeset Printers Cape: Pretoria.

Sport England (2012) *Active People Survey 6 Results.* Available at: http://archive.sportengland.org/research/active_people_survey/active_people_survey_6.aspx (accessed 16 August 2013).

Sport for Development and Peace International Working Group (2006) *Sport for Development and Peace: From Practice to Policy.* Toronto: SDP IWG.

Sport in Action (2010) www.sportinaction.org.zm/youngfarmersclub.html (accessed 18 August 2013).

Sports Development (2011) *Ruff Guide to Coalition Sport Policy.* Available at: www.sport-development.info/index.php?option=com_content&view=article&id=727:ruff-guide-coalition-sportpolicy&catid=54:introsv (accessed 6 February 2012).

State Council General Office of the People's Republic of China (2011) *The National Fitness for All Programme, 2011–2015* (全民健身计划 2011–2015年). Beijing: State Council General Office.

Statistics Norway (2011) *Sport and Outdoor Activities 2011 Survey.* Available at: www.ssb.no/en/kultur-og-fritid/statistikker/fritid/hvert-3-aar (accessed 16 August 2013).

Steinert, H. (2007a) 'Introduction: The cultures of welfare and exclusion', in H. Steinert and A. Pilgram (eds) *Welfare Policy from Below: Struggles against Social Exclusion in Europe.* Aldershot: Ashgate, 1–12.

Steinert, H. (2007b) 'Participation and social exclusion: A conceptual framework', in H. Steinert and A. Pilgram (eds) *Welfare Policy from Below: Struggles against Social Exclusion in Europe.* Aldershot: Ashgate, 45–59.

Stevenson, P. (2009) 'The pedagogy of inclusive youth sport: Working towards real solutions', in H. Fitzgerald (ed.) *Disability and Youth Sport.* London: Routledge, 119–31.

Stone, E. (2001) 'Disability, sport, and the body in China', *Sociology of Sport Journal,* 18(1): 51–68.

Sugden, J. and Bairner, A. (1986) 'Northern Ireland: Sport in a divided society', in L. Allison (ed.) *The Politics of Sport.* Manchester: Manchester University Press, 90–117.

Sugden, J. and Bairner, A. (1993) *Sport and Sectarianism in a Divided Ireland.* Leicester: Leicester University Press.

Sugden, J. and Tomlinson, A. (eds) (2002) *Power Games: A Critical Sociology of Sport.* London: Routledge.

Sugden, J. and Wallis, J. (eds) (2007) *Football for Peace? The Challenges of Using Sport for Co-Existence in Israel.* Oxford: Meyer & Meyer.

Symons, C. (2010) *The Gay Games: A History.* London: Routledge.

Symons, C., Sbaraglia, M., Hillier, L. and Mitchell, A. (2010) *Come out to Play: The Sports Experiences of Lesbian, Gay, Bisexual and Transgender (LGBT) People in Victoria.* Melbourne: Victoria University.

Tacon, R. (2007) 'Football and social inclusion: Evaluating social policy', *Managing Leisure,* 12(1): 1–23.

Taket, A., Crisp, B., Nevill, A., Lamaro, G., Graham M. and Barter-Godfrey S. (2009) *Theorising Social Exclusion.* London: Routledge.

Taylor, B. and Garratt, D. (2010) 'The professionalisation of sports coaching: Relations of power, resistance and compliance', *Sport, Education and Society*, 15: 121–39.

Taylor, C., Sallis, J. and Needle, R. (1985) 'The relation of physical activity and exercise to mental health', *Public Health Reports*, 100(2): 195–202.

Taylor, T. and Toohey, K. (2001) 'Behind the veil: Exploring the recreation needs of Muslim women', *Leisure*, 26(1/2): 85–105.

Taylor-Goodby, P. (2012) 'Opportunity and solidarity', *Journal of Social Policy*, 40(3): 453–70.

Thorpe, H. (2005) 'Jibbing the gender order: Females in the snowboarding culture', *Sport in Society*, 8(1): 76–100.

Tirone, S., Livingston, L., Miller, J. and Smith, E. (2010) 'Including immigrants in elite and community sports: The experiences of athletes, sport providers and immigrants', *Leisure/Loisir*, 34(4): 403–20.

Townsend, P. (1979) *Poverty in the UK: A Survey of Household Resources and Standards of Living*. London: Penguin.

Townsend, P. (1993) *The International Analysis of Poverty*. New York: Harvester Wheatsheaf.

Tucker, V. (1999) 'The myth of development: A critique of a Eurocentric discourse', in R. Munck and D. O'Hearn (eds) *Critical Development: Contributions to a New Paradigm*. London: Zed Books, 13–21.

UNICEF (2006) *Sport for Development in Latin America and the Caribbean*. Panama: UNICEF Regional Office for Latin America and the Caribbean.

UNICEF (2009) *O direito de aprender: Potencializar avanços e reduzir desigualdades*. Brasília: UNICEF.

UNICEF (2010) *Zambia Statistics*. Available at: www.unicef.org/infobycountry/zambia_statistics.html (accessed 30 March 2012).

United Nations (2008) *Achieving the Objectives of the United Nations through Sport*. Geneva: UN Office on Sport for Development and Peace.

United Nations Department of Economic and Social Affairs (UN DESA) (2010) *Analysing and Measuring Social Inclusion in a Global Context*. New York: UN.

United Nations General Assembly (2006) *Sport for Development and Peace: The Way Forward. Report of the Secretary-General* (A/61/373). New York: UNOSDP.

United Nations Office on Sport for Development and Peace (UNOSDP) (2005) *United Nations Sports Bulletin*. New York: UNOSDP.

United Nations Office on Sport for Development and Peace (UNOSDP) (2010) *Case Study: Brazil*. Geneva: UNOSDP.

Vail. S. (2007) Community development and sport participation', *Journal of Sport Management*, 21(4): 571–96.

Valencia Gutiérrez, A. (ed.) (2001) *Exclusión social y construcción de lo público en Colombia*. Bogotá: Centro de Estudios de la Realidad Colombiana, Universidad del Valle.

Valencia Agudelo, G.D. and Cuartas Celis, D. (2009) 'Exclusión económica y violencia en Colombia, 1990–2008: una revisión de la literatura', *Perfil de Coyuntura Económica*, 14: 113–34.

Van Bottenburg, M. (2011) 'The Netherlands', in M. Nicholson, R. Hoye and B. Houlihan (eds) *Participation in Sport: International Policy Perspectives*. London: Routledge, 25–41.

Van Ingen, C. (2003) 'Geographies of gender, sexuality and race: Reframing the focus on space in sport sociology', *International Review for the Sociology of Sport*, 38(2): 201–16.

Veit-Wilson, J. (1998) *Setting Adequacy Standards: How Governments Define Minimum Incomes*. Bristol: Policy Press.

Velho, G. (2008) 'Metrópole, cultura e conflito', in G. Velho (ed.) *Rio de Janeiro: cultura, política e conflito*. Rio de Janeiro: Zahar, 7–29.

Vobruba, G. (1999) 'The end of the full employment society: Changing the basis of inclusion and exclusion', in P. Littlewood (ed.) *Social Exclusion in Europe*. Aldershot: Ashgate, 23–46.

Vobruba, G. (2000) 'Actors in processes of inclusion and exclusion: Towards a dynamic approach', *Social Policy & Administration*, 34(5): 601–13.

Waitt, G. (2003) 'Gay Games: Performing "community" out from the closet of the locker room', *Social and Cultural Geography*, 4(2): 167–84.

Walker, A. and Walker, C. (eds) (1997) *Britain Divided: The Growth of Social Exclusion in the 1980s and 1990s*. London: Child Poverty Action Group.

Walseth, K. (2006) 'Young Muslim women and sport: The impact of identity work', *Leisure Studies*, 25(1): 75–94.

Walseth, K. and Fasting, K. (2003) 'Islam's view on physical activity and sport', *International Review for the Sociology of Sport*, 38(1): 45–60.

Walseth, K. and Fasting, K. (2004) 'Sport as a means of integrating minority women', *Sport in Society*, 7(1): 109–29.

Weber, M. (1978) *Economy and Society* (2 vols), ed. G. Roth and C. Wittich. Berkeley, CA: University of California Press.

Wedgwood, N. (2011) 'Can anybody play? An introduction to the sociology of disability', in S. Georgakis and K. Russell (eds) *Youth Sport in Australia*. Sydney: Sydney University Press, 97–114.

Welford, J. (2011) 'Tokenism, ties and talking too quietly: Women's experiences in non playing roles', *Soccer and Society*, 12(3): 365–81.

Wellard, I. (2006) 'Re-thinking abilities', *Sport, Education and Society*, 11(3): 311–15.

Wellard, I. (2009) *Sport, Masculinities and the Body*. London: Routledge.

Wessels, B. and Miedema, S. (2007) 'Towards understanding situations of social exclusion', in H. Steinert and A. Pilgram (eds) *Welfare Policy from Below: Struggles against Social Exclusion in Europe*. Aldershot: Ashgate, 61–74.

Wheaton, B. (2012) *Lifestyle Sport: The Cultural Politics of Alternative Sports*. London: Routledge.

Wheeler, S. (2012) 'The significance of family culture for sports participation', *International Review for the Sociology of Sport*, 47(2): 235–52.

Wheeler, J.S. (2005) 'Rights without citizenship? Participation, family and community in Rio de Janeiro', in N. Kabeer (ed.) *Inclusive Citizenship: Meanings and Expressions*. London: Zed Books, 99–113.

World Bank (2001) *Attacking Brazil's Poverty*. Washington, DC: World Bank.

World Commission on the Social Dimension of Globalization (2004) *A Fair Globalization: Creating Opportunities for All*. Geneva: ILO.

World Health Organization (2005) 'Denied citizens: Mental health and human rights'. Available at: www.who.int/features/2005/mental_health/en/index.html (accessed 12 March 2013).

World Health Organization (2010) 'Mental health: strengthening our response'. Available at: www.who.int/mediacentre/factsheets/fs220/en/index.html (accessed 12 March 2013).

World Health Organization (2013a) www.who.int/topics/mental_health/en/ (accessed 12 March 2013).

World Health Organization (2013b) www.who.int/features/qa/43/en/index.html (accessed 12 March 2013).

World Health Organization European Regional Office (2013) 'Mental health'. Available at: www.euro.who.int/en/what-we-do/health-topics/noncommunicable-diseases/mental-health (accessed 12 March 2013).

Xinhua (2011a) 'China's "floating population" exceeds 221 mln', Xinhua News Agency, 1 March. Available at: www.china.org.cn/china/2011-03/01/content_22025827.htm (accessed 2 April 2013).

Xinhua (2011b) 'Ethnic games more than a multi-ethnic sports gala', Xinhua News Agency, 14 September. Available at: www.chinadaily.com.cn/sports/2011-9/14/content_13688660.htm (accessed 8 May 2013).

Xinhua (2013a) 'China targets rural issues in central document', Xinhua News Agency, 31 January. Available at: http://news.xinhuanet.com/english/china/2013-01/31/c_132142221.htm (accessed 2 April 2013).

Xinhua (2013b) 'China vows to help migrant workers in urbanization', Xinhua News Agency, 31 January. Available at: http://news.xinhuanet.com/english/china/2013-01/31/c_132142340.htm (accessed 2 April 2013).

Yao, C. (2004) 'Factors limiting the development of sports in poor ethnic areas (贫困民族地区开展体育活动的制约因素及发展对策), *Journal of Sports Correspondence*, 1: 11–12.

Yeich, S. (1994) *The Politics of Ending Homelessness.* Lanham, MD: University Press of America.

Young, J. (1999) *The Exclusive Society.* London: Sage.

Index